Bianca

FE 4º

BIANCA.

A Tale of

ERIN AND ITALY.

BY EDWARD MATURIN, ESQ.,

AUTHOR OF "MONTEZUMA," "EVA," ETC.

Sæva Pelopis domus.—HORACE.

O'Hara, O'Mara, O'Morven, O'More,
O'Donovan, Arran, M'Gillan, Gillore;
All houses so noble, so brave, and so old,
One drop of their blood is worth ounces of gold.

OLD IRISH QUATRAIN.

NEW YORK:

HARPER & BROTHERS, PUBLISHERS,

329 & 331 PEARL STREET,

FRANKLIN SQUARE.

1852.

TO

JESSE W. BENEDICT, Esq.

NEW YORK.

———

Dear Benedict—

Receive the following pages as the best memorial a very sincere friend has to offer. Measured by an intellectual standard, I fear it will be but a weak one. Accept it, then, in another light ;—that of friendship; which, as it is sincere, I trust will be also lasting.

Most truly Yours

THE AUTHOR.

Washington Heights, N.Y.
October, 1852.

BIANCA;

A TALE OF ERIN AND ITALY.

CHAPTER I.

LIFE bridges o'er a dark and stormy sea.
Meetings and partings come, like sun and rain
That lend that sea its passing images.
Like Israël's pilgrims over Jordan's stream,
We fling a stone at every step we take,
To mark, once past, there's no regression. Many
Die ere Life's waters feel their noonday sun ;
While others linger till the eventide
And sink to sleep with the declining day.
       Pledge we the wine-cup then,
The union, flung by the Egyptian Queen,
Is not the *last* that sparkles in its depths.

WE were, indeed, a jovial set. Perhaps never was
known a gayer, more roystering one within the
Elizabethan walls of Trinity College, Dublin ; where
I was entered and matriculated October, 18——. If we
were not sufficiently punctual or accurately prepared
for our quarterly examinations, trust me, dear reader,
it was from the unexampled diligence we made in our
examinations of the City of Dublin, for the purpose
of rollick and fun ; and if there was any complaint at

our peculiar disrelish for Falernian or Massic, believe
me, it was from our peculiar relish for the more native
(and to us equally classic) draught of whisky-punch.
Well—well—those days are past—*omnes composui*—
Light be the dust that Time scatters from her urn on
them!

The Hilary Examination was approaching; and, as
usual with me, the classical authors appointed for the
occasion, had enjoyed undisturbed repose upon the
shelf till within a few weeks of the period—I thought
it treason to remove those hoary sovereigns from their
dusty eminences, they looked such venerable statues
on their spider-wreathed pedestals. The fact is, I had
at school acquired such an early proficiency in the
languages, as to dispense with any very arduous preparation for my academic course.   Thus while the *stews*
(a sobriquet among us for the stupid studious) were
wasting eye and brain over the roots of the Greek or
humanities of the Latin authors, a regatta or a horse-
race, a game at rackets in our superb College Park or
the *àgrémens* of the quadrille with that, perhaps, most
fascinating specimen of her sex (an Irish lady) usurped
the time I should have otherwise given to my *Alma
Mater*—a strange phrase that, by the way!   Whence
do we call this mother beautiful?   I presume on the
negative principle of *lucus a non lucendo;* in other
words, from the frowns and threats she so frequently
lavishes on her disobedient and rebellious sons.   Be

that as it may, the Hilary was approaching; and but
slight preparations made by Morven O'Moore (myself,
sweet reader!) for the stern exactions of the Hall.
Indeed, as the period approached, I think my Æschylus
might have been well taken for one of the seven sleep-
ers of Ephesus (so sacred his repose on my table), and
Anthony need never have feared the fulminations of a
philippic, had Cicero been as silent as he was in my
chambers.

In this rebellious system of idleness I had a most
delightful companion in one of my resident class-mates,
Saville Merton.   Saville's horoscope was cast more
under the influence of Momus than that of the Muses.
Splendid abilities—fine and perhaps extensive acquirements for the very small meed of application he gave;
always ready for a midnight adventure within or without the gates of our venerable mother; whether for a
spree with those wretched martyrs of the night, yclept
watchmen, wrenching or inverting knockers on the
doors of respectable citizens, or mayhap changing the
names on the doors of our fellow students to such
grotesque forms, as to render it impossible for the pro-
prietors to identify on the following morning the names
they inherited from their fathers.   As handsome in
person and fascinating in manner as he was daring and
forward in all our sports or devilments, Saville was
the admired of the *belles* and the envied of his mates.

Scene, Saville's chambers; time, close on midnight

—oysters—punch and champagne; N. B. To-morrow, Examinations; alas! for the ever-to-be-respected mem, ories of Æschylus and Cicero.

That was a festive meeting; but even with the votive offerings we assembled to wreathe on the. *thu-melé* of Bacchus was the cypress to mingle her shade. We were assembled to witness a parting scene, and cry *Vale!* to our generous host, uncertain where or whether we should meet again. Saville had that day received his commission in the —th Regiment, and convoked his choicest companions to celebrate (as he said) the last melancholy obsequies of the few classic authors that, like ghosts, few and far between, haunted his chamber. Saville was to be the hierophant of the solemn services, and we the chief mourners.

A gay and jovial company were assembled when I arrived. The jest, the repartee, the classical pun circulated, the group of roysterers somewhat redeeming their character from the refinement and taste pervading their conversation. It certainly was an anomalous meeting for the purpose specified in our *cartes;* we seemed assembled for any thing most antagonistic to mourning or funeral rites. As I entered, the company were busily engaged in regarding what Saville stated was the funeral pile, erected by his own hands after the most perfect model furnished by the first books in archæology he had consulted for the subject. On the summit of said pile were placed various dusky copies of the classics for cremation; which, had they not been destined for the flames, ran a most excellent chance of being devoured by the spiders—a perfect Scylla and Charybdis case. The pile was surmounted by Saville's cap and gown; from too respectful a feeling, he said, he had for these old gentlemen to send them into the other world without their academics.

Meanwhile the servitors were plying all diligence in arranging his *triclinium* (as Saville called it, who was determined to be classical on the occasion), *anglicé*, laying the table. The atmosphere wafted commingled odors of oysters, broiled bones, &c.; but above all, rose strong, individual, and distinct, the Sabæan aroma of the Irish whisky-punch. Our worthy host brewed it himself with all that particularity and acumen which long experience had imparted to their possessor.

The guests were now seated, the hierophant in the chair, which he filled with a dignity worthy his vocation, and a hilarity adapted to any but the present melancholy occasion. "Gentlemen!" said Saville, "I propose on the present solemn occasion, commemorated by the presence of so many sincere mourners, a sentiment which will, I trust, impress on you the more deeply the many virtues of the deceased, and the unlimited obligations of pain and penalty to which we have submitted in their lifetime—Gentlemen! long have we wandered hand in hand with the deceased through silvan shade and haunted grove. We have threaded

the heights of Parnassus hand in hand, and bathed
together now in the Ilissus or the yellow waves of
Tiber. But whither am I wandering? The tear un-
bidden starts as I recall the by-gone companionship,
the warm pressure of the hand (*subaudi* floggings), the
various mementoes (*subaudi* cuffs and blows), which
survive the lamented departed—

'Labitur et labêtur in omne volubilis ævum.'

Excuse me, Gentlemen! if I be classical. If not now
and here, when and where? If you have tears, prepare, as the poet says, for I have composed an elegy for
the present solemnity, which will, I trust, find an echo
in every heart."

And he instantly darted off, cup in hand, to the
following dithyrambic—

> Away with your Juno, Apollo, and Jove,
>   Good-by to the waters of Castalie's fountain,
> No more with the moonstruck Endymion we'll rove,
>   Or seek with Diana bee-hives on the mountain—
>   Good-by, then, to Homer forever,
>   Of Horace and Virgil I tire;
>   Row them both over Phlegethon's river,
>   *Id est*,—Put them both in the fire!
>
> Fill up then, my boys! and drink deeply to Mars,
>   Hot whisky-punch be our purest Falernian;
> Henceforth be his name the tutelar Lars,
>   That guards the warm heart of each honest Hibernian.
>   With Cicero, then, to the devil,
>   Let Demosthenes, too, share his lot;
>   As for law, either common or civil,
>   Or logic, I care not a jot.

"Gentlemen! permit me to conclude this solemn dithyrambic (as the play-bills say) 'writ expressly for the occasion,' with the sentiment I promised, and which as a tardy debtor I hasten to pay—THE MEMORY OF THE CLASSICS—I have received orders to join—To-morrow I march—*Toga cedat armis!*"

The toast was drunk standing, in solemn silence, with all the honors.

"And now, Gentlemen!" resumed the hierophant of our mysteries, "to fulfill the solemn duties that have convened us, there needs but one more step—The '*Requiescat!*' must be chanted, '*Hic jacet*' engraved, with but little hope, I promise ye, of a '*Resurgam.*' "

So saying, Saville snatched a candle, ignited the pile on the hearthstone, previously prepared for the purpose, while we rallied round the smoking pile, in whose ascending flames we, each of us, read the stern retribution so long due and now finally paid these worthies. The obsequies, thus performed so far, were further solemnized and concluded by a libation performed after the same severe classical model. We emptied our glasses on the half-extinguished embers; and, thoroughly steeping the ashes in whisky-punch, instead of Cæcuban or Massic, we returned to the table, leaving them alone in their glory on the hearth.

We would have protracted our vigils till, perhaps,

an unseasonable hour, had it not been for fear of a late
attendance in the Hall on the following morning at
the summons of that great inexorable bell, whose peal
has smitten with horror on many a Freshman and
Sophister.   Saville had now shaken off the Egyptian
yoke; and, as he expatiated on the terrors of to-
morrow to all unprepared delinquents, a smile instead
of sympathy was all he had for his late fellow-suffer-
ers in bondage.   We parted—it is easy to write that
word; but is it equally so to rupture the ties, bury the
feelings, extinguish the kindred tastes and the many
hours of moral and mental sympathy they inevitably revive?   My friendship for Saville had been long,
strong, and disinterested; nor had it been once interrupted by our various arguments, asserted it might
be with warmth, but never maintained with intem-
perance—where or when to meet again?   But—

I was crossing the brick square in the direction of
my chambers; and, though the company and excitement should have kindled a spirit somewhat hilarious,
the recollection that my friend and I had in one
moment severed the friendship of years, left on me a
deeply melancholy impression.   I was about entering
my chambers, when I observed a form crouched at the
entrance.   The dim moon, which at the moment threw
off her thick mantle of clouds, served the more strongly
to individualize the object.   It was a female, her face
sunk upon her knees.

"My good woman," I said, gently tapping her on the shoulder, "are you aware the bell will soon toll for midnight and the gates be closed? are you in want?"

"Did I ask for any thing, O'Moore?" she said, fixing on me dark, lustrous eyes; that in the full blaze of the moon I knew not whether to assign more of a disordered mind or offended dignity.

"Your appearance and attitude would indicate distress."

There was a pause, during which the familiarity of her address in the use of my surname, which had at first escaped my notice, arose to my recollection. Had it been among my father's peasantry in the country, it would not have awakened any surprise; it being the custom in Ireland to address all those who have any claims to antiquity of lineage in this manner. This style of address is more particularly adopted by the Irish peasantry toward the descendants of the old Irish kings and chieftains, of which former our family claimed to be the lineal posterity. Such they entitle " *The* O'Moore, The O'Connor," &c.

"You seem to know me and mine," I continued, anxious to resume our interview, interrupted by so mysterious a silence.

" *Know* you?" she said, with a melancholy emphasis, starting from her position, and standing to her full height, the more commanding from the disordered

style of her hair and the picturesque manner in which
her dress rather hung than was arranged; "*know* you!
I saw the first glance of the infant that met the light
of this world; who knows but I may close it in its last
sleep? *Know* you?" she continued, grasping my arm
more tightly, and drawing so closely to me as to bring
our eyes almost in contact, "I know the O'Moore too
well—better than the dog his master, as well as the
lover his mistress, and he shall—"

"What?" I ejaculated, almost unconsciously.

"Know *me!*" was the reply; "but only as the
vile—the wretched—the damned know each other, in
chains and darkness, in weeping and wailing—"

"Peace, woman!" burst from me.

"Peace!—and to *me!* I tell thee, O'Moore, I open
the future to thee, and thou refusest to look or enter.
I watch the waves as they pass, the clouds as they
float, but thou wilt not hear the groans that reach
me, or the shapes that gather there, guiding us to what
lies beyond. These are *my* gifts; for, they say, misfortune hath a prophet's eye, and a tongue that—like
our own harp—can give echo to every sound that comes
from a far-off world."

I must confess that, though perfectly free from superstition, I felt somewhat awed in the presence of one
who combined an apparent acquaintance with the
future with that solemn manner and delivery that
seemed to verify her supernatural claims. To disa-

buse myself of these impressions, that I found fast gaining ascendency, I pretended to regard them with contempt, and, brushing by her, said :

" I have neither time nor inclination for your nonsense."

But, though a woman, I found the grasp on my arm was tighter than I thought; and for the spell of her eyes, half weird half frenzied, they almost revealed in their mystic depths those secrets of the future to which she pretended.

" Time !" she iterated; " well may the dying man say that, when the gate is forever closed, and the shadow enters eternity. Time belongs to youth; 'tis for youth to read that page, whether it burns with light and joy, or shrivels with the crimes and cares a guilty manhood hath written there. I tell thee, O'Moore, I have read each character—"

" Woman ! let me pass !" I cried, almost trembling myself at the impatience I dared to exhibit.

" Ay, and I can read *thy* future," she continued, unmindful of my repulse, her voice rising to a scream : " Here—here—here !" as with passion bordering on frenzy she struck her bosom, now well-nigh bare from the earnestness of her distracted gesture ; " *Here*—I know ye, flesh, blood, and all, O'Moore ! I know ye— I know ye !"

At this moment the midnight patrol, previous to closing the gates, was passing. Arrested by the excited voice and gesture of the stranger, they stopped a moment.

"And here," she exclaimed, "are my jailers.—
Well, when we can not break the chain, we must even
wear it. But, by that moon, O'Moore, we shall meet
again!"

She dashed her tattered garments from her arm, and
holding it bare to that light she seemed to invoke as a
witness of her truth, with a docility as unaccountable
as her previous paroxysm of passion, she surrendered
herself to the patrol, and, turning an angle of the
square, was soon lost to my view.

CHAPTER II.

Thɛ Greek in death loved Argos. Nature gives
The heart a two-fold worship. She who bore,
Is scarcely dearer than the earth that lent
Itself to form our clayey mould.—Green isle!
The life thou'st given shall ever bear thine image
Upon its tide; and, when the last pulse beats,
With it shall pass a prayer for Thee and Thine!

        The storm that whelms the bark
May dash an ingot on the shore. We met
Amid the hurtling of the elements:
Can this be prescient of our fate?

IT would be affectation to say that, free as I felt myself from all superstition, and its contemptible train
of phantoms, the strange figure I had encountered, and
her mysterious communications (like the moon that
witnessed them, half dim, half revealed), had not left
on me, perhaps, the deepest impression of my life. I
entered my chamber, and, so far from feeling inclined
for "tired nature's sweet restorer," took my seat by
the fast-sinking embers, whose spectral light but
strengthened the dreamy, ruminative strain of mind
into which the events of the evening had plunged me.
Thoughts rushed through my mind turbidly, discon-
nectedly, resembling more the shifting, fragmentary

phantasmagoria of a dream, than the strong and vivid images presented to our waking moments. She belonged not to that class, in common *parlance*, "fortune-tellers," who impose upon the credulity and purses of their deluded victims, by a pretended solution of futurity; nor was she one of the class—half knave, half fool—where the shrewdness of the one leavens the imbecility of the other. To neither of these classes did she claim kindred. Her emotions too intense and heartfelt, and her distress of that authentic character that disdained relief while needing it, forbade the suspicion—the possibility of her being either. Yet whence her interest in me? Whence her knowledge of me and mine? I had never, to my remembrance, seen her before; and yet, in her own strong language, she had seen the eyes of the infant first open on the light of day. I shuddered, as I thought upon her concluding threat. Thus succeeded thought and suggestion, "in wandering mazes lost;" a Pelion upon Ossa, reared by the mind in its vain attempts to solve the inexplicable, and yet, at the conclusion of its Babel, no nearer the heaven it aimed at than at the beginning.

These reveries, continued till the great toll of the bell announcing midnight, at once acquainted me that I was but a dreamer, while it recalled the rapid approach of my appearance in the Hall, for which I was but poorly prepared. I forbear initiating the reader into the mysteries of a Trinity Examination, and hasten to incidents in which he will, I presume, take a more immediate interest.

The environs of Dublin are among the most beautiful I have seen, and I have looked on many. Nor is their picturesque romance of the wild and terrible, the soft and beautiful, restricted merely to the vicinage of that city. For the space of at least twenty miles, stretching to the unrivaled county of Wicklow, the scenery unites the richest and most elaborate cultivation of a garden with the bold and precipitous character of the mountain. Nor is the eye even restricted to the monotony of land or mountain, for, while on one side it is attracted by the treasure of vale, mountain, and rich meadow land, on the other stretches away to the horizon the grand sweep of waters that forms its bay—suggesting, in their fullness, the opposite images of repose and power. The eye can not but be charmed by the continuity of beauty which at every step arrests it; and the heart and fancy are alike inspired with the thought, that Nature has, in her most frolic and capricious mood, combined those varied elements, which, while they appall by the grandeur and majesty of their form, win and soften by the graceful variety of their alternations.

The exceeding beauty of these environs is, I need scarcely say, a great temptation to the citizen to relinquish, if but for a day, the toils of business or professional care, and enjoy Nature, as here, in all the prodigality of her wealth she has lavished on mountain, valley and lake. One of the most popular resorts on such occasions is that exquisite line of country lying between Kingstown and Bray, with the bold and picturesque hills of Killiney in the interval. Indeed I don't think I ever saw a bay (for its size—some three miles) equal to that of Killiney. It would almost seem an enchanted ground, guarded by its two grim and mighty sentinels (Killiney Hill and Bray Head), frowning on the profane who would dare to disturb its holy and secluded waters.

Pleasure parties to this lovely country are very popular in Dublin, whether aquatic or by land; and when we allow for the plenty of viands furnished on these occasions by the proverbial hospitality of the hosts, and the inexhaustible flow of humor, sprightliness, and repartee they never fail to call forth, I do not wonder that a Dublin pic-nic is among the pleasantest and, perhaps, saddest of our memories. Blent as the present party is with the most mournful recollections, I can scarce find heart to pen it.

A merry party were we as we left the capital that lovely July morning—"Youth at the prow and Pleasure at the helm." Alas! how soon was that helm forsaken, and the prow left to dash itself amid the waves and breakers that beset the sunny sea of youth. A joyous and a merry set were we. The bright lips of the maidens launched their shafts of coquetry and

wit ;' the dancing eye gave out from its unsearchable
depths those jewels it borrows from the heart, as from
a mine, and the voices, sweet as the summer birds that
floated above us, gladdening heaven with their melody,
and wooing earth from its dream of dullness, uttered
those oracles that, like Sibylline leaves, are scattered
from the shrine of youth and passion. A merry party
we ! But the marriage bell may be muffled for the
mourning, and many a bright east may face a clouded
and stormy west.

As I said, we left the capital on our way to Kingstown, from which beautiful harbor we were to take
boats to Killiney, where we proposed to spend the day.
We started with hearts as light as our carriages were
heavy with the hospitable preparations for our party.
Arrived at Kingstown, we took our boats thence for
our romantic destination. We started under as cloudless a sky and golden a sun as ever gladdened the eye
of a Neapolitan, or betrayed the hopes of a Pompeiian
on the day that gulphed his city, and buried him and
his forever. Our watery way was gladdened by eyes
as bright as the diamond drops that glanced from our
oars, and the very waves themselves seemed lulled into
a more than summer stillness, from the sweet melodies of our own dear land, whose echo sank upon
their bosom as a kindred resting place. As day advanced, its glories seemed to grow and strengthen also.
The sky donned a mantle of such cloudless blue, as,

though twin to the sea, they had been parted only by
that destiny which accorded one the sovereignty of
heaven, the other that of earth.   The sun, painted by
inspiration as a giant, seemed with each moment to
rally round his throne fresh glory, and gather new
strength for the day-long race he was to run ; and the
tiny wavelets that met and broke upon our oars, were
like beings called to existence merely for the brief
summer holiday that welcomed their birth, and even
on their last moment flung its farewell of gladness and
sunshine.   So we rowed and talked and ate and drank
and sang.—Alas ! alas ! *Ignes suppositos sub cineri
doloso !*

We had agreed to dine on Dalkey Island ; an island
deriving all its beauty from the varied and commanding scenery that surrounds it.   After our repast, sea-
soned with song and jest and wine, it was agreed to
take again to the boats, and, having enjoyed the lovely
sunset of those hills, to return to Dublin, where we
were to close a merry day by as merry a night in
dancing.   Agreed—we started.

So thoroughly had we been occupied by the pleas-
antries of the dinner that none of us had noted a slight
alteration in the weather ; nor indeed was it till we
had rowed through the rough channel between Dalkey
and the main land, that we discerned in the sky the
prognostics of an approaching storm.   Its first indica-
tions were the heavy drops of a thunder-shower.   We

looked up, and behold a steady array of clouds, like a
host with black banners, gradually emerging from the
horizon, and advancing to the centre of the sky above
us, as to the citadel of attack. Not a moment was to
be lost; with might and main the oars must be plied
for the land, for the breeze that was now rising with
a gusty freshness rendered our rickety little boat un-
manageable under a sail. Meanwhile on marched those
grim, black messengers, with a purpose, it seemed, as
unfaltering and relentless, as though guided by the
undeviating direction of will and action. On they
came, their thick and serried ranks at intervals riven
and broken by flashes that only served to illuminate
their depth and strength. Far off flickered the surrounding hills with the transient gleams, and anon,
as from their very bosom, would follow those heavy
crashes that, while they seemed to rock the hills to
their very base, rolled their echoes over the sea, as a
knell to their work of destruction on earth. Meanwhile the rising waves gave sensible evidence that the
fury of the storm was to come; and our little boat reeled
and ducked, so as to render her almost uncontrollable
either by rudder or oar. We had pulled or rather
strained manfully; for myself I recked not; being
an expert swimmer, the distance to shore presented
but an indifferent obstacle. But what was to become
of the women, of whom we had four on board. Death
is at all times appalling; for age, with its attendant

B

infirmities, it seems to present a welcome and expected
asylum; but where we fling upon his pile youth, beauty, accomplishment—all that can make life a chain to
bind while it endears, to gild while it embraces in its
golden links every thought and passion that can grace
and adorn—we shrink from Death not only as a conqueror who comes to smite with his sword, but a tyrant whose fetter is forged for eternity! As I looked
on those lips now clasped and compressed with silence,
those cheeks even now impressed by that kiss that
freezes up the warmest vein, and those eyes from
which even now the light of life seemed fading fast
and forever, my heart and tongue rose in witness
against me for the rashness that had faced a peril
against which courage and address were alike unavailing. "My God!" burst from my lips, pale and quivering as those I looked upon. As I spoke or rather
muttered, I gave one huge strain on my oar, in which
I seemed to pour out (oh! that I could) heart and
soul, yea, my very life. The oar snapped with the
tug like a reed. We had but two. We *looked* at
each other. Oh! the concentration of that look. All
blasted joy and hope and gladness that rise like a sun
on the world of our life, and all the anguish of the
gnawing worm, the torture of the flame that dieth
not, blent and fused together in that one look. It
might be our last. Then was its fixed and terrible
grimness followed by an expression of stupid apathy

and paralyzed power; the last terrible extreme of human inanition, where we not only *feel* but *look* our weakness.

With that solitary oar (in itself so worthless) perished the last hope that bound so many hearts to life; yes, in the crash of that valueless reed, on which we leant but to find it pierce us, we heard, as it were, our very heart-strings crack, and the last inarticulate farewell burst from lips too faint and pale to utter it. What were we to do? There was but one hope left. Swim for life! And so feeble was that hope, it seemed to die with the very effort that called it forth. The desperate alternative was strengthened by the next moment. A heavy wave struck the boat; she swamped, and in sight—within reach of land! "God have mercy on our souls!" I cried, as, seizing the young lady next me, I plunged and made for shore. I solemnly aver that, at the moment, I was perfectly reckless of the issue as to myself; love—fear—hope—pride—passion, every conflicting feeling that in such an awful instant can swell and kindle in the human heart like lava, burned within me; if I could only lay the priceless burden that I bore—a human life—in safety, and sink dead upon the shore, I were content.

The shriek, the gasp, the paroxysm filled my ear with the terrors of the last trump; the convulsive struggle, clinging in the last moment to the crumbling and delusive; in agony I closed ear and eye; and, with a strength that frenzy and despair only nerved, grasped my prize and pushed for the shore I scarcely dared hope to reach.

Baffled, struggling, and desperate, what was my joy when I felt my knee scrape the bottom! And yet so stunned was I in body and mind, that this joy gave no strength to my arm, no gladness to my heart. It was like a nectar draught presented to a sick man, fatal to the malady that is wasting him; a picture of Paradise brightening the dreams of a blind man, he can not behold with his waking eyes! I had but strength sufficient to reach the shore, and felt that in laying my burden there my spirit, in the violence of the effort, had passed forever.

CHAPTER III.

Socrates had his demon. May not all
Have their attendant sprites to guard their steps,
Like those who, helpless infants, here on earth,
Still have their angels looking upon God ?
There's not a flower but has a destined breath
To bloom or blight it.   Worlds have satellites
To guard their fiery orbits thro' all space.—
Angel or demon, sent to blast or raise me !
She's in the air I breathe ; the very earth
Sends back her image.
                Woman ! what art thou ?
The midnight form that startled her of Endor
Was not more terrible.

FROM the sequel it was evident our disaster had been anxiously watched. When I awoke from the trance, I found myself in the cabin of one of the fishermen on the shore. I was stretched before the cheerful turf fire, and the inmates were administering the requisite attentions by chafing my hands and limbs ; my clothes had been substituted by a blanket. After a brief but sincere prayer for my deliverance, I endeavored to rally my senses in observing the character of my asylum, as well as that of my deliverers.

It was a fisherman's hut, furnished with the different implements of his adventurous trade.   The fisher-

man had (it seems at the imminent risk of his own
life) saved mine. His aspect was such as justified
the presumption of so generous an act. Rough and
weather-beaten as were his features, they served but
as a mask for a kind and gentle nature whose expression was in constant antagonism with their stern and
rugged outline. His good wife was worthy such a
mate; and, as she bent over me, soothing, encouraging, and cheering, in every look and gesture, fancy
could have almost turned that poor Irish cabin into a
palace of delights, and herself into its ministrant spirit.

From their communication I learned that I had
lain in a trance for some hours; and, to my earnest
entreaties respecting the object I had sought to save,
they answered—she was safe.

"Can I see her?"

"She has returned to the city," was the reply;
"but begged your honor not to go there till she has
sent a carriage for you."

"Thank God! thank God!" I murmured; "yet I
should like—"

The kind woman anticipated me. "She has left
this for your honor."

I seized the paper with the little strength left me,
and read:

"You have saved my life! What are words for
such a boon? But *words*. I entreat you to remain

tranquil for some short time till I send a carriage to convey you to Dublin.

"BIANCA ROMANO."

It is an instinct of our nature to prize more highly that which has been acquired by peril and adventure. Such a combination of circumstances will ever heighten love where it exists, and often wakes it to existence in hearts that dreamed not of it before.

It seemed as though this event had opened a new page in that volume which had hitherto presented little more save the monotonous recurrence of duty and study. The little light reading I had pursued had not infrequently united the most ardent passion with obstacles the most impassable and adventures the most hazardous. I challenged any adventure for greater hazard than that through which I had passed. My life was the stake. Can man wage greater? She had been a stranger to me till we met for the party; and now it seemed as though every barrier that had severed us was broken down, and a few moments' peril had sufficed for the familiarity of years. The stone had been rolled from the sepulchre of my heart, and a resurrection, bright, beautiful and new, burst from the trance of years.

Such were the hurried thoughts that glanced through my mind as I lay in that humble cabin. It was evening; and the dim array of thoughts that

floated through my mind was aided by the waning
light of the turf embers that were fast sinking upon
the hearth. The fisherman and his wife, observing my
thoughtful mood, had considerately withdrawn; I was
alone; alone as the devotee with his saint, for my
heart was communing with the image of her I had
saved. I knew not what it was induced me to open
my eyes and dispel the delicious vision that came
down upon them and my heart, like the aureola of his
saint on the worshiper. I started from the helpless
position in which I had lain; a nerve and strength
(stimulated by curiosity, it might be fear) took the
place of utter prostration. There are moments when
in the face of our nature, strength of mind, or even
our religious convictions, superstition, a something of
mystical agency between the other world and the present, forces itself on our fancy, and we feel reason herself totter in the presence of a creed she despises.
Such were my feelings, when by the glimmering embers I discovered whispering to the fisherman, while
her eyes were fixed on me, the mysterious female who
had addressed me as I was entering my chambers.
The shadowy light that dimmed rather than filled the
cabin, seemed a meet accompaniment to one whose
mission and connection with me already bore some
stamp of the supernatural. Nor was this impression
diminished by a closer survey of her figure. Tall and
commanding in stature, her features were cast in a

mould of strict and classic regularity. Their prevailing
expression was that of sadness; but as she spoke,
when memory, like a spirit, descended on and agitated the deep waters within, an inspiration, like that
of the Sibyl, filled eye and feature, abashing the eye
that met her own, and making the gazer feel he stood
in the presence of one who had the power of scanning
his inmost soul, and, it might be, the secrets of his
life. Such was the being now dimly shadowed in the
twilight; and, I must own, I felt no slight misgivings
as our eyes encountered.

"O'Moore," she at length said, "you see there is a
heart that ever beats, and an eye that ever watches
over thee."

"So watches the serpent," I replied, instinctively
recoiling from the strong eye I felt searching my very
heart; "but I know not the victim thanks it for protection. Speak, and say who art thou, that I and
mine are thus known and watched by thee?"

"I saw thee go, in the bright sunshine of morning,
like a bridegroom to the altar; the fair and young (as
I was once,)" her voice trembled, "wore their brightest smiles, and thy young heart leaped, like the harp-
string to the touch, at the sounds that swept it. I
saw your bark launched, I saw the gathering cloud
and the swelling wave, and I saw, oh God—!"

"What?"

"All thy companions perish!"

There was a pause. So stunned and weakened by my exertions was I, as, I grieve to say, to have forgotten my luckless companions. Gone! a prayer broke from me.

"Thou comest of guilty blood, O'Moore; yet is it for such to pray."

"What have I done?"

"Not thou, but thine; were I to tell thee, thy cheek would whiten and thy heart quail, and the waters of thy youth dry up, that manhood should never be freshened by them. I would watch, and guard, and save thee, even as my own life. But, no—I dare not tell thee, for thou would'st hate me. Yet, no, thou might'st pity—"

Her whole character seemed on the instant changed to me, and the fear she had previously inspired was now substituted by a more kindred feeling produced by her tears.

"If thy misfortunes spring from me," I said, "tell me how, and I will remedy them."

"They are beyond thy remedy, yet so blent with thee, as well might sever life from the heart. When I saw thee struggling against the black waves," she continued, dashing aside her tears, "bearing aloft thy burden, I thought 'twere better you and she had sunk with them that perished. And I stood on the shore, looking with gladness for the big wave which might dash thee pale and lifeless at my feet. But the waves

rolled and swelled like chariot wheels to bear thee to
the shore. O'Moore, I stood and wept over thee; for
the life of such as thou can not but be dark and stormy
as the wave that spared thee. And now thou needest
rest. The night falls, ay, and a bleak, black one, too.
'Tis meetest for the wanderings of such as I. The
wind howls—anon the rain will fall; but what are
they to a heart torn by a storm darker, deadlier? Morven, farewell!"

The door opened for an instant, disclosing the bleak-
ness of the coming night; I caught her last glance in
the dark crimson of the embers, heard her departing
step, and she was gone.

CHAPTER IV.

Lady, say on. 'Twas accents such as thine
That brought the angels down from heaven of old
To woo Earth's daughters. Look upon her face!
Art drops the pencil that she vainly seized,
While Earth sends back the image that had strayed
From its bright home in heaven. And then her mind!
A soul like hers, enshrined in such a form,
Is it not like the statue that awakes,
Like magic at the touch of sculptor hand,
From the white slab of old Pentelicus?

BEFORE I was fully recovered from severe physical prostration, I found I had not been forgotten by her for whose life I had risked my own. The carriage promised was in attendance; and the footman carried a generous gratuity from his mistress to the kind-hearted inmates of the cottage, whose unremitting care had contributed to my speedy restoration. With those thousand blessings (minglings of devotion and kind feeling), so peculiarly characteristic of the Irish peasant, I left the cottage; and so great the debility under which I labored, it was with assistance only I was enabled to enter the carriage. We were not long before we reached Dublin. The carriage dropped me at my chambers, whence I dispatched a note appointing an early evening to do myself the honor of waiting on Bianca.

Much had passed since last I sate at my fireside. Death and I had been fellows, and a third had well-nigh borne us company. The rest—where were they? No tear dropped, no grave dug, no prayer said, without even one of those touching rites with which humanity hallows the *fiat* of death, had the young and joyous been plucked from the garden, never to know bloom again. But two of that pleasant company survived to tell the tale of the others. Truly "in the midst of life are we in death." And then that mysterious visitant, the more so for her presence in such an hour! Her allusions to wrong as associated with my name, mingled with affection and sympathy for myself; these were sufficient to awaken superstition not only as to my own fate but her connection with it also. I started from my seat at reflections whose only aim seemed doubt and perplexity: and, like the conqueror of old who could not disentangle the knot, I tore it asunder.

Then would I wander from the darker shades this stranger threw over the picture of my life, to gather a beam, however straggling, from the presence of her I had rescued. We had never met till that fatal morning; but well do I remember the rich Circæan draught I drank from her conversation and beauty. The bold and beautiful outline of feature, the cloudless expres-

sion that seemed to have been baptized in the sunshine
of her own bright Italy, the classic enthusiasm that,
like the buried spirit of antiquity, seemed in its resurrection to have shrined itself in her; all seemed but
as the porch to the high and holy essence that awaited
worship within.   Overwhelmed with thoughts that
became more perplexing and bewildering, I sank upon
my bed and dreamed till morning.

It was some few days afterward (passed in extreme
suspense), that I hastened to fulfill the engagement I
had made.   Bianca's residence was in Kildare-street.
I knocked, and, on inquiring, was informed she was
at home.   The house and furniture betokened wealth,
without that vulgar display which a refined taste will
always endeavor to eschew.

I was not detained long before the fair object of my
visit entered.   An instant recognition, calling up the
painful circumstances of our first meeting, removed
the reserve we must otherwise have felt in so early a
stage of our acquaintance.   With that simplicity of
manner characteristic of her country, more touching
than the most refined artifice, and which while ac-
knowledging an obligation confers one still greater,
Bianca hastened forward ; and, pressing her lips to my
hand, I felt the warm tears of the Italian.

"My blessing on you here and God's hereafter," she
sobbed rather than said, " for the poor life you have
saved— !"

"Lady," I interrupted her, "the boon you speak was but the duty one being owes another—can *we* expect the protection daily, hourly, of that great Being you have invoked, unless we lend our poor aid to those of our fellows needing it? You are safe thank God! But the rest—" My voice faltered, and the sob of the Italian filled the pause more tenderly than words.

"Let us not dwell on so sad a theme," I resumed, leading her to a *fauteuil*, "the livery of life is but dark at best; it is, however, in our own minds to fling a passing ray upon its gloom. Have you been long in Ireland? I was not aware of your residence in this city till—" I checked myself—I was running on the rock again.

"Ah! dear generous Ireland!" interrupted Bianca, with that childlike simplicity which bespoke her sincerity; "I can almost fancy myself again under my own bright sky, for the people seem almost the same. The same in fire—enthusiasm—their love of song—in all save their language—"

"And even there," I interrupted, "I should not deem you had found much difference; your English is as pure as though native; but sweeter for the foreign accent that marks it. So you like the Irish?"

"I love them," she replied, her full, dark eye flashing, as though its very light were freighted with the heart-load; "I love them, for in their character I read the transcript of all that commends my countrymen to my heart—nay, even in our misfortunes we have sympathy—"

" To what do you allude ?"

" The genius of Italy weeps at the grave of Brutus, but the freedom of Ireland reposes in its tomb without a tear."

I felt the blood rise to my cheek, and anxious to evade any thing of a political character, I rejoined, " that if Ireland were now soldiered by a foreign foe, the blame lay in her own sons, whose energies were expended in maintaining religious faction rather than in asserting her independence. The annals of other countries," I concluded, as the subject rose with the force of a taunt, " sufficiently prove, that where the Irish have fought as mere *condottieri*, their courage exhibited in the quarrels of strangers were sufficient by *union* to secure the independence of any nation upon earth. But ' a house divided'—you know the proverb. Have you been long here ?" I continued, anxious to change the subject.

Her dark cheek flushed, and the mournful expression that for a moment supplanted the wonted fire of her eye, gave token that I had touched some chord of sad remembrance.

" Long enough to love her almost as my own—her and her noble-hearted people," she answered, " but not long enough to forget my own. You know what our own sweet Poet says—' *Et dulces moriens,* etc.,' and if

this memory of our native land comes like a setting
sun over our dying hour, what should our *living* enjoyment of that land be, hallowed as mine is by the
enduring triumphs of genius and of art, when the
perishable monuments of the sword have passed away,
and it lies sheathed by the conqueror forever? Such
is Italy. The sword is rusted, the lyre may be silent,
but in the works of her artists we read the epitaph of
the land."

"You speak as warmly as though you had been
inspired a life long with the Delphic air of your native
land; yet you allow me to infer you have been for
some time resident in Ireland?"

I had unconsciously touched the chord again; and
the momentary gleam awakened by the memories of
her classic home was once more shaded by the associations I had touched. She paused a moment, during
which the thick tear started, but was repressed by a
violent effort.

"You have saved my life. To whom, if not to my
deliverer should I communicate the saddest, deepest
secret of my life? It is yours by duty—by affection,"
she continued, with that *naïveté* we but seldom see
amid the cold and rigid conventionalities of northern
society; "by all that can bind one human heart to
another, hear it. My father, an Italian noble of birth
and wealth, had early wedded one his equal in both.
Beautiful and accomplished, my mother was regarded

as the very cynosure of the circle in which she moved.
Her voice was deemed even unrivaled by those who
filled the first *rôles* at the opera, and her conversation
combining the vigorous freshness of an original mind
with the polished grace and varied wealth of classic
lore, you need not wonder that while the wife was
admired the husband was envied.

"Strong as was the intellectual sympathy that
bound them, there was one link needed to render their
union complete—that was uniformity of habit. My
father's early pursuits had rendered him retiring and
studious, while my mother's varied accomplishments,
ever kindled by admiration, required the stimulus of
society to preserve their freshness and attraction.
From the absence of this one link fell through the
chain that bound together happiness and home, and
left me a wanderer in a foreign land, where, but for
your generous heart, Bianca's tale would have been
already told."

"I pray you proceed."

"This difference of taste unfortunately in time produced a difference in temper; disputes and recrimina-
tions followed, and (I tell the tale briefly, to spare you
patience and myself pain) suspicions were not long
wanting to hasten a catastrophe my father could hardly believe while he suspected.

"The manner and accomplishments of my mother
had gathered around her admirers, my father's ingen-

uous mind was for a time willing to enroll in the cate-
gory of those who pay a willing tribute to talents, that
deference and sympathy can not long withhold. So
universal, indeed, were these attentions, that it would
have been difficult even for a mind the most jealous
to centre its suspicions on an individual. But where
this appetite exists it will not long need food; food
produced from our very vitals, like the offspring devoured by the god in the mythology of my own land.

"In compliance with my mother's request, my
father issued cards for a masquerade one night at
Florence, where we were sojourning for the winter.
Such an entertainment, of course, gathered together
the varied groups of gay and grave who assemble for
the pleasure of the scene, or recreation from the pressing pursuits of the day. I have often heard my father
speak of the splendor of that scene, and shudder as he
called to mind the tragedy with which it closed. Not
to detain you, my father's suspicions were fixed, and
all his efforts were on that night, under the dissimulation of pleasantry, to rivet with certainty the link that
had hitherto bound him as with fire. To this end, he
constantly changed the mask he wore; but, amid his
varied disguises, his eyes never wandered from my
poor mother and the miserable *cicisbéo* he suspected.
While the dance was in gay progress, my father's eye,
still fixed on his victims, observed them withdraw.
They entered a small ante-chamber, one wall of which

being covered with tapestry served as a fitting concealment for the intended espionage. The lover (for
such he proved to be) commenced this secret interview
with expressions of the highest admiration for my
mother's beauty and accomplishments, accompanied
with well dissembled sympathy that they had not
found fitter mate than he, who in possession of a mine
of personal and intellectual wealth, secluded both from
the gaze of the world, from a jealousy as sordid as
it was undeserved. He then proceeded to enlarge
upon her happy destiny, cast under higher auspices,
and linked with one whose intellect could appreciate
and his pride lead him to enjoy the participation of
others. ' Leave then,' concluded the impassioned lover,
' a fate, the more like a chain, because worn so pa-
tiently, a sphere where concealment is but a prison,
and a husband who, like a jailer, holds the key of the
treasure he dares not exhibit to the world. Leave all,
and fly with me ;—with me, who perhaps of all, as I
most ardently admire, so can I most fervently adore !'

"This passionate and faithless apostrophe to all my
father most loved on earth, though recently somewhat
alienated by discord, while it appealed to the honor of
the husband, awakened the indignation of the man.
In a second the tapestry was torn asunder, and the
outraged husband stood before the seducer, armed with
his wrongs, keener, sharper, deadlier than the naked
rapier he bore. The cool courage of my father, and

the strict etiquette which always regulated his intercourse with antagonists, were here, alas! forgotten in
the tempest of rage that swept him on to a speedy
revenge. He heard no exculpation, gave his foe no
chance for apology or self-defense, but with one desperate lunge laid him in his blood at his feet. Flinging on my poor mother one mingled look of passion,
scorn, and despair, he dashed his sword, wet with the
blood of her paramour, at her feet, and rushed from the
chamber.

"The narrative of some minutes was but the act
of a second; so incredibly rapid, that before the guests
were privy to the fatal tragedy, my father and I (then
but six years old) were posting, as rapidly as horses
could carry us, to the nearest seaport, Leghorn. For
such misfortunes as my father's there is ever a ready
sympathy, nor was this diminished by the handsome
douceur he gave the captain of a vessel about to weigh
anchor on the following morning for Dublin. The
captain promised concealment, and all the aid in his
power; and, for this purpose, agreed to weigh anchor
some hours earlier than he had intended. I will not
detain you (already too patient) with a recapitulation
of the horrors that thronged and oppressed my fancy,
child though I was, that terrible night. Orestes under
the scorpioned and fiery whips of the Eumenides could
not have suffered more. My father, excited though
he was, had still his sense of wrong to sustain him.

Such is the difference between actual murder and an act of blood, perpetrated in defense of our person or our rights. But with me, the lively fancy of childhood exaggerated the deed and all its collaterals; my father was a murderer in my eyes: for childhood could not discriminate between the bloodthirsty wretch who strikes down his victim for gain, and the husband who exacts blood, as the only penalty that can cancel the stain on his own and children's name. Still he was my father; and, though in my dreams he was arrayed in those grotesque and exaggerated forms with which nursery tales delight to affright the infant mind they should instruct, I loved him—loved him with a deeper, a more enduring passion than before, though that feeling was somewhat tinged by fear.

"I hasten to conclude; for," she continued, with a smile that but faintly played through the melancholy produced by her tale, "though you have saved my life, it is too much to tax you with a narrative of all its petty cares and adventures."

"They can not but interest me. Pray you proceed."

"For some time after our arrival on your hospitable shores (whither it seems the hand of God has guided us, for kinder hearts I have never met since I left my own dear land) my father surrendered himself to the most brooding melancholy, alternated by the most violent paroxysms of grief. This was not remorse; for, while he constantly adjured my mother by name, the name of his wretched victim never once escaped him. Yes, I err :—it did once. I heard him *pray*.

"The night dream and the waking thought, the prayer, the half-suppressed murmur, the sigh ever trembling on the lip, and then seeking relief only in the most violent gush of tears—all these sufficiently attested the fearful penalty my father's rashness had entailed on him, and the passionate fondness even for that name, that seemed to hover like a spirit over the grave its falsehood had dug. Yet no!" (her cheek flushed, and her eloquent eyes by a momentary flash seemed to repudiate the imputation a daughter's lips had uttered against a mother) "no, sir! I trust my dear mother was not dishonored, though the hot blood of the Italian read certainty where cooler temperaments would have paused and deliberated. To return: The small treasure of jewels my father's precipitancy had provided, was in some few months exhausted; but notwithstanding the despair that sometimes pressed him as with a mountain weight, his energies on occasion rose against it, and with a *prévoyance* (as he said, rendered the more anxious by his passionate fondness for his Ninetta Bianca), he looked on the future with a fearless eye, and determined to meet it with his own resources.

"His natural taste for music having been highly cultivated, he betook himself to that as a support for himself and daughter. His sound musical attainments, while they commanded admiration, defied competition. The Signor Rovero (for he had dropped his title and name, the better to preserve incognito) received the largest compensation of any instructor in Dublin, and those families reputed themselves fortunate who could secure his professional services for their daughters. But a phase of life adopted from necessity, and the more distasteful from its strict obligations and punctuality, to one who had hitherto enjoyed the most unlimited independence of time and means, became wearisome, and in time intolerable to my father. His spirits, which had till now supported him, failed; with them sank his energies; and a few months of suffering, by consigning him to his grave, closed the dreadful tragedy in a foreign land. Among his numerous and most admiring patrons were the family whose generosity has assigned me a shelter and a home. The elder members were pupils of my father; and, in consideration of the hospitable kindness that has sheltered the stranger, I have undertaken the education of the younger. My situation in this family is that of governess."

" Such a life," I replied, " must be little congenial with one of your tastes and acquirements. The warm blood of Italy must require a higher stimulus than that furnished by the dull routine of education, and the still duller association of childhood."

"Pardon me; the higher the temperament, the greater necessity for what we term the actual duties and commonplace of life. Ideality may be ambrosia; but you must remember such food requires a god. The early secrets of my life, partaking as they do of the tragic and romantic, might, if not relieved by common daily duties, stimulate to a morbid extent a mind perhaps too much moulded in the ideal."

"You deserve no small praise for reconciling yourself to a lot so much at variance with your early prospects in life."

"There is no praise to be awarded the discharge of duty," replied Bianca, "though its neglect involves censure and reproof. The great Founder of our faith has broadly laid down that unmistakable principle; the fullest discharge of duty leaves us but in the capacity of unprofitable servants, while every believer is acquainted with the punishment that awaits its disregard. But, pray let me pass from a subject, at best unworthy, to a nobler one, for with it are linked gratitude and all the hopes of life. You have not sustained any lasting injury by your adventure in my behalf?"

"Nothing more than a long dream, of which you were the image—a dream so pleasant, that, to taste it once again, I would encounter the same peril."

"Do you remember—? Ah! no, you can not. I recollect you lay in a stupor; but shall *I* ever forget the strange, wild figure that hung over you as they

C

parted us?· Were it not for the frenzy that lit her
features, I could have almost fancied rage was there,
because we had reached the shore in safety.—You
grow pale!"

There was something so chilling in the memory of
this strange being, as almost to curdle my very blood.
A mind naturally strong, and perfectly antagonistic to
the credulous, revolted from any superstitious influence she might exercise over me and my fortunes; yet
her presence in the very hour that death threatened
me, and that in the very face of her own extreme
personal exposure, if it made her not weird or wizard,
at least so blent her fate and feelings with me, as to
degrade whatever I felt of gratitude into fear.

"A slight pain—nothing." I hesitated: "I was
thinking more of your wayward fate than of the mysterious being of whom you spoke. Strange, that one
of her fairest daughters should at so young and shelterless an age have been severed from so lovely a
mother!"

"I have not seen her since that dreadful night. I
think I see her now, as I stood with her before her
mirror, toying with the diamonds with which she was
braiding her hair. Often do I look on and speak with
this," she continued, taking a miniature from her
bosom, set richly with diamonds, and while she gazed
on it, a tear took its place among the gems, pure and
bright as they; "and my last wish will be to have it

rest with me in my grave. I can not, dare not think my mother false."

"Pardon me; I did not allude to your mother," I answered, desirous to evade a subject which had such power in calling up her most painful emotions; "but your country."

"Ah! her glorious nature; her vine-clad hills, and mountain and valley, worthy to be the haunted shrines of old mythology, and even in their desertion steeped in the inspired dreams of Oread, Naiad, and Dryad. These I have but heard of, or gathered from the dull and lifeless lips of books. Imagination wearies in filling up outlines and vivifying records, when the living eye longs to fill itself with the glorious image, the impassioned heart to breathe its worship, and the glowing lip to speak face to face with what has hitherto been a wonder and abstraction. For this reason, as I have risen from Virgil and Horace, a vagueness as to the very identity of the men—the men and places of which they spoke—so bewildered me, that I have almost seemed to have been treading some land of Faërie, and longed to realize all in my own experience. Imagination may embody more than the real, but there is a craving in our nature she never can satisfy. However bold her flight, eagle-eyed her view, creative her energies, still we long to tread the spot where Freedom reared her altar, and the tyrant fell, or the field where countless thousands toiled and bled in vain, because truth, justice and patriotism were the impenetrable panoply of their foes."

"Then you desire to travel?"

"Ardently," she replied, the warm blood of the south beaming in her eye; "but I have much to do before I can accomplish that dearest and strongest resolution of my life."

"As ardent an admirer as yourself, perhaps, of these world-famed lands, it is also my desire to travel. Have you any definite time appointed for this intellectual repast?"

"You shall know when the time comes, for you have made me so much your debtor that I can scarcely conceal any thing from you. But—"

Our conversation was here interrupted by the entrance of the lady of the house, Mrs. Temple; who, in expressing her gratitude for rescuing their "dear child" from so sudden a death, requested me to join a few friends at her house some evenings after. I cheerfully acceded, and withdrew; rejoicing that Bianca was, by the kind manner and expressions of Mrs. Temple, exempted from that painful humiliation and dependence to which the governess is too frequently exposed in the house of the *parvenu* and vulgar rich.

CHAPTER V.

Ho! ho! dame Fortune, wrinklest thus thy brow?
Now, by my grandame! an thou menace thus,
My shoulders are as broad as those of Atlas
To bear your heaviest fardels. Shrink not then,
For heart and hand have flung the gauntlet.

            That voice again!
It sings of death, and yet hath sweetness in it;
Like autumn leaves that lull their mother earth
To her long sleep of winter.

I RETURNED to my chambers. The recent event of my life and the rich casket of beauty and endowments it had opened to me, rendered me but little disposed for that unsympathizing association presented to us within the walls of a college. Add to this, I had but few associates either at school or college. I can not account for this; my disposition is social, my manners not shy; I can but best answer it on the abstract principle of Hamlet, that man delighted not me. Saville was almost the only acquaintance I had ever ripened into a friend. I liked the leaven of the fellow's character, it presented such an admirable blending of the mental and the physical, that first in the athletic sports of the field, he was also unanimously

voted the first in conversation and debate. To poetry
he had particularly turned his attention, and his extensive acquaintance with the art divine could be
equaled only by the high dramatic powers of elocu-
tion he threw into it. Poor Saville, after our parting
Saturnalia in his chambers, had gone to join his regiment, so that I was alone in my glory, and alone I
pleased to be on the present occasion.

If the earlier portions of my life had been cast
in the world of commonplace, the events that were
now fast clustering around, seemed to borrow their
brightest hues from the web of romance. The strange
woman, whose eye seemed to watch my destiny with
as much anxious curiosity as an astrologer would the
horoscope he had cast in infancy, and but waited for
manhood to verify ; and then the high-souled, classical
Bianca, whose life Fate had made an offering to my
will, and whose form had been clasped in an embrace
even more solemn than that of wedlock, who now rose
on me the embodied genius of that far off land, on
which fancy had mused, and eye had wept, and heart
had yearned ; oh ! it was that dawn of the heart's
young life, when we turn with satiety from earth,
and, like the opium eater, seek in the delirium of our
own being that daily manna, that, descending from
heaven, is commended to our lips by angel hands.

As thus I sate musing on such seeds of Time, as
might or might not grow, my servant put a letter in

my hand. The post-mark was that of the town adjoining my father's castle. I felt a momentary pang
as I looked on the missive, from its black seal and
border. I, however, opened and read:

"CLONMUIR CASTLE, *February,* 18—.

"SIR—It is my duty to inform you that an unexpected event has left all the inmates of the Castle in
the deepest mourning. The O'Moore (our father) is
no longer living. While walking in the park last
Thursday evening, a miscreant stabbed him, and, before aid could be afforded him, the spirit had passed.
The knife was found beside him, but all attempts to
detect the perpetrator of the deed have proved unavailing. The body of The O'Moore was consigned
to its resting-place on Sunday, amid the loud lament-
ations of his devoted tenantry.

"From your relations to our deceased father for
some time prior to his death, you must not be surprised that your claims have been wholly overlooked in
the final disposition of his property. Clonmuir Castle,
with its lands, has been left to me, unencumbered
with any charges for the benefit of yourself, the
youngest and only son beside the heir. I regret to
inform you of such a bequest; as it serves for so strong
an indication of the feelings of the deceased, and a
commentary equally unmistakable on the conduct that
has merited such neglect. Your future course in

life, controlled as it must be by your own judgment,
and moulded by your industry, I shall not attempt to
advise. Believe me, however, when I assure you of
my sincere wishes for your happiness and success.

" Yours,   DESMOND O'MOORE."

Forgotten—disowned—disinherited ! Oh ! in the
agony that swelled and embittered the torrent of my
soul, self-injustice, forgetfulness, all were disregarded in the overwhelming conviction of my father's
death and the terrors that must have marked his last
moment. Unshriven, unanealed ; hurried before his
Maker, it might be, in the full flush of sin, without
the amendments of repentance. Yet, no ! Though
outcast and forgotten, I recant the word ; I loved my
father, that few sons could love more ardently; and for
his sins, what right had I, a worm, rotting and trembling in the corruption of my own, to sit in judgment
on another ? To his own master, not his fellow, much
less his son, my poor father stood or fell. Oh, God !
what were the wrongs, real or imaginary, of disinheritance to the sword, sharp and relentless, that lacerated my heart, worse than the assassin's knife the heart
of his victim ? If blood could have called him back,
mine, Absalom as I was, should have flowed ;—could
tears have unsealed his doom, mine—ay, those of the
rebel and the disinherited—should have fallen, till the
iron heart of the inexorable tyrant should have melted,

and his obdurate ear opened as to the adjuration of
words. But what avails grief or prayer when the
narrow bed is closed and the iron-gate shut, that
shall open only once again, when riven by the arch-
angel's trump? "I shall go to him, but he shall not return to me," cried the heart-wrung monarch of Israel.
Vain to weep for the unreturning dead! We can not
recall the thunderbolt that has buried a city, nor number with the sunshine hours of to-morrow those that
are sleeping with the dead they have knelled to rest.

The tide of grief exhausted, reflection naturally
turned to the circumstances revealed in this cold and
formal communication from a *brother*—a brother!
Slander!—a being.

I can scarcely divine a cause for this severe retribution of my father; the more so, as being the last act
of life, it admits neither of appeal nor remedy. What
had I done? Ever an obedient son to my father as
long as I was an inmate of Clonmuir Castle, the first
germs of disobedience or aught unfilial I had ever exhibited was on my first exodus from home for college;
a sort of privileged period with youth, and generally
devoted by them to certain little excesses and eccen-
tricities in celebration of their newly-acquired freedom. I had gambled, drunk—perhaps raced a little;
—what are these? The elegant recreations and facile
accomplishments with which we beguile the few hours
we can spare from the erudite company of the classics.

c *

It is true that I had frequently exceeded the liberality of my father's allowance to me, from the hospitable clique that surrounded me at Trinity. Debts had accrued; creditors threatened exposure to the heads of the college; and, to save credit and character, I was compelled to refer them to my father. The liquidation of the debt as frequently brought reproof; reproof, threats; and, on looking over a file of my father's letters, I found this very menace made in strong and determined language, which I had disregarded at the moment, or since forgotten, but which he had finally enforced as the last and solemn act of his life.

But what were the feelings with which I read so heart-breaking a communication, embittered by the tone and manner of imparting it? They were such as might have been expected from my past relations with Desmond; though I might have hoped that all our past differences should have been laid to sleep with our father, and feelings more beseeming the Christian and the brother marked the melancholy event. But such a reformation was not to have been expected from the flinty and unforgetting nature of Desmond. Our very boyhood had been marked by that spirit of discord our manhood seemed destined to perpetuate. I was the younger; and the occasional partialities shown me by a too-indulgent mother awakened a jealousy in my brother, sometimes bordering on the vindictive. Well, if this feeling had gone no further;

had limited itself as well to the season of childhood
as to the thousand little privileges awarded it;—but,
alas! years but strengthened these evil dispositions,
unchecked by the prudence and affection they should
have developed. It beseems not an autobiographer to
vaunt his own advantages whether of mind or person;
but they are no more objectionable than the egotism
that forms the very staple of the narrative, when they
enter into the elucidation of character, action, or motive. At school, I was awarded the meed over him
for what the world in general calls talent (I suppose
that general proclivity of mind dispensing with all that
is necessary to insure success; industry, and application). And this very superiority, which I neither
sought nor coveted, no more than the invidious com-
parisons it produced, necessarily confirmed the feeling
and widened the breach by what should have been
an honorable competition. The advantages of person
were mine also to a degree far beyond what nature had
conferred on Desmond. He could not endure that the
person that had won the athletic prize, or the fairer
one of the ball-room for the dance, should be admired
for its strength in the one case, or its symmetry and
grace in the other. These fits of sullen jealousy operated so strongly on my brother as frequently to sus-
pend our intercourse. In such cases it would have
been perhaps better to have given open expression to
such feelings, rather than have nursed and strength-

ened them by a savage and morose silence. Be that
as it may, as we verged on manhood, it was plain to
see the cord was snapped, never again to be united.
Like the Theban brothers, we had not stained our
hands in blood ;—but, oh! that daily mortification of
nature ; that denial to her of those gifts she exacts and
claims for her own ; the daily estrangement of feeling and laceration of the heart without the dignity
of a sacrifice !—are not these equal to the dreadful
doom that buried the Theban brothers in the same
grave ?

As I re-read the closing paragraph, however indifferent I felt to the penniless condition in which my
father had left me, I could not curb the passionate
contempt I felt for Desmond's dissembled sympathy
and his sincere "assurances" for my happiness. Oh!
hypocrisy, to present shelterless penury to famishing
lips, and then *assure* us of regard and friendship. As
well might the lion howl a lament over the torn fragments of the body that have served him for a meal!
The very thought made the letter tremble in my hand.
"So perish our brotherhood, Desmond!" I cried ; "and
now to brace myself for the fate in which you augur
me so much *happiness !*"

Yes, I had happiness ; happiness, though but that
of a dream, to which the heart of Desmond, though
lord of an estate that had come down from the old
Irish chieftain, was a stranger ; yes, happiness which

Desmond could not purchase even with the gold of his
land and liveried retainers. With Lear I could say,
"I was more sinned against than sinning!" I had
perpetrated no wrong, I cherished no revenge for what
I fear was an undue influence exercised by Desmond
over my father; one moment of my life had degraded
me from the wealthy lineage of an Irish chieftain to
an alien, a very Ishmaelite, to one in whose veins
flowed the very blood that warmed my own. But I
was happy in my innocence, happy in the strength
and energy that, like the swelling waves beneath the
ship, bear her careering with flying canvas and priceless freight safe to her wished-for haven. Threatened
now with trials and difficulties, at an age that rather
expects the pearl of Cleopatra in its cup than her asp
on its arm, I did not sit down in that spirit of repining
and helpless apathy that would rather suffer than resist; I regarded these coming trials but as the means
of enlisting energies that else might have lain dormant
in my nature. I welcomed them still the more, for
that they were the promised means of giving me independence, and enabling me to fling the heartless sympathy of Desmond back in his teeth, where it deserved
to rest, for it went no further. Henceforth I was to
be my own master, my own pillar of fire, it might be,
through a wilderness; these hands were to earn my
own bread—delightful thought—for bread of Desmond's hand these lips should never taste.

The resolution formed, there was but one way for its accomplishment. I had always maintained a respectable position in my class in classics, and on more than one occasion had received the commendations of my tutor for my answering in the Hall. I determined to avail myself of the character I had made, obtain a tuition, through my tutor's influence, in some private family in the country, and leave Dublin instantly. But then rose Bianca before me, the paradise her hand, as with magic touch, had opened to me, the rich flowers of mind and soul she seemed ready to strew upon my path, coloring, enriching, and etherealizing every object on which had rested before the dullness of life, like a vapor. But should I to such romance as this sacrifice the resolutions, the imperative obligations of a life imposed on me by my thirst of independence? Had Æneas sooner sailed from Carthage instead of dallying in the love bower of the resistless Elissa, he would not, perhaps, have witnessed from the deep the expiring flames of her funeral pile. Away, then, with these boy dreams: life was before me, and I must meet it, as the ship breasts the wave!

I handed Desmond's letter to my tutor (one of the junior fellows of Trinity) who expressed the warmest sympathy for my bereavement, as well as for the unnatural coldness of my brother. He saw the necessity of immediate exertion, approved my intentions, and promised his most ready and effectual aid for their completion. More than this, he insisted on my accepting immediate pecuniary aid for present need, leaving it to time convenient for its liquidation. Not to detain the reader, this zealous friend had, in a few days, performed his promise. A situation was offered me in the private family of De Lacy (unhappy coincidence, not more than ten miles from Clonmuir Castle), where I was to undertake the preparation of the only son and heir for Trinity College. I hesitated for a moment, as I heard of the proximity of the place to Desmond's estate; but pride and dependence came to my aid, and turned the balance. I resolved to go, and accepted. The families had not previously visited, so I apprehended but little chance of meeting Desmond.

The recent domestic events, and the train of associations they brought, were calculated exceedingly to depress my mind, and render my chambers melancholy and distasteful to me. I, therefore, the more gladly anticipated Mrs. Temple's invitation, especially as I wished to inform Bianca of my intended departure from Dublin, and the events that had produced so sudden a resolution.

To Mrs. Temple's, then, I went. The *réunion* was a musical one, and a goodly gathering there was of the *dilettanti* of Dublin. The first object that met and riveted my eye was Bianca; her classic features and superb figure, such as might have inspired the

dreams of Phidias, and transported modern fancy to
the days of Lucretia and Portia, the more characteristic from the national character of her costume, to
which she still adhered with fondness. Her hair, of
the darkest hue, was *coiffed* after the antique fashion
of the Empire; such as we see with the Agrippinas and
the Roman ladies of that day at the Capitol and Villa
Albano, near Rome. The costume was supplied from
the same classic model : her velvet robe hung in loose
folds, gathered together by a diamond clasp, which
bound it to the left shoulder.

As I entered, she was standing by the harp; and
imagination was divided between the risen genius of
antiquity and Corinne improvising her grandeur and
her power amid the crumbling monuments that attested the decay of both. The *bravos* which succeeded
her brilliant execution had scarcely subsided, and the
flush that mantled her brow in answer, seemed a conflict between the pride she felt in the *Thema* (a dream
of Italy) and the modesty that was unwilling to appropriate the plaudits of the assembly.   But even the
momentary vision of her country her music had painted
and the intoxicating tributes her performance elicited,
appeared forgotten as her eye met mine.   She seemed
almost a goddess, weary of the incense and worship,
and descending from her altar to share the joys and
infirmities of humanity.

"*Buona sera, mio caro salvatore!*" she cried; and

with a girlish simplicity of manner she seized my hand, which I as instantly raised to my lips.

"Buona sera, bella Bianca!" I replied; "yet how can we hope the evening would be fair, when its loveliest star has strayed from heaven, and found its way to earth?"

"That star you admire for its radiance might, but for this hand, have shared the fate of Hesperus, and sunk beneath the wave even before night."

"Donna Bianca! it would not have sunk forever; I should have hailed its certain and resplendent resurrection in the words of our own classic Lycidas:

> 'Your sorrow is not dead,
> Though sunk he be beneath the watery floor.
> So sinks the day-star in his ocean bed,
> And yet anon raises his drooping head,
> Retricks his beams, and with new spangled ore,
> Flames in the forehead of the morning sky!' "

"Ah! Signor O'Moore," she answered, recognizing with a graceful bow the poetic compliment, "it suits not poor mortals, in this unmythic age, to wander through those starry heights, lest, like the god spoken of by your favorite classic, ambition may lose its balance, and fall 'sheer over the crystal battlements,' without even a friendly Lemnos to receive us."

"Come and let me present you," she continued, taking my arm; "a wandering Æneas cast upon our friendly shores."

"Perhaps to seek and find a Lavinia."

"Few such suits are prosecuted," she playfully answered, "without the opposition of a Turnus."

The presentation (that awful rite and bore) to the
lady of the house accomplished, and a few words of
usual insipidity having passed, my attention was arrested by the loud importunities for Bianca to take
her seat at the piano. She complied with that ready
confidence and ease, announcing her perfect mastery
over the accomplishment solicited. Her brilliant touch
at once commanded admiration; and the hearer hung
breathless between the matchless rapidity of the execution and the spirit it seemed to awaken from the
instrument, alternating between the softest pathos and
bursts of power and command. But how inadequate
was the admiration extorted by her instrumentation to
that unanimously accorded to her vocal power, when,
bursting into "*Di piacer mi balza il cuore*," her magnificent compass rose like some spirit, awing into submission the very genius of harmony. The clearness of
the voice, the nice articulation of each note, distinct
from its predecessor, yet so blent with it, that the one
seemed as imperfect without the other as the patriarch's ladder without the angels that connected it with
heaven; the brilliant *cadenza*, apparently taxing and
straining every power, yet dashed off with a facility as
though the minstrel, in the most refined labyrinth of
music, were only seeking and embodying the most spiritual tones and abstractions of language; but, above all,

the soul, the inspiration, proclaiming her Italian, that like some flower transplanted from its own, seemed to find as genial a sun in a foreign clime: all these I had never heard so rarely united in the *prime donne* of the day.

Amid the felicitations that greeted her as she rose from the instrument, I hurried forward to utter mine, even though it might be as a neglected garland upon the altar where all were offering oblations.

"Bella Bianca! 'tis well this truant hand saved you from the wave, else Parnassus would have become a desert, and the sweetest pæan of the Muses have been changed to elegy, had they missed so tuneful a sister from their number."

"As great a flatterer as Paris, Signor! *Your* Venus is Melpomené."

Bianca passed on; and I turned to join a small knot of loungers who were canvassing the talents whose recent triumph they had witnessed.

"We have never had her equal," said one; "her success is incontestable."

"Where?"

"At the Opera—"

"Pardon my abruptness, sir," I said to the speaker; "is the Signorina about to appear in public?" and, as I spake, I felt my hurried utterance, and the blood that flushed my cheek, too easily betrayed the interest I took in the reply.

"It is her intention, intimated to her friends, but not yet made public," was the answer.

I bowed and turned. I felt I was no longer the independent, self-relying, self-possessed being that I entered. Oh! well has mythology vailed the destructive power of the Siren under the fable of music; nor can we blame the world-weary wanderer, Ulysses, for binding himself to the mast to escape its fatal fascinations. 'Twas but within the last hour that I had stood within the enchanted circle, and no Circé had ever drugged a more delicious draught for her victim, or more dexterously woven a chain which was now entering my very soul. Yet, like Antony, I had but wooed the bondage; like him, too—I turned from the parallel. I felt myself now no longer my own master, but, like the lion, fretting and lashed amid the very toils my own imprudence had thrown around me. I should have known my own nature better, and avoided temptations calculated only to heighten passion without strengthening principle. But now the die was cast, "and I must stand the hazard of the throw." Then again, the thought of my outcast situation—my *poverty*—came over me, like the sirocco, kindling the hot blood of the fevered patient! What was my situation, that I dared to love? What my hopes, even if I did? Who should be the mate of beauty and talents, both of them unrivaled as hers? Ah! not I—not I!

With thoughts devouring and humiliating as these,

I wandered amid the festive scene like a ghoule, the foulness of the charnel-house still clinging to him amid the loveliness of paradise, and even in presence of its Eve. I had unwittingly plucked of the tree of knowledge; the fruit had turned my eyes inward and bared my own heart before me. I felt—I *knew* I loved. Did ancient philosophy, when it commended self-knowledge as the highest branch of human attainment, know what a desert city it was opening to the eye in the scathed and blackened and desolate regions of the heart? Had that philosophy been evangelized by that Spirit that came to raise and strengthen humanity, instead of turning our eyes to the waste and featureless nature that had forfeited its only claims to divinity, by losing the image of its God, it would have commanded us to raise our eyes to heaven, and in the majesty of day and the starry kingdoms of the night, taught us to adore the antetypes of that glory and perfection from which we had fallen, but to which mercy would restore the penitent. To return : The resolutions I had made, the chilling convictions of my situation and prospects, came to my aid; with a violent effort I tore the chain that was fast coiling its charmed links around me, and, with the self-deceiving Thane, who deluded himself with returning strength and manhood, at the very moment the cheek grew pale and the teeth chattered, I could cry, " I am a man again!"

The very moment my resolution seemed the most steadfast, the temptations appeared the strongest. The classic soul that breathed from and informed her beauty, the inspiration that swayed and gladdened her voice, like the finest vibration of the harp-string, sending back from earth the echo it has caught from heaven, had not enchanted me with a more spell-like fascination than I found the memory of our adventure, and of the life I accidentally rescued, had her. I felt the lustrous power of those Italian eyes, as they frequently rested on me through the evening, their native fire softened by those feelings my presence, perhaps, awakened. More than once I heard her utter my name, joined with the warmest epithets her own sweet language could suggest; and, as she rose from the piano, after her magnificent execution of the grand finale of "*Cenerentola*," I could observe her eye first rested on me for those plaudits my heart had silently uttered before they found their way to the lip. I did not dare to flatter myself; for I felt the cup must be thrown from me untasted.

The guests were fast diminishing as the night advanced, and yet I sauntered and lingered till the very last, like the weary mariner that hugs the shore for its surpassing beauty, though its waters conceal the rock and quicksand. I had a motive in remaining behind—the communication of my intentions to Bianca. I stated my wishes to her; and, apologizing for such a violation of etiquette on so brief acquaintance, she assented, and descending to a lower room, we were left alone. I feared to trust myself to a verbal opening of the interview, so merely handed her Desmond's letter, which she read and re-read; till, stupefied either with horror or incredulity, she stood like one rooted to the spot, the dreadful missive trembling in her hand.

"God help you! God help you, Signor!" were the first words she uttered; and though an alien to her and hers, I could see it was with difficulty she restrained the tears my misfortunes drew from her warm and generous nature. I blushed even more now for the unnatural—the brutal Desmond.

"And God bless you!" I answered, "for the tears your heart is shedding now for the poor and fatherless."

I anticipated the active sympathy my words had awakened, and arrested her hand as it was about to open an *escritoire.* My words were choked, my throat was hot and parched with the keenest self-indignation as I recalled that one word, "poor," and I seized her hand on the eve of raising a purse of gold.

"Lady, lady!" I cried, forgetting the generosity of the act in the anguish it produced; "you can not remember, surely, that this is a taunt to one in whose veins flows the blood of those with whom it is a proverb that, 'to a genuine Milesian every thing is modern save his own pedigree!' Can it be that a descendant

of the O'Moore lives to be a pensioner on the bounty
of a stranger? God! 'tis next to asking bread at the
door of your enemy."

"Deliverer and friend!" cried the sensitive Italian,
dashing the purse to the ground; but, ere she could
proceed, my convictions came to my aid, assuring me
of the error of imputing generosity to the base motive
I had ascribed.

"Lady, 'tis I who cry you pardon; the injustice of
a brother, the forgetfulness of a father, have exposed
me to the shifts and tides of fortune, but manhood forbids I should, therefore, seek alms of a stranger."

"And do you call *me* a stranger? Me, who, next
to my Creator, owe you very life? Oh! when separated (and who can tell how soon?) the sister can not
turn to the brother's name with a more passionate
fondness than I to yours!"

"Say you so, Bianca?" but, scarce had the words
fallen from me, than memory dwelt on the cold and
formal relation expressed in her words, and, like an
enchanter, dissolved in air the palace it had piled in
the clouds.

"Have you no warmer term for me than brother?"

"To your generous hand and brave heart I owe the
enjoyment of that gift first bestowed on me by the
Great Father of all," replied the Italian, her eyes inspired by the full light of adoration and truth as she
spoke; "and with your name shall be connected the

deepest feelings and most grateful memories that Father ever gave our nature to gladden and raise it. But—"

"What?" I cried, breathless with impatience, as the beautiful Italian paused; and, with every moment, felt that I was but more strongly enmeshing myself in the very toils I had resolved on bursting.

"Your father's sudden fate and brother's conduct have made you," she resumed, "an exile on your own soil; my fate has made me no less. Poor and dependent, like yourself, as that letter makes you, I have resolved to break the chain that has bound childhood and the earlier years of the woman, and carve for myself the way that want and indigence would close forever."

"And what do you resolve, Bianca?" but, ere the words had escaped me, the reply was anticipated.

"I am a daughter of Italy; with us song is as speech. You heard me to-night. Music is with me nature; I almost grudge the moments I give to the perfection of its art, for I thereby seem to rob the soul but to repay the sense. But for the solace I derive from this in the proud yearnings of dependence, I could almost desire to die in the land of my exile."

It was, then, true, what I had heard in the evening; Bianca was about to appear upon the stage. Yet what difference did it make in the feelings of one

D

whom uncontrollable circumstances separated from her, perhaps forever ?

"Mine is, indeed, a wayward fate, Bianca," I cried, with an emotion I vainly strove to suppress; "well may it derive its coloring and character from the danger, nay, the very strife with death, that frowned upon our first meeting. Yet, though about to part, let me not wrong my own nature, and the brightest moments that, perhaps, my life has known, by silencing my passion. Bianca, I love you; love you, but to utter that word of ill-fated passion, and see it wither.ere well in being; love you, but to feel I can never call that treasure my own, which so many hearts, while they admire, scarcely dare covet; love you, Bianca, but to say—farewell !"

The Italian stood fixed, as bewildered by feelings she could not interpret and dared not utter. I had, perhaps, touched a string in her nature whose vibration she was unwilling to hear; awakened feelings which, however she might acknowledge, she was yet determined to resist, from the force of circumstances that surrounded us both. I was about to leave the room, when we were both arrested by a voice in the street. It came from one of those ballad singers so common in the streets of Dublin, who, for a passing alms, will, perhaps, stir deeper feelings in the heart of the passer-by, by some simple old ditty, and its touching execution, than was ever felt amid the glare

and *top* of the opera, or the artifices and ornamenta-
tion of the Italian school. Some of the sweetest voices
I have ever heard, I have so heard as itinerant singers
in that city. The present was a voice of peculiar
sweetness, but melancholy to such a degree as to recall to the hearer that passage of the Irish bard,

> "Ah! little they think who delight in her strains
> How the heart of the minstrel is breaking!"

It seemed to speak a sorrow too deep even for the
mystic hand of music to touch ; and yet whose very
intensity seemed to borrow its only alleviation from
the high and subtle modes of harmony. But it was a
voice that petrified Bianca and myself; and while we
heard it, had it been a spectre revealing the secrets of
the prison from which it had but just risen, it could
not have struck more chill to the hearts of both. The
hour, too, was midnight ; the streets were deserted ;
and, above the grave-like stillness, we heard the following words. The voice was that of my mysterious
visitant. At such a moment it fell like an omen:

> "Oh! weep not for the dead, for thou canst never
> Dissolve the spell that binds as with a chain;
> No more than can the waters of the river
> Back to their fountain e'er return again.
>
> "Why weep, then, for the dead? or why recall
> The joy deceptive and the tear that burns?
> And why with ruthless hand rend back the pall
> That shades the silent in their mouldy urns?
>
> "Then weep not for the dead; the evening star
> That hovers o'er the sun's departing ray,

Ere dawn reburnishes her golden car
To light the track of the returning day !

" Weep—weep not for the dead ; for past and o'er
Is every trouble that hath dimm'd the eye ;
The heart shall tremble to its grief no more,
But claim its angel-kindred in the sky !"

At such an hour and from *such* lips ! I flew to the
window, but the singer had gone ! As surely as the
moon and stars were above me, that voice was hers ;
that mysterious woman, whose inexplicable connection with me continued under all circumstances of
death, or, as at the present moment, of passion and
despair. Exclusive of the solemn moment (that of
our parting), the words had a drear and heart-smiting
omen from the connection of the subject with my father's death. Could she—? But no, it was but superstition. Pale and trembling as Bianca herself, we turned on each other a gaze, in which we read feelings too
deep and ominous for language. I felt that the climax
of my fate had come, and that in these sad words I
read a warning to fly from a passion and a presence in
which I read but madness for the present, and for the
future—despair !

" Bianca !" I cried, seizing her hand, on which I
pressed kisses the warmest my nature had ever known ;
" Bianca, farewell ! Should we ever meet again—
But, no ; I care not to taste so delicious a cup again !
Farewell ! farewell ! And when mind and soul lavish
their praises on your genius, oh ! forget not Morven,

whose lucky hand preserved so rich a treasure to the world !"

I rushed from an interview I could no longer endure, leaving Bianca as much overwhelmed as myself by the ill-starred allusions that had closed it. I reached my chambers, and, flinging myself on my bed, strove to forget all—Bianca and myself. But there was one im· age refused to be expelled from my thoughts, whether sleeping or waking—that mysterious woman who filled my eye with a relief the more painful for the melancholy theme of her song and the heart-broken voice that uttered it.

CHAPTER VI.

The world would say this man hath courtliness;
His blood is gentle and his manner cold—
Is coldness breeding ? No. An outward symbol
Is breeding deemed of all the heart contains
Of brave or generous, good or pure. Your foe
May coldly nod or bend a haughty brow;
But, as for this man, warmth, humanity,
Are his Apocrypha.

IT requires no slight metaphysical skill to analyze our own feelings, even with the calm judgment of years and the knowledge afforded by their experience. Judge, then, what was my situation in the hey-day of my manhood, blinded and intoxicated by a passion that had swept on me with the suddenness of a tempest that bears upon its wing the fever of the simoom. In all the after-experience of my life, I can say that there is no feeling that grasps with such harpy power, or consumes and wastes with such relentless implacability as first love. It is the first launch of the soul into those dark and untried waters where life with all its priceless freight may prove a wreck; an initiation into mysteries which the scathed and withered heart would gladly exchange for the ignorance and cloudless hope of its infancy. Certain it is that all the after-strength

of the heart is weakened by this first struggle with
its great antagonist, and the feelings, in many cases,
reserved for marriage are those of calculation and expediency. But my task is not to moralize. My heart
has taken her impress, and I must bear that image
whithersoever I go. Farewell, Bianca! With thee I
seem to leave behind me the very sun of my day!

But a truce to sentiment; she lags, like "a foul and
ugly witch," in the moment that requires action and
energy. The whip cracks—the horn blows—the horses
strike fire from the pavement—I light my cigar, and
surrender myself to the varied dreams suggested by
my anticipated journey and reception; for, reader, I
am on my way to Deer Park, the time-honored seat of
the De Lacys, the Norman ancestry of the present proprietor, Sir Hubert De Lacy.

My ruminations were certainly any thing but cheerful or exhilarating. When I reflected on my present
situation I found it impossible to reconcile it with
fact, or my own convictions of its truth. Had I been
plebeian I could not have found myself more disowned or an outcast; instead of which the blood of me and
mine was among the oldest that flowed in the old Irish
aristocracy; had I been the child of a houseless pau-
per, cradled in poverty, and doomed to sustain the curse
of its heritage through my manhood, my lot could not
have been more forlorn and dependent than now when,
as brother to the heir of an ancient and wealthy estate,

I was about entering the world to bear its brunt and
weather its storms by my own labor and exertions.
" Thank God," I inwardly ejaculated at this point
of my lucubrations, " a good education, while it en-
dorses the gentleman, will on a pinch give support and
honorable independence to the man !" I was on the
very road, too, that led to Clonmuir Castle; that threshold I resolved never again to cross, and cared as little ever again to meet its present lordly owner. I could
have wished to have seen my father before his death,
were it but to receive his last benediction ; for cold
and lost to every high thought and privilege of our
nature is that heart that covets not the blessing of a
parent next to that of its God. That had been denied
me. Next in the sombre train of my thoughts arose
the image of Bianca ; her loveliness deriving a fresh
charm from the high character that marked her, and
her rich endowments of intellect and voice spreading out their golden chain to memory that dwelt with
rapture on each note of linked sweetness. That she
might have loved but for her own proud and independent resolutions, I could scarcely doubt ; that I loved
her I was, alas ! too certain. But as a proud man,
dared I in the circumstances in which I was placed
have solicited the hand of one whose genius and taste,
demanding the nurture of the refined and artificial,
must have required every luxury of wealth and refinement of art?

Such were the floating thoughts that alternately pleased and perplexed me during my solitary journey to Deer Park. Of its proprietor I had heard but little, and knew nothing. I was aware of the nature of the situation I was about to undertake; one which, exacting the education of a gentleman and the highest principles that the man can borrow from the Christian code, is too frequently enrolled by the ignorant and wealthy in the rank of upper servant. Fully aware of this usage, I was determined to act in such a manner as to assert with independence the credentials of gentleman and scholar, for which my situation vouched. In the adoption of an employment so novel to myself, I had but one end to subserve; and that a pecuniary one. I am the more honest in confessing this, from having frequently heard *soi-disant* philanthropists rhapsodize on the charms of teaching, and vaunt their own virtues to such an extent, that I have always met such assertions with incredulity, and the makers of them as hypocrites. For myself, I am free to confess I undertook the office merely as a temporary *savoir faire*.

At my journey's end; the horses are at rest. We have reached our destination, some three miles from Deer Park. I get out, look round. Has the reader ever experienced the *chill* of perfect loneliness pervade his system, when he has reached a strange place? I verily believe that, were it mid-day and the sun shining

D*

with a tropical ardor, still that very sense of isolation would make the teeth chatter. It is then we realize our true humanity; then that we look for one friendly glance or voice; and, oh! with what an overwhelming power come the memories of the absent on us to give, if possible, a greater vacancy to solitude.

I surveyed the scene for some time with that yearning for the sympathies of something human ever inspired by loneliness. My fellow travelers had each some welcome and desired object to greet and fill the vacuum of previous separation; for each there was a warm pressure of the hand, a kindly glance, a friendly word, some outward action or inward impulse that told him he was still an acknowledged link in the great chain; but for me there was none of this; to my own fancy, which I endeavored to cheat and spur into a dissembled cheerfulness, I stood before myself a Marius—on a small scale.

I inquired of the clerk, "Was there any one here from Sir Hubert De Lacy's?" I was pointed to his carriage; and immediately the servant, seeing I was the individual he came for, stepped forward and addressed me by name. Even the deferential tone of that poor menial had a momentary cheering for me. I inquired, "How far was Deer Park?" "Three miles, sir." Behold me, reader, and my solitary trunk installed in the family carriage of the De Lacys; the equipage and horses each most aristocratic in its kind, the hammer cloth and panels richly mounted with the old armorial bearings of the family.

It was sunset, and the slanting beams of that hour fell richly and mellowly on the surrounding country. The bold undulations embrowned with the first sere of autumn, a range of mountains on the horizon, and flanking like an impregnable rampart the treasure of hill and valley that lay at its base, the river that ran, and flashed, and dimpled in the light of the farewell sun, as though, like a parting friend, it anticipated a joyous meeting on the morrow; all these images were calculated to arouse and exhilarate, from my passionate love of nature.

We were already in the lordly demesne that led to the mansion. The huge, hoary trees that, like veteran sentinels, seemed to have guarded that pass for centuries, were worthy the honors of the ancient house that had been confided to their keeping. This thought, however, plumed up my family pride. Why talk of the antiquity of the *Norman?* It made the ancienter blood of the true Milesian tingle. My fathers had trodden this soil as hereditary owners, when the ancestry of the Norman was pursuing the roving life of a sea-king (*anglicé* robber) in the chill northern seas. That was some comfort; so I wrapped myself in the garment of my ancient pedigree, and snapped my fingers at the Norman *parvenu.*

The horses (superb brutes those) stop, the carriage,

as a necessary consequence, comes also to a stand;
and, before well aware of the fact, I find myself
standing on the threshold of the De Lacy. As in most
country houses, the hall entrance lay open; affording
the stranger, as myself, a *coup d'œil* of Sir Hubert's
ancestry; the chronology of each departed worthy
designated by the appropriate costume of his time,
from the bearded, steel clad warrior of Henry II., to
the more modern land owner in his robes of office and
full bottomed wig. Many of them, I observed, had
forsaken the old freebooting propensities by exchanging
the sword for the *toga;* and had prospered by this
great moral reformation, having, by their legal costume, administered the laws of their adopted land.
Though no friend to the Norman, I involuntarily bowed
my head to these images of departed aristocracy; for,
however the *parvenu* may sneer at what he derides,
the antiquity of lineage is to some minds as venerable
as that of ruin. The portraits were diversified with
suits of armor, deers' antlers, swords, &c., and all the
aristocratic appendages of an old Irish mansion. The
images and associations of the latter were familiar to
me at old Clonmuir Castle, where I was born; the
features of Sir Hubert's ancestry merely claimed my
attention.

While I was thus intent on my speculations, a
liveried servant came, with the compliments of Sir
Hubert De Lacy, and showed me to the withdrawing-

room, where he informed me his master would soon
wait on me. Ascending a magnificent oak staircase,
the landings of which were lighted by gothic windows
of stained glass, I reached the room. I need not
weary the reader with a detail of the furniture (combining richness of material with elegance of handicraft),
of which he may have formed a notion more accurate
even than my description. I had scarcely time for
even a superficial glance at the elegance and wealth
that surrounded me, when the massive oak door opened, and presented, in the person of Sir Hubert De Lacy,
a picture as sombre as the frame through which it
emerged.

"I have the pleasure of addressing Mr. O'Moore?"

I bowed—"Pray, be seated sir;" and, in the interval of taking my seat, I will venture a portrait of the
gentleman whose guest I was about to become.

Sir Hubert might have numbered some fifty summers. But there are some on whom the rack of grief
or feeling does more than the work of years—of this
class seemed the individual before me. He was commanding in stature; more bony than muscular; and
his attenuated form, when taken in connection with
the somewhat haggard expression of countenance,
bespoke a frame enfeebled either by grief or disease.
His face was marked to an extreme with the heavy
channels of care or bodily suffering, or something that
gave features, otherwise handsome and regular, an ex-

pression bordering on the ascetic. There was an unsteadiness in the eye, that bespoke him ill at ease either with himself or company; but, when its glance was concentrated on you, it was of that sinister and apprehensive character, that betrayed his fear of your reading his thoughts. As for the *tournure* of the Baronet it was aristocratic to a fault; the stoic coldness and imperturbable ease (those false requisites of *ton* that have banished nature and heart from society), figured in Sir Hubert with such affluence as to satisfy the most fastidious.

Dignity and reserve I observed were the current coin of society at Deer Park; so, like Richard, I resolved not to be out of fashion. I assumed my most freezing manner, gave my most laconic replies; and, feeling that I was there merely for the accomplishment of a certain aim, resolved to repay all this artificial *finesse* of manner by a mixture of the courtesy of the gentleman with the independence of the man. The conversation was short and commonplace, as introductory interviews generally are. He hoped I was not fatigued—that I would like my residence and pupil at Deer Park—complimented me on the high character my tutor had given me for classical proficiency, and finally wound up by pulling the bell, and ordering the butler to show Mr. O'Moore to his room, where I might prepare for dinner, etc.

Myself and that everlasting companion of celibacy,

an old trunk, adjourned under the guidance of the
servant to hold our meeting in my bedroom; in which
I found a cheerful fire, by which I stood for some
moments prior to my preparations for dinner and the
awful process of disemboweling that trunk. Having
donned my best, and rendered my figure, naturally
prepossessing (forgive me, reader; for why attempt a
hero without some description of his person?) very
presentable, I heard the dinner tocsin sound, and
made a desperate plunge from my dormitory.

I entered the superb dining-hall, oak-wainscoted, the
rich Turkey carpet yielding luxuriously to the pressure of the foot. The huge fire-place with its massive fagots, reared as for a funeral pile, heightened the
comfort and chaste beauty of the apartment with its
broad crimson glare. However, accustomed to all this
from my infancy at Clonmuir Castle, I trod with the
self-possession of an *habitué;* of one, who though
young in society, was a veteran to its luxuries and
most refined habitudes. As I entered, Lady De Lacy
and Sir Hubert were standing by the fire-place, to the
former of whom I received from the Baronet a formal
presentation. The lady seemed a mate worthy of the
cold and passionless block to whom her destiny had
united her; possessing, in addition to the stoicism of
her husband, an imperiousness of manner and expression, which seemed to assert whatever dignity of
person and station the ignorance of the world might

withhold from her. An instinctive glance told me her
character, and sensibility whispered me that I was
only a tutor in the eyes of her Ladyship, so I amply
repaid the formality of her salutation by my recognition of the same. She was certainly very handsome ;
but the expression of her mouth was that of the most
withering disdain, of which my subsequent intercourse
showed me Sir Hubert received no slight share.

Scarcely had I returned her ladyship's salute, when
Sir Hubert's only daughter, the Lady Geraldine, entered, leading by the hand my future pupil, young
Connal. Here was a gulp, so I mustered all becoming fortitude to swallow the dose; for, as I observed,
teaching was imposed on me only by the stern obligations of poverty and desire for independence, and the
presence of this youth realized its horrors of dull routine and stupefying inanition. I was, of course, expected to be amiable and insinuating on the occasion
to my future *protégé*. I was as amiable as my
thoughts and repulsive reception would allow me. I
shook his hand, patted him on the head (about ten
years of age), complimented him on his looks (he *was*
a very handsome boy), hoped we should be very good
friends, etc., etc. I willingly raised my eyes from the
boy, the living embodiment of the school-room and its
elementary stupefactions, to fix them on a fairer picture, the Lady Geraldine. Not possessing a regular
feature, but eyes of remarkable animation, shifting like

a kaleidoscope, and betraying every beautiful image
that crossed and gladdened her heart, Lady Geraldine
was a thing of beauty to the eye that rested on her.
There was a joyousness of nature and manner, an
elasticity of mind and soul, that seemed surfeited with
their inward treasure, and longed to make others par-
ticipant of their bounty. The stranger involuntarily
looked from father to daughter, and vainly strove to
fathom the possibility of a connection between them.
Her exquisite *bonhommie* of manner for the moment
disenchanted the freezing impressions left on me by
the worthy Baronet and his lady; and made me feel
that Deer Park was not a monastery, nor was Morven
O'Moore a candidate for the rigid austerity and pious
celibacy of its vows. She welcomed me as warmly as
the delicacy of our relative positions would permit. I
had omitted to mention the more than paternal fondness lavished on and expressed for young Connal by
Sir Hubert. Even in presenting him to me he caressed
and hung over the boy, expressing an almost deeper
and more inexplicable feeling than was, perhaps, war-
ranted by his relation of father. I confess I did not
notice this much at first, but was particularly attracted by it in our subsequent intercourse, in case of any
allusion to the boy or my future relations to him as
tutor. It fell incidentally in conversation, that the
Lady Geraldine and Connal were children by a first
marriage, and that the imperious lady, who well-nigh

frightened me from my propriety, was Sir Hubert's second launch in the great sea of matrimony.

"Any relation to the O'Moore of Clonmuir Castle?" inquired the Baronet, with a suddenness that fell like thunder on me. To give me preparation of a second or so for reply, I addressed myself assiduously to my wine glass.

"Ah! are there O'Moores in your neighborhood?" I answered, as imperturbably as I could, seeking to evade the question.

"Oh! yes.—No relation?"

"Not that I have heard. How far, pray, do they reside from this?" I felt the blood rising rapidly at this conscious dissimulation.

"Some ten miles. Splendid estate—all unencumbered—proprietor recently murdered."

I can not tell the torture I endured at these cold fragmentary ejaculations of conversation, that seemed, with all the dexterity of the surgeon's probe, to be anatomizing my poor father's remains even in the quiet sanctuary of the grave. It seemed that I would gladly have given away both Clonmuir and Deer Park to escape this persecution, as horrible as it was unintentional.

"A sad business that," resumed the Baronet, with the resolution of a hound which has found the scent, and is unwilling to abandon the chase; "very sad, and just as strange. He was murdered while walk-

ing in his demesne. Such crimes are generally
perpetrated from the motive of robbery; but, very
strange, when his body was discovered, his purse (containing several sovereigns) was found untouched."

"Indeed?" I almost started at the temerity of my
own voice.

"His younger son has been, we understand, disinherited, but no cause assigned."

"Dissipation and extravagance, Sir Hubert," interposed her Ladyship.

"Ah! yes, so it was—I remember now."

This was as terrible an artillery as a man could
well be exposed to. I withstood the fire with the
coolness of a French Imperial, wondering where the
next shot would light.

"Did you know him at Trinity?" resumed the
Baronet, following up with unexampled diligence the
victory he was every moment on the eve of gaining.

"But slightly." This reply was followed by a
strong appeal to the wine glass, and a fervent prayer
to some good genius to come to my aid, and relieve
my embarrassment by a change of theme. The Lady
Geraldine, with an ingenuous promptness, came with
the desired reinforcement, in the shape of a pack of
hounds.

"Do you admire the chase, Mr. O'Moore?" and the
sparkle of her eye bespoke the sympathy she felt in
this most exhilarating of all recreations.

"Passionately," I returned; "and there are few sights that present me with a more perfect image of the Amazon than a woman ready mounted for the field."

"We will afford you here every opportunity for indulging your taste."

"It will be the more gratifying if, in your person, I have the pleasure of recalling the image I have endeavored to describe."

I will not weary the reader with detailing the small talk, which, like the *entrémets*, serves to adorn and give zest to the more solid viands of the dinner table. The unlucky subject to which Sir Hubert had alluded, while it revived my own painful and outcast relations to the home of my birth, awakened some degree of alarm as to a possible meeting with Desmond, from the proximity of Deer Park to the Castle. There was but one hope on which I relied to frustrate this fear; that was, the non-visiting terms on which our families lived.

Wine and coffee dispatched, we adjourned to the withdrawing-room, where the brilliancy of a superb chandelier was agreeably modified and relieved by the old oak cases that inclosed a costly collection of books. The first object that arrested me was a magnificent harp. Can any true-hearted Irishman, that loves to wander back to the days—

> "Ere the emerald gem of the western world
> Was set in the crown of a stranger,"

look on this national symbol without regretting the desuetude into which it is falling as a national instrument? And, as I write, I can not forbear reverting to the high and almost extravagant eulogy lavished on the proficiency of the Irish on this instrument by Giraldus Cambrensis, when he visited this island in company with Prince John. Had I his work by my side, I would willingly transcribe it; but I presume my female readers will gladly dispense with the infliction, as the original is Latin. Suffice it to say, I have never read a higher compliment passed on the genius of a nation, than this confers on the musical attainments of the Irish. But the Irish harp, at present unstrung by the rude hand of faction and strife, will yet, I trust, revive those harmonies that have gladdened the halls of her princes, and inspired the souls of her warriors.

With that harp was connected an image and a memory; Bianca and our parting rose up before me, colored with a force and energy time or distance could not efface. What would I not have given to hear her masterly touch and thrilling voice once again? But I turned my thoughts to the fair hand of Geraldine, and the Irish strains that seemed even now to break from the strings.

"This harp lacks a minstrel," I said, turning to the Lady Geraldine.

"Then is it the meeter type of a country that

mourns for her freedom," she answered. "You remember the beautiful apostrophe of the Psalmist to
the silent harp of Judah, when captive Israel wept by
Babel's stream."

"Yet even in that complaint did the Psalmist sweep
the strings, and wake them from their silence. Will
Miss De Lacy follow the example?"

Taking her seat at the harp, and sweeping the chords
in one glorious diapason, that seemed like a wail of
the instrument over the glories of a country it had
once and even now symbolized, the masterly prelude
found such an echo in my nature, that the tears involuntarily started, as though I were under the fascination of a spell I could neither evade nor resist. The
enchantment was completed when the brilliant voluntary was succeeded by a voice of such pathos and
sweetness, as though the very soul of her country were
breathing in and informing every tone. The halls of
Tara, her Red Branch Knights, their martial prowess,
and her present desolation, interrupted only by the
sound that told her "tale of ruin," all were before me;
more than painted, *breathed* into that holy and Pro-
methean being that gladdens for a moment the world
of the poet.

"That melody is even more touching when it comes
from lips like yours, Miss De Lacy. It is the Norman hand has rent the string from the Irish harp."

"But those feuds are now forgotten," she replied,

with a smile that seemed to extinguish them: and
Irish and Sassenach are brothers."

"At least *not enemies*," I returned, seeking to avoid
a subject that galled me.

"Prove that we are friends," she answered, "by
singing within the walls of the Norman one of your
own melodies."

To resist, I must have been more than man; so I
complied by accompanying myself on the piano to one
of the Irish melodies.

On the following morning my pupil and I met by
appointment in the school-room. I was surprised by
an early visit from the Baronet, who, after a more
than paternal caress to my charge, whose tenderness
seemed to combine an apprehension of some peril or
injury to the child in the future, thus addressed me :

"At the exceedingly tender age of Connal, Mr.
O'Moore, I do not desire his faculties to be taxed by
too much application; indeed, it is almost a conde-
scension for one of your high classical attainments
to undertake the charge of one whose extreme youth
can lay no exaction on them."

At this unexpected relaxation of Sir Hubert's stiff-
ness, and implied compliment, I bowed. Sir Hubert
proceeded :

"His health, too, is delicate; another reason why
I should hope his studies would be prosecuted with
extreme leniency." As Sir Hubert spoke, I observed a

slight tremor of the lip, and a pallor gradually stealing over brow and cheek. I found it impossible to reconcile this allusion to Connal's delicacy with the boy's appearance; presenting, as it did, unusual symptoms of strength and robustness. The full ruddy cheek, the bright eye, the healthful physical development even beyond a boy of his years, made me involuntarily turn from the boy to his father, who was not slow in reading the expression of incredulity with which I answered his observations. Seeing that his sudden emotion also had not wholly escaped my notice, he said, with a faint smile:

"It is strange, Mr. O'Moore, that I never speak of that boy, but a feeling seizes me I can neither explain nor resist. *On his life hangs mine,* and when *he* dies all *my* hopes are buried with him."

He regarded me with an expression of anxiety approaching sternness, which I met with one doubtless as penetrating; for I vainly sought from his looks a solution of the mystery I could not find in his words.

"You wonder, sir," he resumed, "but it is true. There is scarcely an ordinary peril to which boys are so frequently exposed in their sports which does not fill me with an alarm bordering on the superstitious."

I started; Sir Hubert sought to retract the words, but it was too late. The shaft had done its work and the archer could not recall it.

"I have been inconsiderate in my language, sir, but

fond parents will sometimes be foolish. Oh God, what a parent sometimes suffers."

As he proceeded I felt more and more bewildered; like an adventurer threading a labyrinth apparently endless in its tortuousness, and to whom the lengthening clew seems to unwind new passages, and but mystify the darkness more. My perplexity was still the more aggravated when I observed the intense emotion of the speaker, amounting to pain, and the momentary weakness that compelled him to lean against the mantle-piece for support. He rallied and proceeded:

"He is the child, sir, of my first wife, and in ether countries might be regarded the child of omen, even of fate."

Now was my turn for alarm; and I need not say the strong expressions of the speaker, coupled with a painful sincerity, inspired me with a feeling so vague and mysterious, that to escape it I would willingly have relinquished the office I had assumed, with all its anticipations of profit.

"I share your alarm, sir," I replied, "to the fullest extent, and beg to inquire, do these solemn circumstances of which you speak in any way influence my relations with your son? If so, I must beg leave to be released from so fearful a responsibility."

I narrowly scanned him as I spoke; for I am honest to confess that my own immediate troubles were

E

of a nature too absorbing to allow me any participation, in those of others.

"Not in the least, sir; not in the least," interposed the Baronet, with a haste that expressed his apprehension; "it would pain me more than I can tell you, should you abandon a charge for which your tutor's commendations bespeak such requisites. I pray you most earnestly, continue your offices to my son, and let your relations to my boy be those of a brother."

"I shall endeavor, Sir Hubert, to the best of my abilities, to fulfill the confidence you so generously repose in me; premising, however, in my own exculpation, that, should any injury befall him during my charge of Connal, you exonerate me wholly from any fault or responsibility in the same."

"Most certainly, sir; and, in anticipation, I thank you for your kind offices."

"Pardon me, Sir Hubert, does Lady De Lacy share these apprehensions for the boy entertained by yourself?"

A stern frown succeeded my question; and I feared that I had transgressed propriety in putting it.

"Lady De Lacy shares none of these apprehensions, Mr. O'Moore; and, I fear, would be perfectly indifferent should the father's worst fears be realized."

So much for the amiability of step-mothers, thought I, and the happiness of the miserable progeny bequeathed to them by others. "Good-morning, Mr.

O'Moore," said the Baronet, " I leave entirely to your discretion and kindness the course you deem expedient to pursue with my son. We meet at dinner," and Sir Hubert bade me *au revoir*.

The reflections left me by his communication were neither very pleasing in their nature nor calculated to incite me to a cheerful discharge of those duties I had undertaken. I sate down and endeavored to solve the problem; but I found it as vain as undertaking one in mathematics without the requisite *data*. The emotion visible in every feature of the wretched father, and the intense sincerity that animated his words, while they excited my sympathy, did not serve to attract me to the discharge of those functions I had assumed at Deer Park. But, while I am lost in these abortive reflections, behold, my little pupil waits.

I found him gentle and tractable in disposition, of rare mental apprehension, and partaking an interest in his little studies far stronger than that usually possessed by those of the same age. To a handsome exterior he united an engagingness of manner and affectionate disposition, that soon gained on me, and tended in a great measure to alleviate the obligations of a task, dull, drudging, and exacting. I felt also an additional tie to my pupil from the melancholy and mysterious allusions made by his father. I began now to regard him with an interest exceeding even the relation that existed between us; and, as day by

day his superior qualities of mind and heart enlisted
my affections toward him, so as to realize the parting
injunction of Sir Hubert, that my discipline should be
that of a brother. I could not resist the evil omen contained in the line,

> "Whom the gods love die young."

It was not for me, however, to encourage this impression, and still less to inquire into the nature of the
communication the Baronet had but partially revealed
to me. As long as my connection with Connal did
not in any way influence the probable dangers or evils
to which his father alluded, I saw no reason why I
should secede from the office I had assumed. As to
the gloomy bodings that arose from the boy's singular
quickness of parts and amiable disposition, I resolved
to drive them from my mind, and address myself to
my duties with kindness and energy.

Under the system I adopted, Connal made great
proficiency, and the extreme dislike I had to the occupation was in part removed by the advancement of
my pupil and the reward it gave my exertion. Meanwhile, as the boy grew in mind, so he waxed in
strength and general *physique;* the bright eye was
not dimmed, the glow on his cheek was supplanted
by no pallor, and as I occasionally would revert to
Sir Hubert's mysterious misgivings at our first interview, the fear they then inspired yielded in time to
impressions of the ludicrous. As he sate at his books

I would regard and analyze the features and expression of the boy, vainly seeking in either for a verification of his father's fears; and, at length, concluded that the origin of these must lie deeper than the health or appearance of my charge.

Our relations of study being terminated for the day, and becoming more agreeable than I had even dared to hope, we would leave the mansion, and pursue together whatever sports or occupations the grounds presented. In these excursions little Connal was my constant companion, and a delightful one, as far as the disparity of our years permitted. Were we bent for the road, by Connal's orders was my horse ready saddled at the door at the appointed hour; if we took to the lake, the boat and tackle were in readiness; or did we choose a walk, my little companion was at my side, his quickness affording a pleasant stimulus to my mind, and his observations showing an appreciation and depth of feeling toward the natural beauties around us, rarely to be met in one of his years. His nature was pure, lofty, and noble; deeply imbued with those higher impulses that originate from strong religious impresssions. Indeed, the latter principle was preeminent in the mental conformation of Connal. In our occasional rambles through his father's grounds or the surrounding country, rich with features to address the contemplative mind or awaken the deepest feelings, I was greatly struck with the influ-

ence of the lovely scenery upon the boy; and where
others would have beheld in it merely external forms
and objects to address and please the eye, I soon discovered in the boy a mental principle going deeper
than the surface, one which traced in the grace and
beauty of surrounding phenomena a directing hand
and intelligence, controlled by beneficence for the joy
and happiness of man. Day by day I discovered (and
with pleasure, for though a hater of cant, I love and
admire *true* religion) a growth of this principle, an
upward springing, as it were, of the boy's mind from
the dim and unsatisfying light of earth, to that perfect revelation of God's glory, seen by the eye of faith
alone, beyond the vail of our own being. His observations argued a deeper spirit of inquiry, and a more
settled and steadfast faith than I have often found in
Christians of matured evangelical experience. Whence
to trace this—I can not call it precocity, for it seemed
not to have that bright but unsteady light, that in-
herent principle of decay that usually marks it—I was
at a loss. It could not be attributed to any parental
care that had been bestowed on the boy's religious
culture; for, though I had observed the Baronet's religious faith bordered on the gloomy and superstitious,
and the Lady De Lacy seemed perfectly indifferent to
the subject, the boy's spiritual welfare seemed to be an
object of care to neither. It was one of those strange
developments, whether of the mental or moral world,

of whose origin we are wholly ignorant, though we acknowledge its existence. Who can trace the first germination (in cases not hereditary) of genius, whose destiny is to dazzle or destroy, and, like the lightning, make men tremble while they wonder? As well seek in the seed for its germinating principle, or in the earth for its fecundity and fertilizing power!

CHAPTER VII.

God's Spirit once did move upon the waters,
And liveth yet on earth; it lingers still
In every lovely vision summer weaves
For her glad worshiper.   Beautiful May !
Thou art an ante-type of heaven !

        The garland's wreathed.
Why twine that envious myrtle with the rose ?
'Tis ever thus ; Life hath her opposites—
Th' Egyptian banquet had its skeleton,
And in the conqueror's chariot sate the slave,
While spark electric wings the frozen hail.

SO passed my days at Deer Park during the winter.
The Baronet's manner was gradually relaxing, betraying symptoms of growing confidence and esteem ;
Lady De Lacy as imperious (I might almost say imperial) and unapproachable as ever ; and the dashing,
ingenuous Geraldine more and more captivating, if not
by the winning kindness of her manner, by the sweetness and heart-power of her voice.   But was I to forget Bianca—her very existence, from the accidents of
her life and her high-toned classic nature, partaking
more of the poetic than the real?   I dreaded the question when put by the searcher, and turned from it in
fear—of myself.

The winter had now passed, and the first burst of spring that, like a resurrection, awakens such an animating influence on the outward world, seems also to extend its talisman to man, calling forth emotions and impulses that through winter have lain dormant only to be fledged by the breath of spring, and borrow its wing for an upward flight. May was approaching: beautiful May!—the bride of the year; her breath all incense, her path of flowers, and her garland dyed of colors that nature seems to have borrowed from the rainbow to deck her favorite child withal. May, beautiful May! The birds chant her epithalamium, earth pours forth her loveliest tributes for bridal gifts, and heaven spreads out her starry curtain to guard the flowery slumbers of her child!

A *fête champêtre* was proposed at Deer Park to celebrate the advent of this sweet stranger; yes, one of those delicious country *fêtes* redolent of the place where it is celebrated, in which hand, voice, heart, every social feeling and gladdening impulse are thrown like incense on the altar to welcome her, whose gifts are those of a God, yet whose greetings are friendly and hearted as those of a sister. From my heart I pity the man who has lost his sympathy with nature; her bold and beautiful forms, her influences of all seasons breathed, as it were, from the very presence of the Maker she represents; her wild and mystic music touched by the hands of invisible spirits that hymn to

E *

earth the harmonies of their native heaven, her gentle
and gentle modes holding communion with all natures,
mourning for the sad and mirth for the joyous;—all
these bespeak her the image of God; and the heart
that can not vibrate to her touch has lost its sense to
the Religion and Being she represents.

The bright and budding first of May has come; and
with it awakes many a sparkling eye and many a glad
heart. The birth of that jocund month was to be welcomed; and we were to join our chorus of gladness to
the loud pæan that chirruped from every tree and lent
music to every breeze. Invitations were issued from
Deer Park the country round; and the first of May
was to be regarded in the neighborhood as a saturnalia of nature, on which the young and beautiful of
both sexes were to meet to welcome the birth of a sister as beautiful, though, alas! more short-lived than
they. And they came, those sweet sisters! The garlands they wore were of May's bright livery; the ringing laugh was but an echo of the sweet hymn their
sister sang from every tree, and hill, and valley; and
the bright eye that glanced forth the heart's purity
and worship was but a reflex of that golden sun and
cloudless sky that showered down ethereal splendor
on the rainbow path of this beautiful child of earth.

At some distance from the mansion lay a beautiful
valley intersected by a lake, to whose borders sloped
high banks rich with luxuriant vegetation and wild

flowers. It was a valley of such sweet seclusion and romantic features that it might have well have served as the prototype to that of Rasselas. It was one of those spots formed, as it were, for the retirement of the world-weary spirit, where in devotional seclusion it might the better enjoy the presence of its God in all the beautiful and benevolent images planted by his love. Such might have formed a retreat for the eremites of the early Christian world, where contemplation might lend wings to the soul fettered by the cares of the world or terrors of persecution, and read in the form of the leaf, or the ripple of the wave, that sublime Providence whose rule extends from the birth of a God to the death of a worm. Such was the spot I have but faintly described, appointed for our happy first of May meeting. Alas! alas! how many eyes have since closed with the bright flowers of that heavenly morning!

From Deer Park behold us then starting; the venerable mansion from mistress to maid is all bustle and excitement: carriage, gig, cabriolet and tax-cart—every vehicle, of every variety and shape that ingenuity can contrive or convenience demand, is put in requisition to convey our merry party to Fairy Vale. But was there ever a joy in this world that had not its leaven? an emotion of delight that recalls not the old Horatian motto:

Nil est ab omni parte beatum?

Ere we start I receive a beckon from the Baronet to attend him in his study.

"Mr. O'Moore," he proceeded, "to detain your young pupil to-day from so festive a scene would appear a punishment for which I could assign no adequate reason. Indeed, a scene of youth and mirth, as the present promises to be, is best adapted to those of his years. Yet I have my misgivings—"

The worthy man checked himself; I observed the same pallor of the cheek, the same tremor of the lip, as on the former occasion.

"Misgivings, Sir! What could possibly befall him in such company and on such an occasion?"

"Death!" answered Sir Hubert, in a tone of such sorrowful depth, that one might have imagined the gloomy image stamped on the very heart that uttered it.

"Death!" I retorted; "it is true, Sir, the sincere Christian should ever be prepared for this most solemn of all events; it is the arrow that flieth by night and the pestilence that walketh by noon, but in cases of extreme youth and apparent health—"

"Apparent!" iterated the Baronet, with a painful emphasis, "it is deceitful always to trust appearances. Who would look for the wasting consumption in the bright bloom of the hectic, or for the full vigor of muscular power in the last violent spasm that precedes dissolution? Apparent!—" And Sir Hubert paused, as seeking for an additional confirmation of his fanciful philosophy.

"I really, Sir Hubert," I interposed, anxious to lend what poor consolation I could, to what I deemed and pitied as a monomania—"I can not see what apprehensions you should entertain in the present case."

"Ah! of course," quietly interposed the Baronet; "I know apprehensions seldom meet sympathy, as they never extend beyond the person who entertains them. But there are hopes and fears bound up in that little life that would, perhaps, as much appall you as me. Yes, appall. Fool! fool! Mr. O'Moore, I pray you, let not your eye wander from him; let him have your care—(as he has had)—that of a brother—"

"Pardon for the interruption, Sir Hubert; would it not be better, under the distressing circumstances you have related, to retain Connal under your own immediate supervision?"

"It would too much resemble a punishment, while to myself it would only serve as a fresh confirmation of my fears."

"In that case, Sir, all I can do is to assure you that Connal shall have my care and watchfulness."

"A thousand thanks," said the Baronet, while he squeezed my hand—and we parted.

"A pleasant situation this!" thought I, as I passed along the corridor; "one of the delectabilities of

teaching. To go to a *fête*, for the purpose of enjoyment, with a boy tied, like the apple of your eye, to
you, is like expecting from a man in chains the graces
and attitudes of the dancing-master. *N'importe ;*
Master Connal must look out for himself."

And now behold us in full career for Fairy Vale :
whips crack, the mettled steeds snort and toss up the
gravel, as though they were about to be participants,
not servitors, in the coming festival. The laugh rings,
the jest passes, the repartee perches on the lip, like
shaft waiting its impulse from the string; the eye
glances its brightest, the heart beats its gladdest, and
" all goes merry as a marriage-bell."

Arrived on the lovely slope of the Vale, we could
not but pause in admiration of the countless and prodigal beauties that nature had lavished on this, her
favorite haunt. It seemed to spread beneath us like
a garden of Armida, heaping together its richest treasures to adorn the palace of the enchantress. The
green slopes, here and there diversified with a bold
projection of rock, looked like sentinels guarding with
jealous fidelity the paradise intrusted to their keeping ; while the lovely lake, that slept in its summer
dreams, resembled a mimic heaven that had transplanted to earth all the unrivaled hues and forms of
its native seat. The eye could scarcely rest on so
sweet a spot without a secret prayer, that such might
be the refuge of our last hour, the resting-place which

would give sanctity to our ashes when the spirit had
fled forever!

But it was not alone the natural loveliness of the
place that arrested the eye, and awoke the deepest
poetry of the heart. Where Nature had been prodigal, Art had not been backward in contributing the
beauties of her creative power. Every natural feature
of that exquisite valley had been seized by the eye
and hand of the artist, to enhance its native loveliness, and bring out new phases and developments
suitable to the romance of the scene or festivity of the
occasion. Arbors had been constructed, festoons flung
their bright chain of flowers, wooing the eye with
their grace and flexibility, and scenting the summer
air with their censer of nectar. The waters of the
lake alternately slumbered in shade or leaped in the
sunbeam, while their bosom was swept with flower-
wreathed boats, that plied their enameled way, like
Peris, allowed to track their beautiful path during sunlight, but at evening winging their flight for their eternal home. There were four principal arbors, whose
rich yet quaint decorations symbolized the myth of the
Four Seasons: it was a happy conceit, and as happily
executed—from the first blossom of spring to the last
icicle of winter; and to each there was attached a
small retinue of lovely children, in their attire allegor-
izing the parts they bore as representatives or tutelar
genii of the respective seasons. To heighten all, a

superb military band, of the regiment quartered near,
alternately swelled or sank with its echoes along the
surrounding slopes or waters, lulling the spectator into
dreams of sky-land.

We had not long descended the hills, at the base
of which were gamboling the little bands of children,
waving their garlands, or twining their flower-chains,
like so many Cupids on the watch for some pilgrim
heart to snare in their meshes, their tiny voices like
so many bells ringing on the ear, when we were summoned to perform the first important business of the
day—the election of a May Queen. The process of
balloting for our sovereign was invested with as much
refinement as our own fancies could suggest, or the
occasion required. Each suffragan attached the name
of his *inamorata* to a rose, and deposited it in a
flower-box. To avoid tediousness to the reader, the
result of the election was the unanimous announcement that " Miss Geraldine De Lacy was Queen of
Beauty and of May, and that all loyal subjects were
expected to obey their Sovereign Mistress !" This important step accomplished, the queen-elect ascended
her throne (of moss, with a rich flower mosaic), bowed most graciously to her subjects (in the toadying
phrase of English journalism), and, crowned and
sceptred in due form by the attendant sprites, was
doomed to the infliction (?) of the following apostrophe to the different seasons personated by the

infant singers. The reader can pass it if he deems it a bore:

HYMN TO THE SEASONS.

I.

How softly rests the sun upon us now,
As though all heaven were open to the view;
And its bright Hierarchy showered below,
From 'neath their waving wings of golden hue,
All light they borrowed from the Eternal throne,
    When vailed before their God they stand,
    Each casting down his burning zone,
The fadeless starlight of that Better Land!
    Lo! Silence every where
Pillowed on downy waves of sleeping air;
    Silence, such as swayed
Creation, when God sent his fiat forth,
Commanding Light to be, and Light was made,
While guilty Darkness fled the face of earth!
Hail, holy Summer! Sabbath of the skies!
Flowers weave thy robe and Beauty holds thy train,
Heaven tesselates thy path with fadeless dyes,
And weaves thy chaplet bright of golden grain,
    Thy locks are braided with the dew,
And clasped the zone with flowers of brightest hue!

II.

What spirit moves within yon holy shrine?
'Tis Spring; the year's young bride that gladly pours
Above—around—an effluence divine
Of light and life, falling in golden showers.
And with her come the sportive nymphs in dance,
Like waves that gambol in the Summer's glance;
Untwining bowers from their winter's sleep,
Unlocking rivers from their fountains deep;
Tinting the leaf with verdure, that had lain
Long hid, like gold within the torpid grain,
Chanting her choral song, as Nature's eyes
First greet the bridal of the earth and skies.

III.

The Spring is past; and blushing Summer comes,
Music and Sunshine throng her scented way;
The birds send gladly from their bowered homes
Their pæan at the birth of flowery May!
From close to shut of day; yes, far and near
The spell of mystic music chains the ear;
All Nature from her bosom pouring forth
Sounds, such as make a Temple of the earth,
Returns in one full stream of harmony
The angel echoes that she hears on high,
Beautiful Summer! fling thy crown of flowers
O'er this dull earth through Winter's weary hours;
Let them not fade; oh! let not sere and blight
Darken thy prism'd couch with shade of Night;
Let not thy music ever break its spell,
Like heaven-bound pilgrim bidding earth—" Farewell!"
Oh! silence not thy music, let thy flowers
Be earth's bright stars responding to the skies;
Wreathing her graves with those immortal bowers
Thy rosy hand twined round the Dead in Paradise!

IV.

Oh! not a vision here, but it must pass,
Like our own image from Life's spectre glass;
Summer is faded, and the Autumn sere
Gathers the fallen leaves upon her bier;
And, like the venomed breath of the Simoom
That turns Zahara's desert to a tomb,
Breathes on the buried Summer's shrined abode,
And leaves a spectre what she found—a God!
'Tis thus ye Woods! your melancholy tale
Hath more of truth than rose and lily pale,
When the bright glories of the Summer vie
To make the earth a mirror of the sky;
In Autumn's time-worn volume do we read
The sacred moral—*all things earthly fade;*
And trace upon the page of every leaf
That first and latest human lesson—grief!

V.

But hark ! that dreary blast that rolls
Like heart-wrung wailings of unburied souls,
    'Tis the Winter's breath
    That comes from the land of Death
    Where the Arctic fetters the main ;
        Like the lightning it darts
        When its water parts
    And dissolves, like the cloud in rain.
    And now pale Winter cometh frore
From the dark North's drear and lifeless shore ;
    And, round his form, trembling and old,
    Hangs his snow robe in drifting fold,   ,
As that ye see on the mountain height;
Like Death asleep in the calm moonlight,
His diadem gleams with the icicle bright,
And his sceptre of ice to destroy and to smite ;
Like a monarch he sweeps from the mount to the vale
In his chariot that gleams with hoar-frost and hail;
His palace the iceberg adorned with spars,
Like a wandering heaven all fretted with stars !

VI.

Temples of eldest Nature, fare ye well !
God-made Cathedrals ! ye whose incense streams
        Like Adoration's soul
    At sound of matin or of vesper bell,
    When the choired harmonies roll
        'Mid the organ's swell,
And heaven reveals itself to Worship's dreams,
Farewell ye Temples, piled and arched by Him
Whose praise for aye shall echo through your tracery dim,
        Not dark ; for, while the sun looks down,
        Image of God's fadeless crown,
            Or, while the holy moon
Lights up her cresset for the midnight noon,
Upon your shrines shall burn that holy ray,
Earth's foretaste of a distant, endless day.
Holy of Holies ! bared to man, adieu !
When Nature consecrates the heart, that heart's with You !

This ode ended, the choir broke up into bands; the green sward peeping brokenly through the mazes of the dance, and the rich natural mosaic of flowers that tesselated it.   On—on they threaded the dance, those gay and happy children, like visitants sporting in the bright pathway of the Summer they were commission-ed to bear to earth.   The dance concluded, they broke away in frolic and mirth, their bright eyes and glad voices the best interpreters to the loveliness of the season they had chanted.

Meantime while these little allegories were disport-ing themselves, we had not observed that a large green silk curtain had been dropped in front of the arbor assigned to the Queen of May.   Nor was the assem-blage fully aware of the fact till the withdrawal of the curtain disclosed a new feature, which, while in perfect keeping with the floral occasion we were cele-brating, lent the scene a new warmth, and ourselves fresh impulses, from its national character.   On the moss throne sate the Lady Geraldine, the wreath she wore was wrought of gold shamrocks, her habit of green silk depending from her shoulders like that of the Roman matron, and studded with golden sham-rocks, swept to her feet.   Before her stood a harp; and around the throne were arranged groups of children, attendant sprites of the Lady Geraldine, who, in this fanciful *tableau*, represented the Genius of Ireland.   A moment more, the Genius descended from the throne;

and, sweeping the harp with an ease and power that
seemed to command and awaken its soul-stirring
sounds, drew forth such tones that their influence on
the assemblage was best proved by the breathless silence that marked the close of the performance.   It was
a bold attempt by music to represent the fortunes of a
country and the feelings of her people; from the first
martial peal that spoke her freedom and defiance, to the
last melancholy wail that, while it bowed to defeat,
avowed a soul would never be subdued.   The curtain
fell and the *tableau* disappeared ; but there were few
hearts to which that picture did not recall the lines :

> "Let Erin remember the days of old
> Ere her faithless sons betrayed her !"

and still fewer who did not hopefully anticipate the
national resurrection painted by the same bard :

> "But onward! the green banner rearing,
> Go, flesh every sword to the hilt;
> On *our* side is Virtue and Erin,
> On *theirs*—the Saxon and Guilt !"

Scarcely had the assembly time to yield to the reflections of melancholy or hope produced by the beautiful
vision on which their eyes rested, when they were entranced by a sweet melody on the harp, with which
she accompanied herself to the following words :

> " There's a land, a bright land, far, far by the deep;
> 'Tis the home of the gallant and brave;
> In its bosom the bones of our forefathers sleep,
> And its dirge is the moan of the wave—

Through weal and through woe 'tis the land I love best;
The last soil the sun blesses—green Isle of the West !

"Oh! can'st thou forget 'mid the joys that surround thee
　　When the lovely her young heroes hail,
Those ties of the country that so long have bound thee
　　In soul to thy loved Innisfail ?
Her harp 'mid whose strings sweet echoes still play,
As the Seamarogue's green leaf woos the odors of May !

" *Her* can'st thou forget, who through absence and grief
　　Still loved as in happier hour ;
And sought thy return as the autumn-dyed leaf
　　Looks to spring for the sun and the shower ?
Oh! yes; there are names we can never forget,
Like the sweet haunts of childhood they cling round us yet !

" Though the path of the sun lies far through the sky
　　'Twixt the dawning of day and its close ;
Yet his last look is turned from his bright throne on high
　　To the Orient whence he arose ;—
Thus the faithful and absent in memory roam
To the land that they love; their cradle—their home !"

The superb military band of the —th regiment now supplied the place of the harp ; and the animating echoes
of the cotillion from the surrounding hills set feet, eyes,
and hearts of that joyous company in motion.　Each
was not backward in selecting his partner ; while I
waited for mine ; the Queen of May having pledged
me the honor of her hand for the first dance.　At
length the curtain parted and disclosed the Lady Geraldine arrayed for the dance.　I caught her eye ; and,
advancing to claim redemption of her promise, found
myself anticipated by the young Earl of ——, an Irish
peer, whom I had often (I can not say) had the pleas-

ure to meet at her father's table. He was very young, recently succeeded to the honors of the earldom, and therefore the more excusable for those ridiculous assumptions we would vainly look for in maturer years. Of the class (and I had extensive observations of them at Clonmuir Castle) I had uniformly observed that they seemed to regard the adventitiousness of title, birth, &c., as quite sufficient indemnity for the absence of every thing of the intellectual or moral that could give a charm to their society. I had frequently at Deer Park met this young scion of nobility, and observed his attentions to the Lady Geraldine, evidently distasteful to, and frequently repelled by her. Nor did I wonder, when I listened to the inane twaddle (y'clept, in *salons*, conversation!) with which he so often dosed her patience. From such inflictions, I observed, she would frequently turn, and address herself to me; which I construed into a stern rebuke to him, but not any indication of favor to myself. This doubtless tended to awaken the jealousy of the stripling lord; for which I entertained as great contempt as the source from which it emanated. It was his turn to play the same card; and I knew not whether to impute it to this cause, or, mayhap, a presumption that the tutor was not an equal to the peer. 'Sdeath! an educated gentleman not equal to a social accident; whose only merit is the hereditary mantle a father has bequeathed him!

As we moved through the dance I was not slow to observe the anger gathering on the "baby brow" of the peer, which in sooth had scarcely force sufficient to express it. I observed his dudgeon with a cool indifference; and assumed for the nonce a triumphant *nonchalance*, by which I hoped to give the stripling's wrath some overt development. The encouragement of this feeling, perhaps, afforded me a satisfaction I should have better suppressed, from the marked personal resemblance of the earl to my brother Desmond. Indeed, they were almost counterparts, and while retaliating the earl's conduct to me on past occasions, I almost seemed to fling back upon Desmond the wrongs and disnature I had experienced from him.

It so chanced that the earl placed himself and partner *vis-à-vis*. His eye rested on me, but his glance (not very powerful, by the way) did not in the least abash me; and, wonderful to say, I survived the thunderbolt. I saw my antagonist irritated and chafed; it was my part, as a skillful tactician, to husband my resources and watch my game with coolness. While, like a chess player, I was intent on the move of my antagonist, my attention was diverted by an observation from the Lady Geraldine.

"Do you see that gentleman?" turning her eyes to another group of dancers; "that is Mr. O'Moore of Clonmuir Castle, your namesake."

I screwed up every nerve, and turning my glance

in the direction, Desmond's eyes encountered mine.
I know not what it was came over me; it was not
fear, but that indescribable revulsion we feel at the
unexpected appearance of an object with which the
worst feelings of our nature are associated. I met
that glance; but I felt my cheek grow pale and my
knees tremble.

"Mr. O'Moore!" I retorted, with as much *insouci-
ance* as I could command; "strange proximity—!"
and my voice sank in the vain effort at conversation
I found myself incapable to continue.

"He came with that party," returned Geraldine;
"they say he is betrothed to his partner."

"Ha!"

"Why, what evil sprite has charmed you, Mr.
O'Moore? You look like a hierophant presiding over
some oracle, while your answers are as monosyllabic
and sententious as those of Dodona!"

"Nothing. Pardon me. The dance waits," and,
thankful for any emergency to escape the theme, I
dashed into the cotillion with all the spirit and enthusiasm I could muster. The earl and I encountered;
his eye was fixed, his cheek crimsoned; *en passant* I
received a violent jostle, for the moment destroying
my balance, but for which the offender deemed no
amende requisite.

"Not very lordlike," thought I, "in the presence
of ladies; but, my lordling youth, you have found

F

your match." Meanwhile proceeded the dance; I
endeavoring by some trifling talk to divert her attention from an incident that could not have escaped her
notice. The eyes of myself and Desmond frequently
encountered; and in the thousand feelings of boyhood
and later events, I, must say, I soon lost all recollection of the earl and his affront.

The sun was now glinting over the green hills,
throwing the entire valley into shade;—and I could
not but recall, as the thick shadow fell on rock, sward,
and lake, the first frown from God that fell on the
Paradise he had created. The summit of those lovely
slopes was now our horizon; and oh! could that sweet
twilight have rested there as the natural light of Fairy
Vale, it seemed to me, it was world wide enough for
me, and I cared not to enter the dreary domain of
passion, care, and struggle beyond. While, as I have
said, the last amber tinge was resting on those green
hills, and in the hilarity of the moment we had forgotten to look on the glorious phenomenon, we observed a slight commotion in the party that formed
Desmond's set; for their eyes were fixed on him, as
he stood rooted and motionless, gazing on an object on
the summit of the sun-tinted hills. In the direction
of that object was soon turned every eye;—what was
my horror, when I recognized the mysterious woman
whose visit seemed to haunt me in Dublin, like the
evil demon of the ancient Greek; her figure, naturally

lofty in stature, assuming now a proportion bordering on the gigantic, as it stood in bold relief against the sky, her hair, as usual, loose upon her shoulders, answering to every breath of the evening breeze, and her arms raised, if not in prayer, at least in seeming deprecation of Desmond, from whom her eyes stirred not. Such was the picture that arrested our eyes. It was but a few seconds that she stood thus, fascinating Desmond with those large, lustrous eyes, like a serpent-charmer. A moment more, and she disappeared; but many elapsed ere my brother was wholly released from the spell her mysterious presence had cast upon him. I observed him quickly retire from the group, pale and trembling, and leaning for support on the arm of his friend the earl.

"*Par nobile fratrum!*" I thought, "the secret of my brotherhood will soon be out to that popinjay."

The sun had now for some time sought his tabernacle in the west; and the shades of evening that, like friendly visitants from a world of rest, come to relieve the eye and whisper peace to the heart, after the monarch has passed on his golden highway, descended now, soothing the turbidness of spirit the closing events of the evening had awakened. The company were now separating with greetings as merry as those with which they had met. Carriages, saddle horses, &c., were soon put in requisition for their respective homes; and Fairy Vale that, in the morning,

bloomed with the light and sweetness of an Eden,
was now left like the same Paradise cursed with the
trail of the serpent.   The Lady Geraldine and myself
entered Sir Hubert's carriage in waiting for us; and
Master Connal preferring the back of his pony to
the softer cushion of the carriage, we were soon in
quick career for Deer Park.

I was not, it may easily be guessed, in plight for
conversation, to which the kindness and good heart
of Geraldine seemed often to challenge me, but without success; and, as I occasionally kept my eye on
Connal, who kept cantering by the window, I felt that
I had utterly disregarded or forgotten the countless
charges imposed on me by the Baronet.

"Connal promises to be a good horseman," said
Geraldine, looking with pride on the dexterity with
which the boy managed a fretful and vicious pony.

"Yes; he will not shame his countrymen in that
regard, who are remarkable for the ease and confidence of their seat.   I presume, some of these days,
he will essay an Irish steeple chase, that *chef d'œuvre*
of horsemanship."

Just as I spoke, the carriage pulled up at Deer
Park; the gate-keeper had opened the gate; when a
figure, that had hitherto been crouching, rose up suddenly to the full extent of its stature in the twilight,
from which it seemed to emerge as a kindred shade.
The figure was that strange woman; but oh! what

was the mystery or fear of her former visits to the results of her presence here? The pony, fretted and chafed by the ride, plunged violently, flung Connal over his head, and dashed away at headlong speed up the demesne. There was a faint scream from the boy, that sank to my very heart; the pale cheek and trembling lip of the father rose before me; was it a prophecy; or this woman or myself the wretched tools of its fulfillment? These were the burning and agonized thoughts of a second; as bursting from the carriage, Geraldine and myself were in a moment kneeling at his side.

"My God—my God!" cried the woman, "what have I done?" as she flung herself on the boy, alternately kissing him and pressing his senseless form to her bosom.

"Death—death," I returned, as I assisted the men in raising him from the ground; who, in company with Geraldine, whose hand clasped that of Connal as she walked, proceeded to the mansion.

"What hast thou done?" I iterated, fixing on the woman a gaze that must have concentrated all the fire and passion of my nature; "what the serpent does when he whets his fang, what the owl does when it croaks death at midnight. Wretch! avoid me. The sky above thee is black, and the earth beneath thee cursed."

"Oh God! oh God!" fell brokenly from the woman

in such heart-piercing pains as, for the moment, to divest me of all anger, and almost change it to pity, if not tenderness.

"Why call on God?" I asked.

"Should I not pray for mercy on the soul I have sent Him?" she answered, the thick tears choking her utterance; "it was not he I sought, but you— and I have murdered—murdered—murdered him!" in this heart-broken iteration, she staggered against a tree, and buried her head, now heaving with violent spasms, in her hands.

I waited for some moments: there was an earnest intensity of grief about the poor creature, that disa-bused me of any superstition or evil influence I had hitherto associated with her presence. There she stood against the tree, her hands strained like cords to her face, her whole body trembling with a convulsive shud-der, and the very voice that refused its utterance, show-ing by its stifled sobs an agony deeper than could ever be expressed by words. Was this a creature of ill? No. Such sorrow never harbored with guilt for its partner.

"Woman, speak!" I at length said, in tones as mild as my situation, and the recent catastrophe, would allow.

"Morven—" The poor creature could go no fur-ther; and there was such tenderness in that one word, that it seemed to revive the buried ties and thousand affections of home, now passed from me forever.

"They seek thee wrong—ay, they of thine own blood. I have heard them. That is thine own they seek to tear from thee. You saw how he watched to-day that fair-faced Norman. Anon he'll come—"

"Sir Hubert, Sir, requests your immediate presence," interrupted a servant.

"I attend him." And heedless alike of myself, the woman's desultory allusions, or whatever evil they involved to me, I left my companion for the mansion.

"Morven—!" Again that word—again that tenderness; but I waved my hand, for every thing was now merged in Connal's fate, and the ominous warnings and fears of Sir Hubert, that circumstance seemed to convert into prophecy.

CHAPTER VIII.

Lord, lettest now thy servant part in peace!
Ay, servant truly; for his angel looks,
In guardian vigils, on his Father's face.
When children die, it is as 'twere so much
Of God's pure spirit taken back to heaven.
They are the only doves in this huge ark;
The only righteous in this doomed Gomorrah!
Sucklings and babes He maketh towers of strength.
The widow's mite glowed like an ingot in
The treasury above; and God revealed
The might of Egypt in a widow's cruse.

WHAT pen can describe the scene that awaited my arrival in the grand hall! The boy was extended on an ottoman, by the side of which knelt the affectionate Geraldine, bathing his brow with her kisses, and straining his clammy hand in hers; on the other side stood Sir Hubert, on whom a few moments seemed to have wrought the work of years. The perspiration stood in thick beads on his brow, his eye had the cold rigidity of spectre rather than of living man, and the wanness of the cheek seemed even more livid from the hollows these few seconds had plowed there like the ravages of years. His arms hung listlessly by his side; his head was slightly inclined forward, and his eyes were bent upon the boy with that keenness of penetration, and glassy aspect, that seems to extend the visual powers of this world to the mysteries and terrors of that beyond the grave. At the foot of the ottoman stood the Lady De Lacy, with that imperturbability of demeanor and expression that seemed to deride the ravages of disease, and challenge even the power of death.

My footsteps seemed to dissolve the awful spell that enchained the party as I entered. Sir Hubert started from his stupor, and, as I encountered his piercing eye, I felt my very heart transfixed as by some influence beyond the sphere of men. In that gaze there was a mixture of melancholy that seemed to wring out the very last drop from the heart with a sternness of rebuke, as though in the sad picture before him he read the fulfillment of those warnings I had disregarded.

"Sir Hubert—"

"It is over, Sir," interposed the Baronet; "there is the first victim—the other must soon follow."

I waited not for any further intercourse at a moment that so sadly influenced us both; but, in a moment, was with Geraldine kneeling at Connal's side, soothing a hand that hung insensibly in mine, and whispering to an ear that seemed no longer capable of hearing.

"He is dead! my brother—my brother—dead—

F *

dead"—groaned Geraldine, as she sank on the boy;
"Oh, Connal, dear child—would I could die for thee!"

"He is not dead, Miss De Lacy," I answered,
stammering out the consolation I scarcely felt myself.
"He is not dead; his pulse beats, and—see here!—"
and, as I spoke, as it were to bless the hope I strove
to give others, the boy opened his eyes slowly, but
almost as soon closed them.

"He is dead! Oh God—my darling little brother.
His eyes are closed," screamed Geraldine. "Connal,
dear Connal!"

"For God's sake, Miss De Lacy, be calm!—here
comes the physician;" and, while I spoke, the family
physician, for whom a servant had been dispatched,
entered. Miserable beings of hope that we are! There
never was a case, however defiant of time, skill, or
knowledge, to which the presence of the physician did
not lend some aspect of relief and consolation. No
devotee ever turned to his oracle with an eye more
questioning, or a heart more credulous, than we to
that man who, in his person, seemed to represent the
issues of life and death. He felt the boy's pulse, ex-
amined his head where he had received the injury—
but all in silence. During these manipulations of
awful suspense, there was not a word spoken, not a
question asked; for each read his answer in the
unmistakably legible features of the physician. The
man of medicine proceeded to apply the requisite rem-

edies. During the operation, I raised my eyes to the
Baronet, who, in the anxiety I felt for the safety of
our little patient, had wholly escaped my recollection.
He was still standing there, his eyes bent on the
child; but so ghastly an expression had in the interval possessed his countenance, that I felt myself in
the presence of a dead man standing in the attitude
of life.

"Is there danger, Sir?" at length inquired Lady
De Lacy, in a tone that betrayed not curiosity, far
less interest. The question or the voice seemed to
rally all the torpid energies of her wretched husband.
The pallor gave way to a transient flush; the eye
which seemed for ever to have closed on the light and
passion of life and heart, was suddenly rekindled with
a fire that shot up, as it were, from the expiring pile
of nature.

"Danger!—oh, God! for her I have suffered all!"
were the words of the distracted father, but shrieked
in such a tone that the voice of the maniac alone could
equal it. He tottered from excessive faintness, and
was borne to his chamber.

But I had scarcely time to heed the father, or his
terrible allusion to Lady De Lacy, in my intense and
increasing solicitude for dear little Connal. Dear and
loved as he had been before by me, it seemed, as I bent
over his pale face, and pressed his hand from which
came no answering pressure, that I would willingly

have bartered my own life to recall that high-souled,
noble boy to the sweet world and lordly home I feared
he was leaving for ever. With every day had that
dear boy strengthened in my favor, and knit himself
with my very heart; the exactions of education were
lost in the gentler obligations of affection, the ties of
tutor in those of brother; and now was that relation
so soon to be severed which shed so happy a promise
over the future? Was so bright a morning to darken
with the wrath of the tempest and the cloud ere it
traveled its golden way to as bright a noon? And was
I, or rather she—? Oh! madness, madness! Connal
—dear child! when I think of thee thou art as a noon
ray sent for but a few hours to gladden the path but
for thee dark and cheerless! Thine early fate seemed
a recompense to thee for that religion that spoke to
thy young days of " a home not made with hands,
eternal in the heavens!"

The poor child was at the request of the physician
removed to his bedroom, for the greater comfort and
quietness demanded by his situation. He was accord-
ingly laid on that bed he had left in the morning, all
joy and happiness, to meet ere night the fearfulest visitant that can summon even the prepared. From that
bedside his sister, the physician, and myself scarcely
stirred the whole night, anxiously watching the operation of the remedies, or any change in our little patient that might minister to our hopes. The child lay

calm, almost motionless; and, but for a scarcely per-
ceptible respiration, we would have already numbered
him with the dead. But no change was there to cheer
the hearts of the watchers through that dreary night;
no light in that glazed eye, as from the rekindled energies of life; no quickening of the pulse from that
mystic hand that directs the ebbs and flows of life;
no returning flush to that cheek growing paler, would
seem to say the guest of life had not given over to
tabernacle in the heart! We were like questioners at
the oracle; but the shrine was deserted, and with the
priestess all hope had fled! :

In the course of that sad night I had occasion to
pass to my chamber in search of something required
for our dear little patient. In passing a narrow corridor of the castle, not much frequented, but forming
a shorter means of access to my own chamber, I was
arrested by deep groans, alternated by prayers and the
solemn mention of the name, *Mary*. The voice was
that of Sir Hubert. As to the groan and the prayers,
they awakened in me no surprise, so consistent were
they with the distress that seemed to involve the whole
castle as with a funeral shroud; for so loved was that
dear boy, there was not a servant whose eyes were not
wet as they looked on their young master stretched in
the mockery of death. What riveted my curiosity was
the iteration of the name—that passionate iteration,
seeming to combine all that was recollective of hap-

piness with all that was anticipative of misery and
despair. I was standing outside a very small door
communicating with the chamber; so small, I had not
hitherto observed it, though I had frequently traversed
the corridor. I know not how it was, but some slight
bodily motion, to myself imperceptible, attracted the
sorrowful inmate of the chamber. The voice was
hushed; in an instant all was still as the grave;—one
huge spring—the door was torn open with a violence
that staggered me some paces backward, and Sir Hubert stood before me!—not as last I saw him, pale, col-
lapsed, and speechless, but with an eye of fire, a cheek
of flame, a form that seemed from intense excitement
to have borrowed for the moment a stature and dimensions I could not reconcile with those of the Baronet.
So we stood; I crouching and timorous, for all manliness and self-possession seemed to have fled, not more
from the terrific appearance before me than the suspi-
cious attitude in which I had been discovered. The
blood-hound and the stag, furred by its pursuer, were
not apter illustrations of power and cowering weakness than I and Sir Hubert De Lacy.

"Excuse me, Sir Hubert—" I stammered. Some
moments elapsed ere the Baronet could summon repose of manner sufficient to reply.

"All *listeners*, sir, need excuse," he returned, with
a causticity that stung my heart's pride to the very
core. I was on the point of retaliating, as became

a man laboring under a disgraceful imputation; but judgment and pity for the wretched situation of the father interposed.

"Pardon, Sir Hubert! I have heard nothing can inculpate you, or give me any power over you," I at length said, with as much calmness as I could command; and was on the point of leaving when the Baronet stayed me.

"Stay, sir! You have heard—oh, God! what have you heard? Her name, that years have buried in the grave and silence of my own heart, only to be dragged forth now to the eyes of a stranger!" And the wretched man clasped his hands over his eyes, as though to exorcise some spirit visible to himself alone.

"I have heard but the name of Mary," I said, endeavoring by the simple avowal to mitigate those violent emotions I saw were gaining the ascendency over him.

"In that you have heard what none other ever has; what I had purposed to carry with me to the grave, but never thought to disclose to mortal ear." His manner became more subdued; a melancholy succeeded his former violence; the tears fell copiously from him; and, taking me by the hand, he led me into the apartment of which I had previously but a small view, and closed the door.

The chamber in which we stood was of small dimensions. My attention, on the instant, was riveted by the style of the room. It was hung with black; and in the centre stood a white marble statue of a female, the exquisite proportions of the form, and the beauty of the face, showing additionally from the relief presented by the black tapestry. Alone at such an hour, the boy dying under the same roof, my companion, a man but now wrought to the highest pitch of passion all but revengeful, the dark associations of another world, and the overwhelming feelings they awakened from the sable hangings of the room and the statue of the beautiful dead it contained; all this, I must confess, unmanned me for the moment, and called for the support of nerves stronger than I could command.

"Well, Mr. O'Moore," said Sir Hubert, fixing on me an eye whose searchingness made me quail, "you have sought for the heart of my mystery—behold it!" These words were spoken with an irony that restored my sense of equality, from the wrong they implied; and I answered:

"Sir, I *sought* nothing but what your own freewill or unguardedness has chosen to disclose!"

"Mr. O'Moore, a thousand pardons! God help me! God help me!"—my child dying;—all is fulfilled— God help me!"

From such broken ejaculations it was impossible to gather any thing connected; any thing that might

solve an enigma he seemed unwilling to unriddle and
I incapable to fathom. There was but one allusion at
which, in my bewilderment, I could catch.

"What is fulfilled, Sir Hubert?" He regarded me
for some moments; and then, as it were, satisfied that
I was worthy of confidence, he took my hand.

"Can you be faithful? For years have I trembled
with the burden of a secret, that has haunted me by
day, frowned on my sleep at night, and now—now—
trembles on the eve of fulfillment." I remained silent,
unwilling to be the depository of a confidence I had
unwittingly solicited. "Yet," he continued, "you
will smile on me for superstition, or condemn me for
my fear."

"Neither, Sir Hubert, as long as you enlist my sympathy."

"At my father's instigation I married an heiress,
while yet but twenty. His object was policy. Yonder is her statue, and this room consecrated to her
memory." Sir Hubert paused, as he looked at the
statue, and shuddered. "I can not say that our life
was happy. But for that I am myself to blame. I
acknowledged this marriage merely as a stroke of
policy; one that would supply my tastes for extravagance and dissipation; to which alas—alas! I was
then more devoted than to my home or wife. In time
two children were born; the Lady Geraldine and the
boy who now—" His words faltered, he turned to

the statue, and his cheek resumed its accustomed
pallor. "Excess soon brought embarrassments; creditors pressed; my stud, pictures, etc., went under the
hammer; Lady De Lacy's fortune was squandered; I
was bankrupt, and she broken-hearted. At this part
of my narrative I blush as man and husband. Creditors persecuting me, my estate passed to others, bail-
iffs prowling like so many harpies, the very articles
that had formed part and parcel of my fireside swept
away by the remorseless hand of the law, there was
nothing in the future but want, and no possibility of
retrieving that social influence and position I had
hitherto maintained by wealth and rank. I now began
to taste that bitterest of all cups the world can com-
mend to our lips—that cup mingled by the hand of
Misfortune and presented to us by Ingratitude. Of the
legion who had daily sported with my hounds, drank
of my cup, and regaled themselves at the luxuries of
my table, not one was there who had sympathy for my
distress, not one generous soul to interpose between me
and the power which was hourly crushing me to the
earth, shivering the very gods of my hearth, and turning me out to the gibes of man, poor and outcast.
Well has Shakspeare styled Ingratitude a marble-
hearted fiend. See me then in the very hey-day of life,
born to a baronetcy, wedded to a fortune—what? a pau-
per! Then my children—; but let me turn from that.

"Now comes the part of my narrative that makes

me blush, and oh! how has it made me tremble! The
feelings which swept over and threatened to bury me
in their desolation I basely retaliated on her who, I
must say, with the constancy of a true wife, clung the
more closely to me for my very distresses, but from
whom I recoiled with that strange perversity of feeling
that made me regard *her* as the cause of the misery
my own imprudence had entailed on us all. Yes, I
regarded the whole thing with that obliquity of vision
that turned my eyes from myself, the immediate
agent, to the fortune Lady De Lacy brought me, only
the remote cause. My home became to me a howling
wilderness; sentiment, affection, sympathy—all that
can make our fireside a Paradise had fled; and the
Tempter that had blasted all, planted thorns and evil
passions where he had found flowers and happiness.
From coldness and reserve I proceeded to censure,
censure in its turn rose to recrimination, and violent
passion soon came to the aid of angry and vehement
words. Children and wife would try their little arts
at soothing; but the evil spirit was not to be charmed
away; I yielded to the Tempter, and his yoke was the
more easily stretched over his victim. I will not
weary you with domestic details of exacerbated temper, morose language, and those aggravations of gloomy
and ascetic moods, that spread like a pall or a noxious
vapor, making the shrine of the fireside a very charnel-
house. Let me hasten on.

"I saw that the course I was at present pursuing was exercising a most baleful influence on my wife's health. She was sinking rapidly under the double infliction—poverty and my own treatment of her. At this I was devil enough to rejoice—you start. 'Tis right—none but one imbued with the malignity of a demon can rejoice over the miseries of a fellow being, or triumph in the anticipation of that death his own hand may be said to inflict. I saw her day after day pine and droop. Did I weep? No. I inwardly gloated at the prospect—oh God! This is truth. May its confession in part atone!" The wretched man clasped his hands in such an agony of prayer as seemed, while it expressed the whole burden of his soul, to implore pardon in the anguish of repentance. There was a moment's pause, in which he appeared to rally his shattered energies and then resumed.

"But why do I speak thus to you—a stranger?" While he asked this, he fixed on me eyes, in which glared the fierce and wandering fires of the maniac.

"Sir Hubert, assure yourself of my warmest sympathy. It is true, I am but a stranger; yet a stranger's heart beats sometimes with those humanities we in vain look for from those of our own home."

"True. I have observed your friendship for that boy—Connal—" here his voice became broken, and I was obliged to use some expressions of kindness to reassure him in the continuance of his narrative.

"Mythology itself has represented tears of iron coursing down the cheek of the king of hell; but for me, who pretended to be a man, warmed with the same blood, animated with the same impulses as my victim, there was no tear; nothing to tell me, I came from the Creator's hand, moulded of the same clay as my fellow, that bounds to the rapture of joy and bows to the weight of grief. I saw her sink daily; and (I repeat it with remorse)—with gladness; for, in the prospect of her death alone I read the means of extricating myself from the shame and poverty that seemed as with a shroud to wrap me. Devil that I was, it was not sufficient that grief, like a slow worm, was gnawing away the very soul of her life and blighting the bloom on her cheek; no, the work of the miner was too slow for one who sought the lowest depths of the mine for the paltry soul-bought treasure that glittered there. I repeat, the work of the Destroyer was not sufficiently rapid for the devil who watched and directed the movements, and anxiously waited for the moment when the fatal blow might be struck and the bloody triumph secured. No—I plied my own demon arts to accelerate the last moment, and place within my grasp the treasure I coveted. But has it brought me happiness? You shall learn.

"The family of a wealthy Irish peer resided near my estate; our lands joined. They had but one child —a daughter; she was an heiress. To secure her

was my object. I need not say that I was incited to
this union by affection; no, you will easily anticipate
the base and sordid feelings that formed my project.
Of my dying wife I never thought, and cared as little;
her place would soon be vacant, but a guest more unwelcome still, was prepared to enter in and dwell;—
that guest was Poverty. To escape his presence, I
would have bartered, I believe, my soul. The founda-
tion of this desperate project was pride, family pride;
I was born to rank, and must maintain it; never thinking that the true rank of the man depends on the
fortitude with which he encounters reverses, and not
on the gewgaws or accessories with which he gilds
his earthly state. Pride—pride:—it is indeed the
reigning sin that angels in their fall have brought
from heaven to earth!

"It was impossible that my wife's system, debilitated as it was by the rapid inroads of disease, and can-
kered by my own brutal treatment, could much longer
withstand the strife that was now passing between
life and death. Not to detain you, the last moment
arrived which, as I thought, was to blot out the hand-
writing and the penalty, restore my fallen pride and
family honors, and finally emancipate me from all the
shame and trials that threatened to crush me and
mine forever.

"The funeral procession stood before the mansion;
I see it now; the black plumes of the horses, the

weepers of the mourners. Ay, even now I hear the wild scream of her children, as they look their last on the coffin, containing in its narrow compass all they shall ever know of mother on earth. For myself— But why place before you the tearless, heartless marble? Look on me! Have I not atoned?

"Consigned to the family vault with all becoming decorum, I felt I had but to wait a short interval (prescribed by the forms of decency) ere I should welcome a new bride to my house; whose presence, like the touch of Midas, would turn all to gold in the dreary and desolate mansion of Deer Park. And now change the scene (for such and as instantaneous is the panorama of life) from the funeral to the bridal— the grave to the altar." He paused a moment; there was a strong shudder, and he resumed—

"Now commences *my* tale of suffering. But God in his retributions is just. I had mixed the cup for another—why should not I drain it myself? The marriage train has passed; the bride is the present Lady De Lacy, the rich dower, for which I had hurried an innocent and affectionate soul to the grave, is mine—ay, mine; but, like the shekels of Judas, only to curse the soul that sought, and the hand that grasped it!

"We had not long been united, when one evening walking in my grounds with Lady De Lacy (I know not how others might account for it, as the child of

remorse, or the uncertain twilight stimulating with
its shadowy power a mind unstrung and overwrought),
I suddenly started; for there, before me, in her grave
shroud, stood the form of my deceased wife. Till this
hour I had ever resisted the prominent characteristic
of my countrymen—faith in the reappearance of the
dead. But there was a reality in the present, coupled
with the circumstances of her demise, which made
me feel I really stood in the presence of one who had
passed the bitterness of death. You are, doubtless,
familiar with the admirable portraiture of Banquo's
apparition, which is seen by the guilty alone, though
invisible to the guests of the Thane. The present
was visible to myself alone; I stood petrified; a marble coldness pervaded my whole frame; and, chilled
and trembling before this risen monument of my own
guilt, I stood motionless, speechless, and more the
image of the mysterious object before me than of
aught living.

"'Why do you tremble? What do you see?' said
my companion.

"'My God—my God! have mercy on me!' I remember was the incoherent reply; as, sinking on my
knees, I implored pardon of my Maker, and adjured
the presence to leave me.

"'What do you see?' iterated my companion, vainly
striving to raise me from my humble attitude.

"'Herself—herself!'

"'Fool—idiot!' exclaimed Lady De Lacy; and while she spoke, she dashed from her the trembling hand that clung to her as the only assurance of something human in that terrible hour.

"I sprang to my feet. I felt the echo of that taunt ring through every nerve like the scorpion's venom; my manliness had been assailed by even more than woman;—my own wife. I clasped my hands to my eyes, and employed various artifices to prove to myself that I was not in that sleeping state in which dreams mock us with the assumptions of reality. But it was vain. When I withdrew my hands and strained my vision, the object was still there; and oh! what a change in her expression; not the mild, uncomplaining one with which she had passed from me; but on that brow sate a sternness and reproach speaking trumpet-tongued of the demon heartlessness that had sent her thus early to her tomb.

"'I am no fool,' I cried, 'nor idiot,' bursting with passion the chain these words seemed to forge for me; 'but as God is the Maker and Judge of both, I saw the wife I have murdered—ay, murdered—and for you.'

"'For me!' iterated the lady; 'then it is fitting you should feel remorse. Judas hanged himself for his avarice; and with my dower you purposed to rebuild the fallen honors of Deer Park.' These words were uttered in so measured a tone, so frigid a manner, so

G

cold and caustic an eye, as to rankle like so many
shafts in the heart but now bleeding from her words.
You are aware that extremes meet; and there are
occasions, when the heart, stung and lacerated so as
to quiver from its very acuteness, may on the instant
become so blunted as to become capable of bearing all
in silence and without reproof. My eyes were still
strained toward the object which, without moving,
gradually faded away, like a mist wreath, from the
spot it had occupied. This was the origin of those
difficulties you may have observed in the demeanor of
Lady De Lacy toward myself and children. Had I a
right in the motives of our union to expect aught else?

"It was not long after the appearance I have described that—"

"You tremble and grow pale, Sir Hubert."

"Ah! you will not blame me when you have heard
all." After a moment, he resumed:

"You observed the charges I gave you in reference
to Connal?"

"They appeared to originate from a fear bordering
on the superstitious," I observed.

"Superstition! Well, well! It may be so; but
when we hear whispers from the grave, when we stand
in the presence of death itself, and feel its icy breath
on our cheek, we can not surely deem it superstition;
no more than we can the very fact of our existence,
the air we breathe, or the light we look upon. But to

my tale. It was not long after this appearance or apparition (as you please to term it), that in my sleep I was visited with the same image, with this aggravation, that the apparition was accompanied by a distinct prophecy that Connal should die while yet a boy; and, oh, horrible! the demon is now upon me, and ever follows in the track of that terrible thought," (as he spoke he seized me with a hand, which, though it trembled, grasped mine with the strength of iron); "and that on the anniversary of my poor boy's death I was to be laid by his side."

There was a fearful silence, during which we regarded each other. I felt a cold shudder steal over me: like the fallen king of Israel, I stood before one who was revealing to me the secrets of the unknown world, while the wretched man vainly searched my countenance for that sympathy which must have passed away from features I felt were becoming cold and marble as his own.

"Judge now," he resumed, "of the injunctions I gave you about the boy. This, you say, may have been a dream. True; but not a solitary one, else would it have passed from me as a waking vision of the morning? No; this was seen in my sleep three times distinctly; the last, the night before you went to the *fête champêtre;* the next day saw it fulfilled—Connal is on his death-bed, and the grave opens for—"

" Be calm, Sir Hubert," I interrupted, pressing his
hand with what assurance I could command ; "the
boy's life is not despaired of ; and even were it so, I
see no reason for your indulging in such fears, which
are, after all, but the idle offspring of a dream."

"A dream, sir !" iterated my companion ; "oh !
never was truth writ in characters more legible and
appalling than that dream you deem so idle.   No, not
the dream of the Egyptian king which made the monarch tremble on his throne, and the jewels of his diadem but worthless dust in his eyes.   But I must abide
my fate ; it is, as I have deserved, but a visitation
from a retributive Providence : through her I should
have cherished as my own flesh, yet whom my cruelty
regarded but as a clod of the valley."

I will not dwell longer on the terrors of that night ;
—the boy dying within the castle ; the deepening and
overwhelming fears of the victim, who reckoned the
prophecy now half verified, the other half suspended
over him, like the sword of Damocles, and the vain
consolations I endeavored to administer under circumstances too appalling for the mere tones of human comfort.   Let us return to the chamber of little Connal.

The morning saw but little if any improvement in
the condition of the little sufferer.   The stupor continued ; for the physician said his brain was seriously
injured by the contusion ; and in the despair we read
in his monosyllabic replies to our earnest inquiries, it

was impossible that any hope could linger with ourselves. But, Geraldine—the noble, affectionate Geraldine! Who can speak the devotion of that sister to
the dying boy? As well might we count the tears
that fell on her little brother's cheek as she bent over
him, mingling her murmurs of affectionate endearment
with prayers to the great Father of all.

With her I kept constant watch in the chamber ;
carefully and punctually applying the remedies prescribed, with but little hope, alas ! of their final effi-
ciency. As I looked on the pale, quiet boy, now rapidly passing as under the curse of a dead mother, the
communication of the Baronet, with all its aggravations of mystery and terror, frequently rose before me.
I strove to push the whole thing from my thoughts as
the delusive shadow flung on a susceptible mind by
the passing image of a dream ; but vain ! There are
moments, I believe, when the mind, it matters not
how fortified by truth and religion, will yield to the
abortive phantoms superstition conjures from the
depths of the grave, or the solitude of midnight. I
was willing to deride the whole as a dream, produced
as in the case of Macbeth, by the guilty and suffering
state of mind ; but, nevertheless, the latter tending
to the fulfillment of that which its own condition made
a prophecy.

The depositary of this secret, however unwillingly
so, bound me by a still stronger tie to poor little Con-

nal. There was something in his fate that linked him
the more strongly with the other world, now that it
had been a distinct subject of prediction by his departed mother. As I looked on the little sufferer, it seemed
as though I could trace there the dark lines of death
furrowing those features that had never known impress deeper than the smile of boyhood, and hear from
those locked lips of the child words that communed
with his mother and the world to which he was hastening. Ever kind and endearing, our intercourse had
been one of the closest affection; but there was something now hovering over my poor pupil, which, while
it threatened immediate and irrevocable separation,
bound our hearts (at least mine to his) by that cord it
seemed death had no power to loose.

At length came the crisis. The physician despaired;
and the sting of his death was, that he might pass
away in a stupor;—no word of parting, no look of
recognition from the pilgrim to those he was leaving
behind and forever! Oh, how I wept!—how my heart
groaned inwardly, as the thought that a few months'
intercourse was to end in the incommunicable silence
of the death hour—our brotherhood to pass away without a single remembrance or word of blessing on its
happy hours from the dying!

He had lain thus silent and helpless, when the first
symptom of consciousness he had exhibited since the
accident was on the following day. His eyes slowly

opened, wandered about from object to object in the
room, as though in search of something, and as slowly
closed. It was to us, as we anxiously gazed on him,
as the closing of the window of life forever; the ex-
tinction of a light that, once passed away, could never
be relumed. Again they opened, and his lips were
slightly parted; and I thought I heard a sound like
my own name; I bent over the dear boy: it was my
name he pronounced. But, as I bent, the tears came
fast and heavy, though I strove to stifle them.

"I am going, Sir," he said, with evident difficulty,
"to that sweet place of which we have so often
spoken. Oh! how I thank my Father that, child
though I was, he has given me thoughts and feelings
perhaps withheld from others."

"Do you *feel* you are dying, Connal?"

"I *know* it, Sir," was the answer; and the words
were uttered with that collectedness of tone, that
would even say the thought of death brought comfort
with it: "and though but a child, I would not forfeit
the dreams I have had, for all a return to life and the
world could offer me."

"Then you are happy, dear child?"

"As I never was before, Sir. If we must pass the
valley of the dark shadow, yet there is a hand to cheer
the fainting heart, and strengthen the feeble knees. I
feel, Sir—oh! I feel," he repeated, with a burst of
joy that called a momentary gleam to his eye, "I feel

that hand is with me; and He himself has told us if
He be for us, none shall be against us."

The boy paused; his eyes closed, as in contemplation of the dreams of which he spoke. I was glad;
for the tears I could not restrain were thus unobserved. As I looked on my little pupil, had it been
the will of God, I should gladly have changed places
with him. How different the objects that brightened
and gladdened his path, to those whose gross forms
and shadows hovered like foul demons over mine. He
was, perhaps, looking on the burning throne, from the
great centre of which burst that Eternal Light, that
flamed in the crowns or sparkled on the wings of his
angel ministers. Harps, too, were there—lulling the
sense and wrapping the soul in such ecstasy, that the
clay of the mortal was even now being informed with
the spirit of its God; while I—

" You remember those lovely walks, Sir, we used
to take together? I now feel the comfort of those
holy truths that spoke through you from every object
we met. You said that though God was visible every
where, from the creation of the great mountain even
to the smallest seed, yet was he seen only by the eye
of faith—I think, Sir, that was your word?" I nod-
ded. "I remember your explaining faith to me also,
as a debt the least we could pay to one who could not
lie and would not deceive us. I feel, Sir, that now I
am paying that debt; and paying it by that entire

confidence in God that would make me even now unwilling to return to life, were it possible. Oh! Sir,
I feel so happy—" Connal stopped again, as for
strength. So choked were my words, I could scarcely
find sufficient strength to entreat him not to overtax
himself by speaking.

"You speak now, Sir, of the flesh: that is indeed
weary; but remember the spirit has wings that tire
not, though they spread on earth to fold only in
heaven. Oh! Sir, I have more than hope. This morning I think I saw my Saviour; and his smile was that
of him who encouraged little children to come to him;
and, as I looked on him, I remember a prayer broke
from me, that I might be among that happy little band
he suffered to come."

"And was your prayer answered, Connal?"

"It was, Sir; for I thought that Jesus smiled, and
an angel parted from the bright company that surrounded him, and spreading over me his wings, so
white that I turned my eyes from their glory, in a
moment I was caught up to Jesus's feet, and was welcomed among the little band of children."

The little sufferer's eyes again closed, and his lips
slightly moved; and the words of sweet religion that
broke from them at intervals showed that his fancies
were not exaggerated, but that his eyes had but closed
on earth to open them in heaven.

"Where is Papa—and Geraldine? ah! dear sister,

G *

you are there." He looked on Geraldine, whom he
had not before observed. Their eyes met for a moment, and the affectionate sister, overpowered by her
feelings, sank her head on the pillow.

"Well—well—dear sister," he said, regarding her,
while his eyes slowly filled; "here it is all tears, but
there all joy; here the wing is ever spreading, but
there ever folded. Geraldine, we shall meet again. I
have heard it all. The doctor says I must die—I
heard him. Ah! that wicked little pony! Your
young master, that used to feed you. Ah! Ambler—
I thought you loved him better—better—that woman—!"

I found his senses were wandering, and proposed to
the physician an anodyne; but he replied that all
remedies were unavailing—the brain was irrecover-
ably injured.

"Do not be afraid to tell *me*, doctor; I know I
must die," he said, with an unexpected rally both of
mind and body. "And I rather wish it; for there I
shall meet that little band of children that Christ so
much loved, when he said their spirits looked on the
face of his Father. Ah! that calls to my mind—"
and, checking himself as in the effort to aid his memory, he beckoned to me. I approached, and bending
my ear, he whispered, the purport of which was, that
from the neighboring school to which he had gone
before placed under my charge, I should summon his

quondam class-mates. The request struck me as in perfect consonance with the boy's character—so full of affection and kindness; and I doubt not that in poor Connal's mind there was a deeper motive for this than that supplied by the old recollections of the school-mate—a desire to exercise a religious influence on the future lives of his companions by his own death. The boy's request met instant compliance. A servant was dispatched; and it was not long before the feet of his little mates were heard upon the stairs, gently approaching his chamber. It was as touching a scene as I have ever looked on, that last meeting between the little school-mates. Possessing all that was simple and pure in our nature, it irresistibly raised the heart, by uniting all that was good and as yet unpolluted on earth, with the holy and the godlike of a better world. I could not resist the tears that gushed from me, when I saw those little class-mates gather round the bed of their former fellow. There was a gentle rivalry among them to touch his hand—to kiss his cheek ; an effort, as it were, by each to claim the treasure, were it but a moment, for his own—so soon to be snatched away forever.

"My little friends," said the dying boy, "God is calling me home ; and I sent for you, that you might hear from me of that bright home I have seen in my dreams, that Christ has prepared for those who love him. Not long since, we ran, and rode, and sported together. Yet see me now. Oh! would L give one moment's dream of heaven and Jesus for all the short-lived joys we have followed together?" He stopped a moment, and his voice faltered with the tears that rose at every word. " Think not," he continued, with a strong effort mastering them, " that I cry because I am dying. Oh! no. They are tears of joy for that dear home. Oh! sing me that sweet hymn we wel-comed every Sabbath with; I loved it then, let me hear it now. Now is the time, for I shall soon be there." He sank back upon his pillow, apparently exhausted with the effort of speaking, while his little class-fellows began the following hymn, in so low and sweet a tone that it seemed rather the echo of distant voices stealing through the chamber, than music itself. The Lady Geraldine was kneeling by Connal's bed, her face buried in her hands ; and, for myself, I never felt the very depths of my nature more powerfully stirred than by those sweet voices of childhood as they sang the following

HYMN.

"Fear not, my child! for Jesus saith,
'Let little children come to me!'
Fear not to pass the vale of Death,
Beyond, thy Saviour thou wilt see.

"And He will take thee by the hand,
As shepherds do the lambs they love;
And guide thee onward to that land
That lies those star-bright worlds above.

"And Jordan's stream before thy feet
 Her silver waves shall part in twain,
And angels with their harpings greet
 The pilgrim child to Zion's plain.

"And oh! what visions then will burst
 Upon thine eye, thou ransomed one;
When thou shalt look on Christ—the First
 The Last—upon the burning Throne!

"And on that band of Spirits bright
 That Jesus said, do aye behold
Thy Father's face, in radiant flight
 The throne of Adonai enfold.

"Fear not, then, child! though from thy birth
 Oh! very few the years were given;
Thy little lamp was quenched on earth
 To burn eternally in heaven!"

"Thank you, thank you," said the dying child; "I feel happy now. It was that hymn first gave me thoughts of Jesus's love and heaven; oh! I shall not forget you all when there. Good-by, good-by—" The effort of hearing and speaking had exhausted him; his eyes closed, and he seemed to sink into a stupor. Slowly and sadly wound that little procession of mourners from the sick chamber; and as one by one they looked upon the dying boy, so much earnest affection did each exhibit, it seemed as though he felt he was looking his last on his little class-mate.

During the remainder of the day he did not awaken from the lethargy which succeeded this interview. Once or twice a broken string of words escaped from the poor boy, evidencing the utter divorce of the mind

from earth or the sufferings of the body. The sun
had already set; and the glorious light that seems to
follow like the homage of heaven in the wake of its
descending god, streamed into the sick chamber, bathing every object in a flood of gorgeous amber. The
solemn tint of twilight was now succeeded by that
stream of tender light the moon poured from her fountain of silver. Between that soft light and the melancholy scene within there seemed a mystic sympathy,
raising the mind from the suffering body before us to
that world whose spirituality found its holiest type in
the light that streamed on the death-bed. To the
pilgrim soul returning to its native heaven and its
Father it streamed like the pillar of fire that guided
the way-worn Hebrew through the wilderness. The
casement lay open, and before the eye stretched the
magnificent demesne of Deer Park, with its giant
trees, whose shadows stood forth in the moonlight,
like mourners for him whose funeral array would ere
long pass beneath their branches. We looked forth
and upward in silent worship at the stars that seemed
to hold watch with us, and that unearthly light that
best symbolized the hour in which Life was fast passing into Death. It seemed as though the same cord
bound our thoughts, the same sympathies twined and
guided our hearts. On that moon, now in her midnight majesty ascending the midmost depths of heaven,
the eyes of both were fixed; as though the heart turns

all its hopes and instincts to that world that promises
eternity, when this, with its dreams, shall have passed
away forever. And well for some hearts, closed against
the convictions of revelation, that God has spread out
this wondrous map, that ocean of blue—those isles of
gold—types these of a world brighter and more lasting
than themselves; for they shall pass, and their ruins
but give place to a home eternal in the heavens.

"He can not survive the night," at length murmured Geraldine, her eyes glistening with tears in
the moonlight, on which they were fixed; "and now
that we have felt the worst I would scarcely recall
dear Connal. What an anomaly is the heart? We
cling to a life we know to be but a vapor, marked at
every step by some chance that makes us weep or
laugh from contempt; and yet we profess a Faith
that tells us of happiness, endless and unspeakable,
after death."

"This is but the instinctive love of life, chaining
us and all our feelings here, while religion points the
pilgrim, like the prophet, to the Land of Promise."
I turned. Connal was apparently sleeping. His
breathing was heavy. "He will soon be there," I
said, almost unconsciously, as the visage of the boy
conjured up that of death.

"What is that?" said Geraldine, extending her
finger in the direction of something that seemed to
flit, like a cloud just dropped on the moonlit plain.

"It moves—and now—it stands still—strange. It
has something of the human form—!"

We both strained our eyes in the direction of the
object; so wavy and fleecelike it indeed resembled a
cloud in texture, while in form it bore the semblance
of humanity. Now it moved—anon it stood still. In
an hour so solemn as the present one, superstition was
not slow in evoking her phantoms. Was it a supernatural visitant—? I rushed to the bedside—bent
over the boy—he lived! I returned hastily to the
window, against which Geraldine had sunk for support; her hands were outstretched toward the object,
the cold moonlight fell on features as cold and white
as itself, and scarcely could she articulate from lips
horror had parted: "It is the Banshee—! all—is
over." *

This broken ejaculation rooted me to the spot, and
seemed to freeze my very blood with that spectral influence, against which prayer and convictions are for
the time unavailing; being but the vain resources of
man against the terrors of an invisible world. These
fears now the more overwhelmed me, as we heard a
low wail or moan reach us from the object which had
now taken its seat on the moonlit sward immediately
opposite to the window at which we stood. So deep,

---

* Every family in Ireland is supposed to be attended by its own
Banshee, a spirit foretelling, in the manner described, any impending
calamity or death.

so heart-breaking that wail, it never came from mortal lip, but in its tones of unearthly modulation seemed
to embody the mysteries of the world whence it came,
and the fate of those it was appointed to predict.

"My God—my God! It is the Banshee!" burst
from me; as my eyes remained immovably fixed on
the figure, and my ears entranced by sounds more
mystic and unearthly than ever lured Ulysses and his
companions to their destruction. The figure was robed
in white, its long hair streaming on its shoulders;
and, while sitting, it kept time by a long swaying
motion with the following melancholy, irregular ditty.
The air had more the character of a chant than a
song. It was but the precursor of death to Geraldine
and myself, as we stood and listened.

"Ochone—ochone
To the sod and the stone!
To the grave with your dead, for his chamber is laid
Deep down in the earth with the sexton's spade;
And ye never need weep, for the silver cord
Of life is parted, like flash from the sword!
"Ochone—ochone

To the sod and the stone!
Then weep not De Lacy; he'll never return;
No more than the glimmering stars that burn
On the mariner's way, o'er the ocean's breast,
When they sink deep down in the midnight west.
"Ochone—ochone
To the sod and the stone!
Thou seest yon cloud; ere the midnight hour
'Twill shadow your boy with its grave-like power;
Ay, blot out the moon, like a spirit from hell;
For the presence of death is invisible!

"Ochone—ochone
To the sod and the stone !
Yet weep not, De Lacy ! 'Tis better to pass,
Ere the image of life hath polluted its glass,
Than to linger 'mid crimes, amid sorrows, and tears
That canker, like worms, the core of man's years !"

The Banshee (let not the reader be incredulous, I have
but described an object of popular belief in Ireland)
slowly rose, gazed for some moments toward the room
of the dying boy, waved its long arm, as white as the
moonlight that streamed upon it, and moved as slowly
away. As my eyes were strained on that retreating
figure, it seemed as though it concentrated on itself
every sense of my being; I knew not that I lived, or
breathed, or heard, or saw, for the mystery of that
presence and the terrors it wrote, as with the pale
hand of the dead, on my very soul. I felt that I had
held communion, though momentary, with the dead;
that the very form I had looked on had passed that
murky, impalpable atmosphere mortal lip could never
breathe, and that that voice, whose echo still pressed
down ear and heart with a chain forged by no human
hand, had communed of those secrets that were never
allowed to pass the dark barrier of its world.

It was some time ere Geraldine recovered from the
spell cast on her by the Banshee, and the fatal message it bore. Her eyes were wild, her whole form
visibly trembling, and her face had in those few moments assumed a haggard and distorted aspect. I

:rove to rally myself, to reassure her.   It was, after
ll, but the rally of the physical; the minds of both
ere overwhelmed, stunned by a blow for which time
id hope had neither a remedy.   In silence we con-
nued to gaze listlessly on the spot but now filled by
e Banshee; the dread tripod from which that Sibyl
  death had delivered her prophecy; the eye was
ell-bound as that of the victim by the serpent.
iat was a breathless and a terrible moment; there
is a weight in the air, a luridness in the sky, a
solation and a curse on the silvered sward beneath
, that made every breath we drew a poison, every
rd we might utter a seal to the dread tidings that
1 been sent us from the grave.   We turned to look
the poor little boy; and read in every moment that
sed amid the stillness that hung round the uncon-
us sleeper, the terrible fulfillment of the prediction
  had heard.   The death hour, too, had its approach-
  sign; for a deep and slumbering shadow now
ipt in its advancing wings the dying boy, and every
ict within the chamber, that had but now been
hed in the pearl-like glory of the midnight heaven.
  looked; and lo! a thick and murky cloud was
  usurping the throne, but a few moments past
ving and radiant as though from the presence of a
  .   We trembled at the omen.   Presently all was
:, save for the dim light of the little taper that
cely pierced the depths of the sick chamber.   There

was a slight movement in the bed-clothes. We rushed to the bed. At that moment the door opened, and Sir Hubert entered, supported by the Lady De Lacy. But I can not now dwell upon that feeble, emaciated, and haggard form; for, as I turned from him to poor little Connal, death seemed more to have set his pale seal on the father than the son. It was but a moment; as the father, fixing on the boy eyes of unearthly light, tottered to the bed and sank on it.

"The dead can not lie. My God—my God! he is dead!" he cried.

We seized the light, and held it over Connal. There seemed to be a slight convulsion, a clenching of the bed-clothes. I bent my ear. He was dead.

CHAPTER IX.

I do not deem myself a Bobadil
To decimate our planet man by man,
By scholar rules of nice arithmetic;—
But when a man traduces all life holds
Honored, beshrew me then, his taunts are counters
He'd better reckon, or woe upon the issue! ~

MY dear little pupil had been consigned to his resting-place. I had now space to reflect on the
mysterious agency that had caused his death. But
the more I reflected, the more inexplicable seemed
the whole event; from my first meeting with that
woman to that last dreadful one, that had clothed a
day of happiness in the saddest weeds that ever death
wove for the mourner. I had not seen her since.
The events, too, of that fatal day crowded on me.
The taunt of the young earl, the presence of Desmond,
the recognitions that passed between the woman and
himself, and the terrors her presence seemed to inspire
in a heart I had deemed callous to all human influence. But I turned from myself, and began to regard
with a deeper interest the inmates of Deer Park.

The death of poor Connal had produced a strong
influence, on the Lady De Lacy especially. Whether

in the death of the boy, she recognized the truth of
the mother's apparition, I know not; but certain it is,
from that event her manner toward the Baronet, and
doubtless her feelings, underwent a miraculous change.
Instead of the haughty and reserved being I had met
on my first arrival—cold and inaccessible in address
as insensible in feeling—now that tenderness (at once
the prerogative and distinctive trait of woman) borrowed a new depth and strength from the affection
and alacrity she gave to the duties of the wife. Indeed the change seemed the result as well of an affection long subdued, as of a repentance poignant and
sincere. Ever at Sir Hubert's side, she had always a
word of sympathy, a look of kindness, for that irre-
pressible grief, which finds its balm alone in faith in
Him who has sent it. From religion she borrowed
her chiefest sources of consolation; and while I heard
her endeavoring to comfort the disconsolate, by com-
paring the joys of heaven with the sorrows and temptations from which that pure spirit had been removed,
the hand of mercy that had changed the burden of
flesh for the crown and harp of the spirit, I could not
but hope that affliction had, in her case, been the
bearer of that priceless message—faith in the healing
power of that hand that doth not willingly chastise.
The poor husband observed this change, and it seemed
to affect him with joy and gratitude. As she quoted
passages from that book to which the afflicted never

seek in vain, the tears would start, and the heart
seemed to share its gratefulness between the Father
who had indited these records of comfort for penitent
and returning children, and the affectionate lips that
read them now to him in his hour of distress. Privy
as I was to the anguish of the father, and those mental causes that had produced it, it was with joy I
heard the consolations both of wife and daughter, and
the gradual cheerfulness he assumed under their influence. I say, assumed—for I fear that mind had been
too fearfully unbalanced, and that heart too deeply
wounded, to hear of comfort from human lips. He
would smile and apparently cheer as they read passages from the Bible suited to the comfort of mourners; and, as that divine volume spoke of the joys that
God had prepared for those who love him in an after
state, his eye would brighten as though by faith he
already viewed them, and his hands would clasp in
the strength of prayer, as though he asked to be found
worthy of them. But no sooner was the volume
closed, and the voices hushed, that spoke from its
pages as from the mercy-seat where God yet dwelt,
than the poor man relapsed into his comfortless gloom,
and, like the mother of Israel, would not be comforted
because his child was not.

Deer Park was, indeed, now a gloomy place. The
little boy had been laid in his grave; and every spot
throughout the stately mansion presented that chill

and dreary vacuum we feel, when a form and voice of
daily familiarity has been snatched from our midst.
Ah! where is the morning greeting, the day intercourse, the evening companion, and the night parting?
—the kind word that flung oblivion over the painful
past, that gave hope to distress, and enhancement to
our joys, by sharing them? Where the form, alas!
we no more expect to miss than the sun in heaven—
that form that seems part of our own existence, twin-
ned with us at a birth, like two flowers springing from
the same stem? Such was little Connal to me. I felt
myself indeed alone.

A few mornings after the interment of the little boy,
I received a message from Sir Hubert to attend him
in his study. Thence he led me to that dark chamber, where I had heard his terrible confession, and
witnessed his agonies.

Closing the door, he said: "It was this room, Mr.
O'Moore, that witnessed the outbreak of a passion I
was unable to restrain; this room should also witness
the most ample reparation one gentleman can make
another. Sir, I ask your pardon, and with it your
sympathy."

"The latter, Sir Hubert, you have a right to claim
in its most extended sense; but for my pardon, I know
not in what you have offended."

"The death of my dear child releases you from
the obligations you assumed in coming to Deer Park.

Pardon me, Mr. O'Moore," interrupting me as I was on the eve of announcing my readiness to take my departure; "you are released from all duties to my beloved child, but not to myself." I fixed on him an interrogating glance, as I was at an utter loss to divine the meaning of words, exacting from me duties where I could recognize none.

"You are surprised, Sir, as your looks denote. Permit me to explain. An accident, or, it may be, my own unguarded passion, has made you alone familiar with a secret I have studiously, nay religiously, concealed from my own family—a secret, which not even yourself, however uninterested in the result, can possibly deem a trifle. My son is dead, and dead in childhood."—He rested for a moment, and resumed, with a voice trembling with the deepest emotion: "The latter part remains—*the father is to follow the son!*"

These words were uttered with such painful intensity and emphasis, as sufficiently to show the effect the dream had left on the speaker's mind.

"Think not I tremble, Sir; it may be an inexplicable and mysterious phenomenon of our nature has revealed that at which the boldest would shudder, and a merciful God has in that mercy wrapt in secret. No. I expect my fate, and await it, I trust, with the same boldness as the soldier, who knows not whether the termination of the battle may enroll him among the

H

slain. But to the point : You are the sole repository
of a secret I have hoarded, as the miser his treasure.
I regard you alone as my confidant. Your kindness
to my boy has won my esteem and gratitude, and that
confidence reposed in you, whether forced or voluntary, has raised both to the standard of friendship.
My request is, that you still continue an inmate of
Deer Park. I know your spirit, naturally proud and
independent, will at the first regard of my request,
make me appear as conferring an obligation, when my
object is to demand a favor. In few words I have
stated my situation and my feelings, and expect the
compliance of a friend."

I started such objections as occurred on the instant;
not those originating from myself, but based on public
opinion, and the observations it must inevitably draw
upon me. I stated to him, what he himself had anticipated ;—the termination of my engagement by the
death of my dear little pupil, and finally wound up
my objections by the difference of our rank, which, in
the eyes of the world, would naturally deepen the relation of dependence involved in his request. But my
objections were overmastered, not so much by the
reasoning of Sir Hubert, as by the fervent spirit of
entreaty with which he sought compliance—at once
shifting the obligation from myself to him. I consented at length. " Thank you—thank you, a thousand times," said the Baronet, squeezing my hand,

while the tear started; "thank you; you have seen the beginning, but—" and here he paused, while his lips blanched and quivered—"*the end is not yet!*" * * * *

I pass over some six months in this sketch of my life, presenting nothing worthy of my own memory, or the attention of the reader. Indeed life at Deer Park (to a true Irish spirit ever on the *qui vive* for the various and the exciting) was fast degenerating into the mechanical routine and periodic dullness of a monastery. With a punctuality worthy the monks' refectory, we (that is four of us) assembled in the great oak dining-hall for breakfast and dinner; at the former meal our stinted number frequently dwindling into the dual, in the persons of the Lady Geraldine and myself. The huge hall might have feasted knight and vassal; and with its chivalrous portraits of the bygone day, looking down on us from their grim frames (Sir Hubert's ancestry), the memory of whose stirring deeds and times strangely contrasted with the silence and quiet of the party, we might well have deemed ourselves assembled at a funeral feast of the ancients, were it not for the stern armor of the Norman knights, that pushed on fancy some years into our own era. I found the *têtes-à-tête* with Geraldine far preferable to the presence of the worthy Baronet and his lady. There was a common effort to drive from our minds the absorbing theme that at other times paralyzed our intercourse. Music and poetry, in both of which Ger-

aldine wás a fine proficient, formed the frequent theme
of our conversation. In the former she was highly
cultivated ; the finest singer of the ballad school I had
ever heard, and imparting to the Irish melodies that
simplicity and tenderness so eminently characteristic
of our national airs. Her taste in poetry was ex-
quisitely fine, and her familiarity with the best writers
extensive. Her power of quotation was wonderful ;
not as in many cases arguing a poverty of thought
or expression in herself, but summoned adventitiously
for the purpose of maintaining some original position
or suggestion. I need hardly say, that such society
made me soon forgetful of the monastic monotony that
surrounded me at Deer Park. Still I did not allow
this feeling to obtain, as I felt that, in the present
circumstances of Sir Hubert, my sojourn was dictated
by those philanthropic feelings that are their own best
and most certain reward.

Thus at Deer Park one day-told another ; we alternated (that is Geraldine and myself) between conversation and reading, and the sedentary feelings inspired
by these employments we occasionally relieved by the
more stimulating one of riding. A good horseman
myself, I must hide my diminished head before the
more masterly prowess of Geraldine. Her seat was
at once firm and graceful, and her boldness equal to
both. Indeed I have seen her face leaps which, perhaps, experienced horsemen would rather have left

undone. In the beautiful grounds of Deer Park I was not infrequently her companion. On the occasion I am about to relate I was absent, as the reader shall hear.

In a remote part of the garden and at some distance from the mansion, Nature, in one of her frolic moods, had formed a bower, which art had not been slow in improving. I knew this to be a constant and favorite resort of Geraldine; and, when not in the mansion, I seldom failed in tracing her steps to this bower. The natural mould of the bower, interwoven with creepers and wild flowers, and commanding a grand and extensive range of mountain in the distance, with the flashing waters of a river between, presented features naturally attractive for the mind of poetic musing and meditation. As usual, the dullness of the castle making me rather *ennuyeux*, I felt desirous for that change I knew I should find in her society. As I approached the bower my attention was arrested by a voice. I stopped and held my breath. It was repeated. The voice was Geraldine's. It was one of distress, with a tone of reproof rising to passion. On the instant I darted from the spot. I heard another voice. I felt for the moment as though some spell rested with a chain's weight, paralyzing will and motion. That voice—that voice—it pealed, not sounded in my ear. I rallied and rushed forward—I tore aside the falling curtain of the creepers that drooped over the entrance of the bower; and in a moment, oh, horror! I stood confronted with Desmond.

"By heaven, I love you—!" were the words that fell from him as I entered. In a moment he started to his feet; relinquished the hand he had clasped in his own with the evident reluctance of Geraldine, and fixed on me eyes in which it was hard to say whether rage for the present or vengeance for the future predominated.

"Morven, you shall repent this," he cried.

"Desmond, to your teeth, I fear you not," was the instant answer; as clenching his fist with fury at me, he hurried down a wild path that led to the bower, at the foot of which stood his horse. In an instant he sprang to his back. The spur was dashed into the flanks of the poor animal, that he reared and plunged before he could be put to his headlong speed. I heard the wild and clattering hoof in the distance. The steed seemed to partake the momentary madness of his master.

I conducted Geraldine to a moss seat. She trembled violently in my arms as I supported her. With much difficulty I restored her to equanimity. The insult she had received and the momentary alarm it had produced, were, in the eyes of the generous girl, as nothing compared with the deadly defiance that had passed between brothers. Till that moment she had never known of the relationship existing between myself and our neighbor of Clonmuir Castle. I can

not now state my motive, but, as the reader may remember, on the first inquiry, denied it.

"Why did you not tell me," said Geraldine, wring-
ing her hands, as she contemplated the probable consequences of this *rencontre;* "and a formal introduction at Deer Park or—something might have obviated
an incident so dreadful as the present."

"I beseech you, Miss De Lacy, be not alarmed at
his meeting, or any gloomy bodings it may throw
over the future. Desmond's words were but an empty
threat, and mine as empty a reply to what I deemed
an unmerited insult. I have known Desmond from a
boy; and, trust me, he is not likely to be guilty of
any act that might result in danger to himself."

We returned to the mansion, having pledged each
other to silence on the incident that had just transpired. Easy though it be to lay a fetter on the tongue,
it is not equally so to restrain the wanderings of the
mind. Though protected by a sense of my own innocence, that night I found it impossible to sleep for
thoughts of Desmond. His presence at Deer Park
could have been accounted for only on the principle of
carrying out some evil designs against one who had
ever injured him. If so, he had, so far, succeeded, by
the collision that had taken place, and the challenge
mutual enmity it had produced. There must have
been some motive of this kind in his appearance on
the grounds of the De Lacys, for previously there had

existed no intercourse between the families. Whatever might have been my brother's motive, I felt
resolved to abide the issue, with the calmness of one
who had done nothing to provoke, and would, therefore, take but little trouble to avoid it.

Some months passed at Deer Park after the above
incident, on which Geraldine and myself preserved an
inviolable silence, and to which we never alluded, even
between ourselves. Our life passed much as usual;
presenting but little, if any, variety from without, and
therefore rendering dependence on our own resources
the more necessary. My interviews with Sir Hubert
(at his own request) were more frequent, proceeding
from the dreadful communication he had made me at
Connal's death, and the increasing confidence he appeared desirous to repose in me. About the period of
which I speak, I observed a growing silence and depression in the Baronet I could not fail to impute to
the fate of his son and its mysterious connection with
his own. I endeavored with whatever resources of
conversation and amusement I could master to divert
his thoughts from this absorbing theme, and remove
from his mind that single oppressive thought that
brooded over it like a vampire, exhausting its nourish-
ment and healthfulness. But the voice of the charmer
was unheard in those dreadful hours that now returned with periodic regularity and aggravation ; and the
task of consolation I was compelled to abandon as

vain, as the mind was too strongly preoccupied by
that fearful tenant that kept possession with the ob-
stinate malignity of a demon. On the part of the sufferer, there was no struggle; no, not an effort to throw
off this incubus that was withering up the very roots
of life, and dragging down the spirit of the man to a
level with the dust that encompassed it. It was but
an illusion; but one delivered from the lips, and moulded from the form of the dead. It was, therefore, as
implicitly believed by the impressible mind as though
the words had been spoken by the lips of the living,
and the illusion itself charactered in the infallible
light of noon-day, and not in the shadowy uncertainty
of midnight. The demon might be exorcised for a
moment by the resources of society or conversation,
but only to return with a stronger retinue to tenant
the house his temporary absence had left swept and
garnished. 'Tis thus the mind, easily a dupe to supernatural agency, becomes by its own imbecility and submission, the fulfillment of that it deems as prophecy.

But Desmond's threats were not as abortive or
empty as I had deemed them. The web was woven
by a dexterous hand; the pit dug by a strong and
determined one; and the victim snared!

As I was one day wandering near the bower (the
scene of my unexpected and fearful interview with
my brother), I heard a stir among the branches, and
thought that I observed the motion of a human figure

H*

among the thick foliage. The circumstance did not,
at the moment, attract my attention beyond a mere
passing incident, and I continued, without any further thought of it, to pursue my way to the arbor. As
I entered, my eye fell on a paper closed in the form
of a letter ; and, without raising it from the ground,
from recollection of the figure I had seen, I hastened
forward and looked above the declivity by which my
brother had escaped. There I spied my young friend,
the earl, just taking to horse. His secrecy, the place,
the reflections awakened by his intimacy with Desmond, all smouldered and kindled in my mind on the
instant. Suspicion was not long in lighting her demon train. With brain and heart both on fire with
contempt and indignation, I was in no very moderate
vein to peruse the following, evidently meant for the
eyes of Geraldine, though chance had submitted it first
to mine. It bore no superscription; and, notwithstanding the feigned hand, the authorship was undeniable :

"In Morven O'Moore you harbor one who, by connection with one of the ancientest families of Ireland,
owned by his birth the character and pretensions of a
gentleman, he has since, by his own dishonorable conduct, forfeited. Society disowns the disinherited son;
while his present dependent position on the bounty
of Sir Hubert De Lacy, fills up by his meanness the
measure of that fate his father's wrongs and his own
misconduct have partially awarded him."

Stung to madness, and on fire at the cowardice and falsehood of this furtive assault, will, thought, action, were paralyzed. I seemed to myself, on the instant, transformed to stone—thoughtless, motionless, soulless. Amid the inane and dreary wilderness into which my being was converted, I could trace but one sensation that bound me to the earth I could not feel beneath me; but one that told me I yet held a life, in my bitterness I almost cursed! That was the burning throb that, as with a single cord, bound brow and heart together. But one pulse animated and pervaded my whole being; a pulse, to which the thrusting of my naked hand into the flames would have been a relief; one, which pealed upon my ear with a demon's voice —Revenge! while it unnerved and prostrated every energy to achieve it from the thought that its object was—a brother! The whole scene swam around me; my mind had lost its balance, my whole being its sense, save the torturing one that, like the Furies of old, goaded Orestes to vengeance with whips of fire and scorpions. I twined my hands in my hair—I tore the leaves from the trees—I stamped my feet upon the earth, to give myself the painful assurance that all was real. It was; it was! The leaves lay scattered and torn at my feet, and the earth gave back its dull and heavy echo to my fury. It was no dream: I was slandered—belied—robbed of my honor, and by him who should have cherished; painted as an outcast by

the hand that should have clothed and fed me, and
disowned as an alien by the very lips that had drunk
at the same fount of nature with myself. But even
the slander of my conduct to my father I could have
borne; yes, perhaps with patience, every word of that
poisoned missive, except the closing ones, that branded
me with a *dependence*, the taunt of which I had anticipated from the sometime heartless, harsh-judging
world, and in which I had involved myself only from
the entreaties of a despairing man, and a heart that,
perhaps, too kindly submitted to what my convictions
utterly condemned. It was this that stung me far
above any calumny that had originated from my filial
relations. I dashed from me the cup of passion and
madness that every moment was filling with poison;
rallied whatever reflection I had in that agitated moment, and sought out, with the best of my judgment,
the course I should pursue. It was plain from the
drift of this infernal writing (in which it was difficult
to say whether falsehood or malignity predominated),
that Desmond was a lover of Geraldine, that this sentiment was the cause of our meeting, and that in this
slanderous letter he sought to undermine the pretensions of one he had reason to regard as a more successful rival. What was I to do? Action—instant
and vehement—was to be taken by me; but my own
feelings, however wrung, lacerated, and almost extinguished by Desmond's conduct, had yet too much of

the brotherly leaven to permit any exhibition of hostility to the delinquent. There was but one course to pursue—to hold the bearer of this hated missive responsible. This would afford me a double opportunity of retribution; the present and the past, which, though intermitted for the time, yet had never been forgotten. The Irish, they say, never turn back on friend or enemy. I hope I have never been ungrateful to the former; and for the latter, as a commoner, I was doubly resolved to hold the young noble to account. I left the bower with this resolution, and turned my steps to Deer Park. The letter I inclosed in my bosom, determined that no eye should look on it save he whom the law of honor was about to make my peer.

CHAPTER X.

Honor, forsooth! 'Tis thus in polished phrase
Men guild a murder. Would this hand of Cain
Had rotted piecemeal, ere this guilty soul
Had wrought it to the deed!

MY purposes were, however, for the moment diverted by the intelligence I received as I entered the
mansion. Sir Hubert had been suddenly indisposed;
so alarmingly as to require the immediate attendance
of the physician who was now in the sick room of his
patient. I lost not a moment in acceding to the request
communicated to me by the servant, that I would
wait on his master. As I entered, the physician,
Lady De Lacy and Geraldine were requested by the
sick man to withdraw. I trembled for the coming
interview; for I saw by the preternatural light of the
eye and wanness of the cheek, that the suicidal energies of the mind were at work, and even now more
destructive and wasting in their effects than the inroads of disease.

"You remember," said the Baronet, fixing his eyes
on me, and with a strong effort shaking off the languor
that oppressed him; "what our great poet has said:

'The greatest is *behind!*'" I shuddered at the freezing emphasis he laid on the last word; placing in
visible relief before me the appalling terrors of an un-
revealed future.

"I do; but recollect, Sir Hubert, that was in application to the enjoyments of honor and sovereignty."

"You are kind thus to render it; but in *my* case it
means—*Death!* Do not start. The grave has been
dug, and Death has clasped its first victim. The
second part of the prophecy hangs on a thread. Break
that thread, and the hecatomb is complete. Ha! what
say you?" continued the wretched man, discerning
some cheering expression in my countenance, and
catching at it with the eagerness of a sinking swimmer
at a straw.

"That the death of the son implies neither the death
of the father, nor even that event within a specified
time, that seems thus to awake in you an unearthly
terror. My dear Sir Hubert," I continued, pressing
the subject with an interest and ardor I sincerely felt;
"you must rally sense and will on this subject. The
poet, of whom you spoke, has in the very character
from which you quoted, made Macbeth the slave of
his own mental and imaginary fears, and thus in part
ministrant to the fulfillments of that dreadful prophecy,
that crowned a life of bloodshed with temporary
success only to close it by an end as bloody. You now
tremble under the fearful visitation of a dream, which

after all may be the reflex of your day-thoughts. You
have expressed to me the extreme remorse you felt for
the differences between yourself and Lady De Lacy."

"Which I have endeavored to atone," groaned the
sufferer.

"But not yet forgotten," I interposed; "and the
memory of which still exists to aggravate that morbid
sensibility, which once conquered would dissipate the
fear it creates. For your wife's and daughter's sake,
Sir Hubert, I pray you cast this thought from you."

He seized my hand, locked rather than pressed it
in his own; his eyes were fixed on mine; but their
glassiness was fast being dimmed by the tears that
gushed from them. "You are my friend—my only
one," he, at length, said; "for to you alone have I
confided a secret I have breathed to none save yourself and—"

"Whom?" I had scarcely courage to ask, from the
pause that followed.

"God—God—before whom I must shortly stand;
who has searched and tried my heart; who regards my
conduct to the dead as sin to Himself; ay, to Himself; for has not this weak hand of wormy flesh dared
to put asunder what God hath joined together? Oh!
here—here—" he continued, straining both hands in
the violence of his agony to his head; "oh! here—that
the worm dieth not and the fire is never quenched—!"

A long silence ensued I felt myself incapable of

breaking, from my utter incapacity to minister to the
consolation of the sufferer.

"Yet that sublime Teacher, sir, whose words you
have quoted gives us hope that repentance may kill
the one and extinguish the other."

"Oh! sir, you know not the bitter agony I have
poured forth in my prayers to God, as every word,
while it convinced me of my guilt attested the sincerity
of my repentance—nor have those prayers been uttered
alone amid the frigid formalities of the church, where
worship partakes more the mechanism of habit than
the devotional rapture of Faith; no—not there alone
have my prayers been offered; but in the silence of my
own chamber, on the mountain, in the valley, by the
river side, by the lone and starry watches of midnight;
wherever nature, with her thousand voices, told me of
a God who created and protected his works, with the
same tongue she also told me that He heard. But it
was vain, I prayed, but the prayer turned to my own
bosom, and where I might have expected the balm of
trust and repentance, I but felt the more poignantly
the adder of remorse. It is vain, sir; the hand is on
me that no mortal could ever combat or evade. The
pile is built, why should not the sacrifice ascend?"

That night as I retired I could not help brooding on
the melancholy circumstances by which I was surrounded, the result of which was as undefined as the
future that encompassed it. The death of Sir Hubert

would at once dissolve a connection the more revolting from the confidence that forced it on me, and the taunting allusion made to it in the anonymous paper I had found. The satisfaction I was bent on exacting from my dastard opponent (albeit an earl) might terminate fatally to him—in which case I would occupy the delectable position of a criminal—or to myself. Well, for the latter I recked not. Life had not, at least for me, laid on her brightest colors or wooed the eye with her fairest forms. Like Pierre, "This vile world and I had long been jangling, and could not part on better terms than now!"

"So stood the great account," as Zanga says. On mature reflection, however, I saw nothing to shake my resolution. I had been first insulted, under circumstances peculiarly aggravative of the offense—the presence of a lady. That offense had been now tenfold enhanced by the degraded character assumed by the opponent—defamer of my character. Circumstances screened the principal, but the agent of so dastard an act I was resolved should not escape its accountability.

I was instant in search of my antagonist, who seemed as lucky, as I doubt not he was desirous to elude me. I frequented those haunts where I deemed a meeting most probable. But my pursuit seemed baffled. I traversed the roads for some distance round; but some good spirit seemed to have taken charge of

s lordly godchild, for nowhere was he to be found or
sen. Had I been superstitious, I could have almost
eemed him a second Curtius—steed and man both
wallowed up. No hound ever trailed the scent with
1ore perseverance; no general, fresh from victory,
ver exhibited more vigor in the pursuit of his flying
1emy. At length, one day, when almost in despair
t being thus compelled to bear insult with impunity,
espied a horseman on the road at some distance, but
it sufficient, however, to prevent identification of my
1ble friend. I clapped spurs to the blooded mare,
1d in a few moments she brought me to his side,
ith fiery eye and distended nostril, almost partici-
iting the purpose of her master.

"My Lord! I have been diligent in my quest of
1u. You may guess the motive. For fear of any
isapprehension on that subject, your Lordship is
obably aware of the contents of this missive."—I
ew the letter from my bosom, and handed it to him.
he color forsook his cheek as he mechanically opened
and riveted on it eyes so fixed, they seemed to take
note of its contents.

"Your Lordship need not hesitate in making your-
lf acquainted with the characters before you. The
ter is neither a papyrus from the chambers of Ghizeh,
r a calcined manuscript from the ruins of Pompeii."
1is ironical taunt roused him from the momentary
hargy that had supervened on our meeting. A

violent effort restored the blood to his cheek, and manliness to his whole bearing.

"It is needless, sir," he replied, "to inform me that
the characters are English. I am aware of the occasion on which they were penned, and have the honor
to be acquainted with the writer—"

"As well as the bearer of them, I presume?" re-
pressing scarcely the choler I found mastering me at
his imperturbable answer.

"I was the bearer of them, sir," was the answer.

"Then, sir, I hold myself free of choice between
the writer and the bearer. The law of honor holds
you, I believe, endorser?"

"I presume so, Mr. O'Moore."

"Then, sir, you have but to accede to the course
your own conduct has forced on me." I proceeded
then to appoint a place of meeting, time, and weapons.
All arranged, we parted with that polite etiquette
characteristic of true diplomatists, who are never so
courtly and polished in their correspondence as when
their respective nations are on the eve of war.

The few days that intervened before our appointed
meeting, were marked by a visible and increasing
decay in poor Sir Hubert De Lacy. He was impressed
with the certainty of his death; and it would have
been as easy to disabuse him of that fatal impression
as to have given a material existence to the phantom
dream that had thus awed and prostrated his mind

wounded me to the heart that at such a time my
ord was pledged to a meeting, which, however it
ight terminate, would more or less affect the inmates
' the mansion. But all minor considerations were
sorbed in my own strong sensibilities, and the fear
at the calumnies set forth in the letter would be
t aggravated by rendering myself amenable to the
arge of cowardice. My course was taken. He who
s courage for the throw should stand the hazard of
die.

So secret was I resolved this meeting should be,
m pure regard to the inmates of Deer Park, that I
s determined to face the chances of the field alone,
l without a second. The conventionalities of the
eting I could arrange to my own satisfaction, and
uld the result prove fatal, I trusted to the humani-
of my antagonist. It was indeed a gloomy morn-
, as I took leave of my room for the appointed
e. Every trivial object on which the eye rested
arting, endeared by so many years of possession,
such varied recollections, assumed a domestic
heartfelt interest they had never had previously
ne. As I passed unobserved from the great gate
e De Lacys, I looked back on the massive pile,
cely looming out from the impenetrable mist that
shrouding it. Huge tower and buttress seemed
to betray the eye with illusions that stood forth
spectres amid the vapor that had waited on them

from their own mysterious land. It resembled more
a cloud-built palace than the solid masonry of human
hand. A vague and shadowy feeling overpowered me.
To my own fancy I was, on the instant, as visionary
as the objects that met the eye. I had issued from a
fabric piled in cloudland by other than mortal hand,
bound on a mission that, mayhap, ere a brief hour
was past, might number me with those of the spirit-
land. Ere another sun had beamed on those towers,
my very life might mingle with that vapor that seemed reeking with the oppressive weight of the grave,
my name fill a few moments' memory, and my place
be forgotten even by him who would soon succeed me.
How associative is place! The whole tableau of
events that had transpired within those walls rose
with a painful precision before me, as for the last time
I fixed my eyes on them. In certain conditions, what
a keen anatomizer is the mind. Never did surgeon
with probe or cautery ever search and lacerate the
wound with such a careful tediousness as will the
mind revert to the past, read the epitaphs and memories of its buried events, and impart a painful vitality
to the ashes that heart and memory had sepulchred
forever. Our past life is then the valley of dead
bones; and our self-torturing minds the cunning arti-
ficer that invests the grinning skeletons with the
aspect and very motions of life. Poor little Connal
was visible to me amid the thick mist that curtained

hat huge pile. I saw the love and grief that spoke rom his pale face ;—the thin and wasted hand that beckoned me back. I could almost, amid the dreary stillness of that dark morning, hear his voice. But his was unmanning me at the very moment that demanded all my energies. .I tore asunder the net the mind was but too dexterously weaving, and hurried orward with such speed that a few moments rendered he mansion altogether invisible. But there were two within those walls who still haunted me ;—the owner f that lordly mansion, now on his death-bed, and Geraldine. I put my hand to my pistol. The touch raced me.

Hastening to the appointed spot, I found my adversary was before me. The ground was measured. The mist, in the mean time, increased to such a degree as to render it somewhat difficult for me to discern my opponent. We took our ground. At the word I readily raised my pistol and fired. I heard the ball my antagonist whiz past my ear. A moment elapsed after I fired. I heard a groan, and saw my opponent sink to the ground. Remorse as strongly now seized me as wounded pride and a retaliative spirit previously. I dashed away my pistol with a violence bordering on frenzy, and rushing up, beheld good God! it was my brother I had shot, while the girl was kneeling by his side, supporting his head in her arms.

"Desmond—Desmond—" I cried; but could say no more; I sank upon his neck as weak and powerless as my wounded, perhaps dying brother.

"No more—no more—" feebly ejaculated Desmond, turning on me his swimming eyes that seemed fast losing the power of vision. "The fault is mine. Fly —fly—lest worse than that I have done befall you—!"

"Fly—fly—" said the earl. But it seemed an iron band bound me to the spot of blood; and, like Cain, the demon of remorse chained me to the body of my victim till I should hear the thunder of Divine denunciation. I clung the more firmly to Desmond. I covered his cheek with kisses and tears. That awful moment canceled the bond of enmity forever. He was still my brother; ay, a thousand times more, now that I had murdered him! "Oh God!" I exclaimed in my agony, "strike me dead—dead even here by the brother I have murdered!"

"Fly—fly—" again murmured the dying man. "Fly—" iterated the earl. I started to my feet, gazed round wildly. The scene seemed on the instant transformed. The mist had been raised as a curtain from the earth. The sun seemed to glare on me—and me alone—with that concentrated power, as though it would bury my victim in the ashes of his murderer. The air was hot and parched; and through its burning wilderness there howled but one echo—"Murderer— Murderer!" I twined my hands madly in my moist

hair, and cast one withering look on the craven peer.
" Coward—coward—coward !" broke from me unconsciously. ' I flew from the spot, unknowing whither,
save that instinct I presume directed me to Deer Park
is the only refuge for the murderer. As I rushed
orward with the blind impulses of passion and despe-
ation, another voice broke through the mist. " Fly
—fly—fly—Morven !" I turned ; it was that strange
roman whom, it seemed to me, the changing scenes
: life could not divorce from me. Her arms were
ised ; and her figure stood out in bold relief from the
ist that like some spirit she had raised to mantle the
rrible deed of the murderer. I heard no more, but
ntinued to pursue my way with that reckless blind-
ss, that only seeks for shelter and cares not if it find
in the depths of the earth. I reached the mansion,
I was hastening through the hall to bury myself in
' chamber, when the servant addressed me.
' Sir Hubert De Lacy, Sir, is dead."
' My God—my God—death—nothing but death !"
ashed up the stairs, closed the door of my chamber.
> thought rushed on me. That fatal day was the
iversary of Connal's death.

I

CHAPTER XI.

Is Cain's brand set upon my brow, that thus
I am a wanderer? I would the Fiat,
To spare the guilty, were with me-reversed,
And they, who meet, might kill!

          Antiquity,
All hail! a kindred spirit moves among
Your ruins; one whose broken heart can weep
Ay, tear for tear, with Niobé. All hail!
Thy prostrate fanes and columned loneliness
Are temple meet for worship such as mine.

Beshrew me, these be catacombs indeed!
Oh! for an Ariadné's clew to guide
Us through these windings, where the Minotaur
Might seek his Attic sacrifice in vain;
Darkness and Hunger hold their carnival—
Oh! for one ray of light!

I PACED my room some moments, agitated, bewildered, and unconscious of all save existence. The sense of that still clung to me as the fearfullest penalty Divine wrath could inflict on me. I tried to disengage my thoughts from the one image that, like the angel of retribution, still haunted them, my brother—my dying—murdered brother. But ever as I sought to fix my mind on my perilous situation and the action it

required, that image would interpose its bleeding front,
its bloodless cheek, its quivering hand. It was the
spirit of Banquo, haunting the guilty Thane with a
remorseless perseverance, which ever side of the banquet table he turned. I tried every resource to calm
my mind and nerve myself for any requisite future
course of conduct; but all was vain. The bleeding
form would not down at my bidding. But in so terrible an hour, vain is the help of man; heart and mind,
at other times as bands of iron, in such an hour are
but broken reeds. I knelt. I prayed. I rose—was
calm and strengthened. My course was taken. If a
murderer—thank God! I was an unintentional one.
I resolved to leave Deer Park instantly. Circumstances forbade a farewell to Geraldine or even the
remains of my deceased friend. I took ink and paper
and wrote as follows:

"DEAR MISS DE LACY.—Circumstances I can not
recapitulate, but which will doubtless in short space
transpire, compel me to quit Deer Park in secresy.
God bless you for your kindness to me, and comfort
you in the severe visitations of a single year. I dare
not trust my pen further. There is a power on me—
a conscience—a madness that constrains me to fly. I
trust we may meet again, and that you will not
wholly discard from memory the wretched but grateful   MORVEN O'MOORE."

This note dispatched, I superscribed it and left it on my table. I was not long in reaching the adjoining post-town, whence I hired a post-chaise for Dublin, giving the driver a good *douceur* for putting his horses to a greater speed than usual. Arrived in Dublin, my determination was instant for the Continent. The watering places of Germany presented too social an aspect for one whose feelings were too gloomy for the enjoyments they offered, and for the same reason the frivolities and excesses of the French capital were equally disagreeable. I reflected for some time on my future whereabouts, and decided in favor of Italy. There is something talismanic in the name of that fair land, whether to the antiquarian or the sorrow-laden spirit that seeks sympathy from outward types or the sad memorials of the past. How had the soul and imagination even of boyhood glowed and kindled at the memories of her heroic grandeur and the sombre tale of her ruins, that time had spread like a shroud over the majesty of her temples, the shrines of her poets, the groves of her philosophers and the graves of her heroes! And as advancing years brought familiarity with the classics, I found the glory of her memories but gathering new light and strength, as manhood felt stronger sympathies with the heroic, the intellectual and ideal. Yes, amid these mighty symbols of the past, I might find some balm for a wounded soul—some still voice amid the silence of that great tomb might charm the adder, whose hourly sting was upon me—some source of outward mental diversion might minister to the mind diseased and tell me I was not a murderer!

Rapidly passing through England and France, I found myself aboard the steamboat bound for Civita Vecchia, the port of Rome. We took Genoa *en chemin;* and, as it is not my purpose to substitute travels for autobiography, I will content myself by observing merely on the aspect Genoa presents to the eye when viewed from the water. She stands on a magnificent declivity sloping down to the blue waves of the Mediterranean, in her very attitude (so to speak) justifying her title ; *Genova Superba*—like a queen commanding the tributary waters that lay their treasures at her feet. But I am too desirous to advance with my story to dwell on any irrelevancies. Suffice it to say, that our evening departure from the port of Genoa, for the first time, realized my early dreams of enchantment in the Arabian Nights. As we stood out to sea, the broad bright moon showered down her richest flood of light on that city of palaces. There seemed to be a holy affinity between that evening radiance and the massive piles of white marble that the magic light on the instant converted into so many temples. It was heaven, as it were, doing homage to earth. As we stood off and the city receded in the distance, the whole was softened down so as to resemble one vast city of the

Dead over whose marble sepulchres the moon held her holy vigils.

But on—on—the vessel heaves, and the waves dash their diamond showers around us. Farewell, thou city of the noble and the palace? Thy daughters in lofty port and gait are worthy children of so regal a mother. With their queenly vails they tread thy streets, and in their haughty brow and eye you may trace the descent of a line of kings.

At last the pilgrim has reached his Mecca; and never did Moslem bow to the Caaba with more devotional homage than did I look on the massive towers and battlements (old as Trajan) that encompassed the port of Civita Vecchia. The town itself is mean and inconsiderable; presenting no attractions but those of association; its proximity to the Niobé of nations, Rome being about fifty miles distant. But here I found myself in the vicinity of old Etruria. I could not resist the impulse to visit Tarquinii, the ancient seat of Lars Porsena, to descend her sepulchres, and stand amid the ruins, whose pride and power had sheltered Tarquin from the rage of the insulted Roman. A party of us took a vettura from Civita Vecchia, and were soon in rapid way for the remains of Tarquinii. I need not say that, on such an expedition, my mind was as much inspired with the *genius loci* as ever was the sibyl with the *afflatus* of the god. But, strange to say, the first image that arose to my

mind was the *Pulverem Olympicum* of Horace; for,
had it not been for my own convictions of the classic
soil beneath me, I could have almost deemed myself
a Howadji in the desert, so huge and impervious the
clouds of dust that rose on every side. There was
one consolation, however, I was breathing classic air
and *soil* simultaneously. The road through which we
passed commanded a fine prospect of a champaign,
richly cultivated country, flanked by a low range of
mountains in the direction we were going; among
which we descried Corneto, the appellation of the
modern town near Tarquinii, on which my eye kept
fixed with all the fervor of the first love of travel. At
some distance from us rolled the blue Mediterranean;
the sparkles of golden sunshine that glanced on its
waters, cresting them like stars that, like the rebel
angels, had fled the glories of heaven for the surpassing loveliness of earth. Oh! what memories rose from
the depths and floated on those blue waves. On every
wave had history, with her pen of iron, writ an im-
perishable record. Phœnician—Phocœan—Greek—
Roman—Goth—Moor—the prows of all had brushed
her surface, the sails of all had wooed her breath;
and, whether in the enterprises of civilization, or the
iron march of war, these hoary waters had served as
highway from the purple dyer of Tyre to Tarik the
Moor, who brought death to the Goth and supplanted
his power by his own.

We arrived at Corneto, which presents but one narrow street and a square, into which we drove, followed
by all the ciceroni, eloquent of their services, and
every variety of lazzaroni in the town. Our vetturino
set us down in a stable-yard utterly neglected, it might
be from its very filth. What was my surprise when
I saw in the centre a beautiful white marble fountain,
and the basement of the Soderini palace that rose
above me, supported by elaborate white marble columns, and converted into a stable!—" To what base
uses may we come at last!" But the modern Italian
is a creature of present expediency, animated by but
one sentiment, the most craving appetite for extortion,
an alien as well to the heroic birthright of his ances-
tors as to the sentiments that should mark their children.

Amid the unintelligible Babeldom of these modern
Etrurians, I ascertained that there was *one* (*par ex-
cellence*) cicerone of Tarquinii; but that this oracle
was taking his siesta. Availing ourselves of the self-
welcome of travelers, we followed a small crowd of
village hangers-on to the abode of the cicerone. We
found him refreshed from slumber, from which his
cara sposa had aroused him, and busy in arranging a
little ornament of wax tapers, which I afterward found
was the universal prelude to any subterranean expedition in Italy. His little hovel contained every variety of Etruscan vase, presenting all those features of

authenticity we find attached to the different specimens of the *true* Cross scattered throughout the world,
and about as genuine. Travelers should be much on
their guard against these modern manufactures of
antiques. Like true pilgrims we followed our self-
appointed Moses; and, passing through a phalanx of
barns and stables, found ourselves on the high road;
the Mediterranean, like a summer sky dropped to
earth, bounding our right with its breathless calmness,
while somewhat onward to our left lay a large grassy
plain, broken and undulating. "*Ecco Tarquinii!*"
said our cicerone, pointing to the plain. Breathless
with those thousand ineffable emotions the scholar
feels on first visiting the scenes of classic history, I
stopped a moment, and fixed my eyes on the plain.
"Tarquinii!" thought I, "can I be treading the ground
that echoed to the chariot wheels of the flying Tarquin? The ground that has been pressed by the foot
of the martyr patriot, Scævola?" I felt the warm
flush on my brow, a throbbing of the heart, a quickening (so to speak) of my whole nature, transporting
me into an existence I had never known before save
in dreams, yet now as vivid as truth herself, as sensu-
ous as life. Away with those dull, practical spirits
whose intellectual ken never stirs beyond the actual
purposes of life, and whose soul, unwinged by imagination or feeling, never lifts itself above the clod that
envelops it! Such are like men, who see but a golden

speck in a star, but are lost to all speculations on
the hand that could launch a world into space, and
call forth its myriad life from a wandering *nebula*.
" Tush," say they, " these are but stones !" True ;
yet imagination, in those stones, can disentomb the
past, awake the dead, clothe them in their deeds, or
eloquence, or virtues, and read the epitaph of the
patriot or the tyrant.   History rolls back the stone
from the sepulchre, while antiquity bursts forth in
her resurrection.

The plain, as I have remarked, was broken and
uneven ; the latter characteristic, however, on nearer
inspection, attributable to the countless *tumuli* that
dotted it like so many tombs.   These *tumuli* are supposed to have been the burial places of Tarquinii, where
also the inhabitants (if we may judge from the frescoes we afterward saw) held their funeral feasts prior
to interment of the dead.   It was here that some (I
believe) German explorer had his adventurous spirit
gratified by seeing the shadow of a *Lucumo* (Etrurian
prince) as he had lain for three thousand years.   After
delving for some time with spade and pick into the
side of one of these *tumuli*, he beheld the warrior reposing in his armor, who, straightway on the admis-
sion of air, crumbled and vanished !

Quitting the road, we entered on the plain.   But
a few of these sepulchres have been opened, three of
which we descended by steep flights of stairs.   The

first two were small square apartments, very little exceeding the ordinary stature of a man; the floor was
of *terra cotta*, and the ceilings richly tesselated into
white and black compartments. The walls were ornamented with frescoes, Egyptian alike in their subjects and execution. Chariot races—funeral feasts—
the dead on his bier, surrounded by mourners, formed
the principal groupings. The third was of ampler
space, and presented more variety in its details. It
was surrounded on three sides by what appeared altar
steps, on which were laid huge stone sarcophagi. The
centre was supported by a very large buttress, rather
than pillar, and at the entrance was a monstrous figure wreathed with serpents. The frescoes on the walls
of this sepulchre were almost effaced. There was but
one face visible: the features were Greek, and the
complexion very swarthy. From the mournful splendor and superior elaborateness of this chamber over
the others, might we not conclude it was the resting-
place of the *Lucumo*, or chieftain? We returned
to the plain; and were glad once again to greet the
sun, albeit overpowering and sultry, as the sudden
transition from upper air to the cold, damp atmosphere
of these vaults is liable to produce fever. Along the
plain stretches an aqueduct, the chronology of which
is uncertain; while in the distance, separated from us
by a deep valley, lay the crumbled walls, whose pride
and strength had once harbored the fugitive Tarquin

from his incensed countrymen.   In their prostration I
read a commentary on all human passions, our affections and enmities.

Returning by a different route, we descended what,
at first sight, presented the aspect of an amphitheatre,
but is supposed to be the vast excavation that supplied the materials for old Tarquinii.   Adjoining this
apparent arena was a huge cave, whose depth and
dimensions were calculated almost to deter the timid
from exploring it.   We entered, however, beneath the
colossal portal, which, at the extremity of the cave,
dwindled to an almost invisible hole, scarcely admit-
ting a ray of light to the spot whereon we stood.   Independently of the associations attached to it, the
excavation itself presented the most perfect image of
the Sublime.   Without it lay the *columbaria*, or re-
positories for the urns of the dead, as I saw afterward
at Pompeii affixed to the wall.   I fear, however, to
dwell on these ancient relics, or the classic enthusiasm
they awakened, longer, lest the reader might lose the
thread of my narrative, and find himself in the perilous situation of Theseus, when he lost his way in the
labyrinth.   We returned to Corneto, dined at the Soderini Palace, and drank the memory of Lars Porsena, in
a cup of genuine old Etrurian.   Evening had just donned her russet mantle, as we reached Civita Vecchia ;
thence by daylight, next morning, to Rome.   Nothing
worthy of note on this road, except the everlasting dust

of an Italian road, condensed—palpable. The road
was the one frequented by Gasparoni and his *condottieri;* but no adventure of romance or brigand
stayed our way ; for Gasparoni, we heard, was quietly
doing penance in the prison of Civita Vecchia for all
his piracies on rich and defenseless *voyageurs.* He
pleads guilty, I understand, to the charge of having
murdered his tens, but not the wholesale heroism of
hundreds. And now St. Peter's is in sight; its matchless dome swelling out beneath that cloudless sky,
like a temple suspended from heaven, as alone worthy
to tabernacle the majesty of God.

All hail, old Rome !

Thy pilgrim's foot should, indeed, be unshodden,
for thou art holy ground—holy with the memory of the
living, holy with the ashes of the dead ! There looks
down a deity from thy seven hills as from a heaven,
at whose base slumber the mighty, whose deeds and
genius ascend forever as incense. Thither all ages
and all nations bring, as to an altar, the voluntary oblations of intellect and soul; and here, while old Tiber
sounds his dirge amid thy ruins and thy dead, shall
the devotion of the pilgrim blend with his voice of
mourning ! Like Niobé, thou seest thy children dead
at thy feet ;—yet weep not, they have not lived in
vain ; nations have bowed to their sword, and kings
have worn their yoke, and on language have they impressed and charactered their own. The genius of thy

sons sits, like eternity, throned on the Coliseum ; for
their deeds are inscribed on Time's old column, that
shall crumble and fall only with the world. Old
Rome, all hail !

We entered Rome by St. Peter's ; and, as I looked
upon the Vatican, I could not but smile on the timid
credulity of kings and people that had trembled at her
Bulls, and rejoice that intellectual light had strangled
the serpent of superstition, and silenced the fulminations of this self-styled Vicar of Christ.   On we drove
through a street terminating in the round tower-tomb
of Hadrian (*moderné*, Castle of St. Angelo), and turning to the right, crossed the Ponte San Angelo arch-
ing old Tiber, whose yellow waves were sentineled, as
it were, by the huge statues of apostles and others
that crowned the buttresses of the bridge.   It would
be tedious to trouble the reader with any further description of this portion of (modern) Rome, than by
saying that it is dingy, dirty, and narrow.   Arrived
at the *Hôtel d'Allemagne*, I hurried to my chamber ;
and never did I find more oppressively the sense of
solitude, deepened by melancholy, than on my first
attempt to realize the place in which I stood, and the
mighty memorials that surrounded me.   Antiquity is
at all times melancholy and imposing; in her remains
we are but reading the epitaphs of the builders, and
treading on their very dust that has helped to pile the
vast mausoleum.   But, in my case, these feelings as-

sumed a still greater depth and gloom from the circumstances that had forced on me this voluntary exile. I endeavored to throw off the terrible thought, however, with the hope that Desmond might still be living, and self-acquittal, in case the *rencontre* might have proved fatal.

I had, in the mean while, diligently employed my time, and, above all, diverted my mind from the allengrossing theme, by visiting the ruins, commencing with the Capitol, and the sublime *coup-d'œil* of remains that stretch thence to the Coliseum, at the opposite extremity; the sides of this imaginary square filled with temples to the left, while from the right looks down, in the desolation of its buried majesty, the Palatine hill, the seat of the Cæsars' palace; in which, alas, for the modern Roman that I should have to say it, I saw—*a hay-stack!* What a homily was there on king and people! But I can not dwell longer on the details of ruins, which have already furnished a theme for volumes, and are yet exhaustless. I must forward to an unexpected incident that befell me soon after my arrival.

I had retired one evening to my usual haunt, the *Café Grecq*, in the *Via de' Condotti*, the favorite *rendezvous* of artists, from whom I derived valuable information on the sublime objects that had occupied my attention for the day, and found an agreeable recreation after that most fatiguing of all occupations—

sight-seeing. What was my surprise one evening, as
I sate enjoying my cigar, to see my old college mate,
Saville Merton, enter!

"Saville! my dear fellow," I cried, grasping his
hand, "can it be that we meet in Rome? Do you
remember the last night we parted in old Trinity you
wrote your abhorrence of every thing Roman, ay, and
Greek, too, by the holocaust you made of the classics?"

"True, my dear Morven; but, blest by the gods
with a taste classic or anti-classic, as the case may
be, I must at least thank the good fortune that has
revived our college friendship."

"But what make you to Elsinore, Saville?"

"I do honestly assure you," he replied, "that it was
an admiration neither for the Cæsars nor their city,
nor yet a veneration to the Pope, has brought me
hither. You know we must have change; I tired of
the daily routine of regimental drill, country quarters,
and country bumpkins, so I applied to the Horse
Guards; obtained my furlough, and here I am, ready
to wander by moonlight through the Coliseum, apostrophize the Capitol in strains that would rouse Cicero
from its halls to look after the safety of his birthright,
kiss the Pope's toe, or dance the cachucha with any
of your modern Agrippinas or Messalinas—*à votre
service.*"

The voluble and dashing character of the reply
assured me that Saville was the same rollicking,

reckless, good-hearted being I had parted from in Trinity.

"But I need not ask what has brought the classic O'Moore to this Delphic shrine."

I then proceeded to epitomize the circumstances that had transpired since our parting, closing with the terrible event that had compelled me to the shelter of a foreign land.

"My dear boy," said Saville, squeezing my hand with the warmest sympathy, "I am delighted that a good fairy, as we say in dear old Ireland, has brought us together. In your present situation you need more than a companion—the strongest sympathy and consolation; both you shall find in me to the extent of my friendship for you. You must fortify yourself with the strong conviction of your entire innocence. It is very plain that some devilish feeling induced your brother to substitute himself for your real antagonist. Are *you* to blame, who sought in honor and fairness your enemy?"

The strong resemblance between Desmond and the earl, to which I have before adverted, rushed to my mind. But, independently of the delusion favored by this resemblance, that dark and ominous mist was before me, almost concealing my opponent from me. These two thoughts comforted and supported me. Conscience acquitted me—I was innocent.

"Have you been to Venice?" said Saville.

"No, I entered Italy by Genoa."

"My dear fellow, I have paid my respects to the four million shrine of Cardinal Borroméo at Milan, and gondoliered at Venice. Ah! Morven, Morven, we talk of the 'poetry of motion,' but what in this world can better realize the poetry of *repose* than a gondola gliding between those giant palaces of the Grand Canal? I verily believe it was in those waters the Italian conceived his exquisite *dolce far niente ;* that indescribable peace of body and mind, which seems to still the very pulse of life itself. But where shall we go to-morrow?"

"Have you been in the great vaults of San Sebastian on the Via Appia?" I said. "Every moment to the neophyte brings up in this wonderful place something to challenge the mind and awaken admiration. It was only this evening I heard of them from an artist."

"No; but you may calculate on me for the enterprise. I am a perfect Roman in my present humor of travel; 'when in Rome,' &c. Command me O'Moore. You'll find me pliant in all things."

Appointing the following morning for our rendezvous, we parted. I retired to my hotel much cheered not only by my meeting with Saville, but also by the friendly consolation he had imparted in our brief interview. In his friendship and association I anticipated the strongest hope of dispelling that one awful

thought that so much overwhelmed me, and which
first impelled me to travel as a mental remedy of diversion, for actual enjoyment in my situation would
have been as impossible as unnatural. I retired that
night much soothed, and partly free from the terrible
influences of past thought and feeling. Hope, the
strongest, filled me, that by novelty of scene and object the mind would be relieved of that one fearful
thought, that, with its subtle essence, filled every
chamber and avenue, and that at length I would find
peace from the recollections of an act that, even in its
most fatal phase, could not be regarded as a crime.

A lovely morning dawned like an omen of the happiness of the coming day. The bright sun and the
unclouded sky, lifting, as it were, every weight from
the spirit that had hitherto cumbered and oppressed
it. Saville was punctual to the hour. I entered the
carriage, and soon our wheels were rattling along the
Corso for the *quartier* of ancient Rome. We passed
the magnificent *Forum* of Trajan, but partially excavated, and the centre occupied by his pillar; *en
passant*, the model of the splendid column of Napoleon
in the *Place Vendôme* at Paris. Thence to the Capitol, from which passing beneath the arch of Titus,
almost immediately facing the Coliseum, and under
the arch of Constantine, we soon found ourselves on
he old Via Appia. Here I could dwell on the magnificent remains that meet us at almost every step,

from Caracalla's baths to the tomb of Cecilia Metella;
but I must on to the vaults of San Sebastian, nearly
opposite this lordly mausoleum. Alighting we were
received by a monk in cowl and full canonicals, who
greeted us with that cringing, sycophantic politeness
of the Italian, that recognizes the traveler only as a
legitimate object of taxation. The wax taper was
kindled with that alacrity with which the hope of a
little gain never fails to inspire the Italian. We descended by several steps to those far-famed catacombs.
I may premise, however, that these vaults are supposed to have been excavated by the ancient Romans,
and in the early ages of Christianity appropriated by
the Christians, not only for the celebration of their
worship, but also as a refuge from the terrors of persecution. These wonderful vaults are supposed to
encompass a space of sixty miles. We passed along
through a perfect labyrinth; the windings so tortuous
and complicated as to require an infallible clew for
the security of our guide. The passages are broad
enough to admit only one person at a time; while
the sides of these narrow avenues supply to the traveler the most gloomy and sombre images, being mere
excavations for the dead, rising three tiers from the
earth. Such is a brief description of these wonderful
vaults. They were the first objects that ever impressed me with a correct notion of a labyrinth.

On a very sudden turn by our guide, desirous to

point out to us an inscription outside one of these re-
ceptacles, he stooped abruptly. I presume it was the
suddenness of the gesture, but on the instant the feeble
taper became extinguished. We called to him, in
whatever Italian we could command, for another; but
the poor man's only reply was a deep groan, and a
clasping of the hands so violent, it seemed to concentrate all the adjuration of prayer, and the agonies of
immediate death. I found it impossible at the instant
to realize our situation to the full extent of its horrors.
Indeed, so insensible was I when the accident occurred,
either to itself or the consequences it might involve,
that my mind was for some moments occupied in
communion with the melancholy memorials of the
dead that surrounded us, their tortures, their persecu-
tions, and that endurance of the Christian, towering
far above the heroic, that sought and was contented to
bide a refuge scarce fitted for the lairs of beasts. But
soon was I aroused to the real terrors of our situation;
too soon in the passionate groans—the prayers—the
violent gestures of the Italian—*audible* if not visible
—did I feel that dark and paralyzing power of despair,
that withers on the moment every energy of mind and
body, and leaves us but passive slaves, where a moment's strength of will would make us conquerors.
" *Santo Dio! Santo Dio! Misericordia! Misericordia pel amore di Gesù!*" This solemn invocation to
God, in the name of His Son, from the lips of the

Italian, at once acquainted me with the extent of our
peril. We were in an utter state of darkness, in one
of the most tortuous labyrinths in the world ; the guide
had lost the clew, and—we must die ! On the instant
of this conviction, deep and piercing as death itself, I
felt the pulses vibrate through my frame like a torrent
of fire, then suddenly stop in their lava flood, and a
sensation cold as ice shoot through heart, and brain,
and vein, as though death himself had by a single
touch congealed life's warm stream forever ! Oh! it
was horrible ; that complication of sensations succeeding each other in the petty frame of man with a meteor speed that defied analysis and challenged death
for an ordeal of deeper torture. Then followed the
overwhelming conviction of the slow and agonizing
pangs of starvation that must precede dissolution. The
creeping gnawings of hunger, the wasting fires of
thirst, the rapid collapse of all physical strength, the
idiot prostration of the mind, the last groan, the skeleton ;—all these different phases of the terrible future
darted through my mind with a rapidity that almost
defied sensation, and yet with a precision that mocked
reality. "Can you not save us ? Can you not find
the clew ?" were the impatient questions that ground
like curses from my teeth. "*Dio sa ! Dio sa ! Santa
Maria ! Gesù ! Gesù sia nostro Salvatore !*" were the
fragments that he uttered, half in desperation and
half in the dependence of prayer. I roused myself by

a violent effort from the torpor that was fast pervading
mind and body, making me nerveless and helpless as
a child. "Saville—Saville—this will never do. This
blundering, superstitious priest will leave us here to
die. We must seek some way of escape ourselves."
The extreme self-possession of Saville, and that imperturbable good-humor that seemed his birthright, reani-
mated my confidence and nerved my exertions. "Follow, Saville!" And so they did, both Saville and the
priest, whose prompt obedience to the command snapped forever the slight reed on which I had leant. I
led the way; but alas! there was neither hope in my
heart nor strength in my step. I led the way; but
whither? We were but groping our way; without
the advantage of a single ray to prove to us we were
not retracing our steps; for it appeared, as we groped
along the walls, that they diverged in small circles.
Thus, instead of advancing, our course might be retro-
gressive. "Oh God! Saville!" I exclaimed, "I feel
the sentence passed—the hour come!" A cold, clammy
sweat burst from my brow—my throat was parched
—a fire seemed raging there and in my brain that the
" multitudinous seas" could not slake; I grasped the
clay wall by which I stood for support—even that
seemed a presage of my fate—it crumbled at my touch.
I fell to the ground.

I must have sunk in a swoon; for the first thing
that aroused my consciousness was the voice of Saville,

whose equanimity seemed at last to have been exhausted, and who was now indulging in the most
bitter and abusive reproaches of the wretched monk.
Faint, and sick, and overpowered with those emotions,
indescribable because they borrow their equivocal
character from the future to which they relate, I had
yet some little sympathy left for the unfortunate man
whose carelessness had brought us face to face with
death.   His prayers were rather agonies—heart-sweat
(so to speak), than partaking that equable and solemn
communion of the creature with his God.   I would
hear him smite his breast—stamp the earth—grasp
the clay, with an infuriate hand, that had once coffined
martyrs, and scatter it around him madly, as though
it were the wall that barriered out the bright world
beyond us; and then the frantic defiance and abortive
efforts of mere human strength would be succeeded
by a groan, whose echoes through the long winding
passages started like the phantoms of the dead to
welcome us to their ghastly company.   In one violent
paroxysm of despair, I heard him tear out his hair,
trample it under his feet, and clasping his hands above
his head with a force that shook the whole man, apostrophize the Deity in words and tones that partook
more of blasphemy than prayer.   Wrung with the
agonies of the poor creature, I could not but feel my
sympathies enhanced by the violent reproofs of Saville.

" For God's sake !" I cried, " let the poor creature
pass. The death that awaits us is for him too." It
was with a difficulty bordering on pain, I remember,
that I could utter these few words, so parched was my
throat and so utterly feeble seemed vitality within me.

" Can we not make some clew for ourselves ?" suggested Saville, somewhat calmed by my remonstrance;
" can we not drop stones, or pass a cord, or something— ?" but the poor fellow seemed to lose the momentary confidence inspired by his ingenuity.

" 'Tis vain," I answered : " the passages are too
intricate and—" the words died on my lips, for I
found my thoughts wandering.

" I'll try," said Saville, " we must not die without
an effort." So saying, he groped for some space, found
a stone and set it on the ground. Indeed, Saville was
now our only guide, for the monk had, in despair,
abandoned his office, and together with myself, followed Saville with that acquiescence that disclaimed
for the future all hope or effort on his part. The expedient, as suggested by Saville, was adopted; our
guide groped along, picking up a stray stone and dropping it as he went. In such a situation our feelings
are the only monitors of time, and under their deep
and caustic influence minutes are, perhaps, magnified
into hours. I can not, therefore, tell how long we
were employed in this project; whose hope was so
weak and fragile when we commenced as scarcely to

K

differ from despair. The part of the labyrinth in which
we now were was of a tortuous character that paralyzed us, and mocked our efforts at the very com-
mencement of the undertaking. Thus had we toiled,
groping our way and dropping stone after stone for
some hours; when, to our horror, we came in contact
with the first stone Saville had dropped. "*Dio!
Dio! Misericordia sulle nostre anime!*" groaned the
monk. "My God—my God!" echoed Saville, "have
mercy on our souls!" These words from Saville, on
whom all my hope had hitherto rested, shot like an
ice bolt on my heart. I felt the words on my lips,
"Surely the bitterness of death is past!" * * *

Yes, death had no sterner trials, nor disease more
wasting pains than those through which I had already
passed. Expedient after expedient was proposed—
some adopted, others abandoned. One was, that we
should separate in search of some outlet, some ray of
light;—a something, an anything, that to men in our
desperate circumstances might tell us Death was not
so near us as we feared. The lunatic in his cell was
not so wild and fantastic in the various imaginary
characters he assumes, as we in the different plans,
suggested by fancy, hope, terror, and despair, for our
escape. Our plan was, to part each in a different direction, still within so limited a distance that our voices
might serve us for clews. We parted, but alas—alas!
it was to meet again as we had parted, despair on our

lips and death already at our cold—cold hearts! This
was but one of the thousand expedients; but what will
not frenzy conceive and despair impel us to?

The worst feature now began to exhibit itself;
hitherto, we had never stirred from each other's side,
as though bound together by some cabalistic chain
on the same terrible venture. We looked on the very
worst, and, as the worst, resolved to meet it. Prayer
had sunk to adjuration; that, in its turn, was super-
seded by groans; and these had, at length, sunk to
silence. Despair has reached its climax when discon-
tent no longer seeks its ordinary expressions of word
or gesture. So were we in that charnel house: the
ashes of martyrs around us; the groan of the dying
Christian, and the shout of the exulting Roman,
hurtling through those narrow passages, and awaking
the silence of centuries from her trance to knell the
wretched wanderers on their fast journey to join the
canonized bones around them. I have said we had
hitherto kept close together; it might have been from
the ghastly terrors of the place, or that, mayhap, the
conscious touch of humanity lent us hope of protracted life. Fools! Can it be the instincts of this world,
or the terrors of a future one, that bind man to life
under such circumstances as burden each passing
moment with the pangs of a living death? Be that
as it may, each one clung to life with that violent
tension of hope that seemed to exhaust itself in a

single paroxysm, and leave not a rack for the future
But the worst feature was, that while previously we
had indulged this hope, warmed by the touch and
word of our neighbor (for, thank God, here was no
light to show us the ghastly expression and bloodless
face), now the ties of fellow-wretchedness and equal
fate that had hitherto bound us, were gradually being
loosened; the touch of our fellow but reminded us of a
duplicate of misery, and his words, however feeble in
consolation, registered our doom, as with a voice of
thunder. Like lunatics in their cell, we separated from
each other at least for some little distance ; and each
in silence gnawed his own heart by alternate brooding,
prayer, ejaculation, or, it might be, sullen silence.

I know not how long a time had elapsed when this
phase began to exhibit itself. It must, however, have
been some space ; or hours must have wrought the
work of days, judging from the extreme debility of
body, and that wildering confusion of mind that found
it, at times, impossible to identify place, circumstance,
or any thing connected with my fate. I have a strong
recollection of something like an intense ray of light
shooting through my mind, bearing on it, in bold and
luminous relief, the single word, "PRAY!" I started
to my feet, but as quickly sank to the earth from the
suddenness of the effort and the utter prostration of
the system. I strove to utter the Lord's Prayer ; but
I rather muttered than repeated the first passage ; and

then I checked myself with the blasphemous conviction that shot through my brain like a shaft of fire—
that God was not *my* father; and that, if in heaven,
He could not, or would not look to the depths of my
den! The thought was blasphemy; yet I felt it not
as such. I turned to the depth and strength of my
despair, to the intense conflict between infirm nature
and the preternatural horrors that threatened to crush
it, and found a palliation in the reflection. The monk,
though ignorant of the language I muttered, was not
insensible to its meaning: he answered me with a
deep groan; it was a prayer, but one which in its
very agony seemed to abjure the help he implored,
and avow its impracticability in the circumstances
under which it was offered. Not a word was uttered
by Saville—not a sound escaped him; it seemed as
though death itself, by his final release, could not
more benumb the senses, more utterly extinguish the
very last spark of consciousness.

. The operations of the mind had with me for some
time been suspended, and the animal, faint and exhausted though it was, took up the terrible thread
of suffering that had been relinquished by the mind
I was comparatively insensible to the pangs of hunger; but the thirst—oh, God! the thirst that ran riot
through every vein, burning, burning, like a stream
of fire that demons had kindled, and but one hand
alone could slake—Death! How I longed for that,

and brooded on the thought! The conviction it could not be distant once again aroused my mental powers. But the thought, kindled by the wish, was that of annihilation. There was joy in that thought; a wild and frantic exultation, that defied religion and derided every fear of judgment. The utter annihilation of consciousness was a triumph to one who groaned with the burden of life, and whose tortures had already transformed the grisly terrors of death into the radiant robes of an angel. But how long must it be, I thought, before that final and happy release? Through how many phases of suffering, how many grades of prostration and debility must I pass before I felt the blow that was to sever the chains of clay that bound me? * * * *

Consciousness seemed now, as I dwelt on this thought, to fail me. A numbness and a torpor, most like a dreamless sleep, possessed me; and I seemed to have passed into death without a feeling of his approach. Time, place, and even the memory of the sad fellowship that suffered and lingered with me, were alike forgotten; and, I know not how to express it, I experienced the condition of one who stands on his own tomb, and reads his own epitaph. I *felt* (if the expression be not anomalous) *that I was, indeed, dead!*

It must have been a long and terrible dream. But the curtain was rent asunder, and the chain broken,

by a scream. Oh! it was more than was ever uttered
by human voice. It rang like the scream of a lunatic,
whose superhuman strength has burst his chains, re-
storing him to the liberty he mistakes for reason: yet
strange to say, it had scarcely power to remove my
torpor, or stir me from the position in which I heard it.
Again that scream! Then burst upon me the thought
it was that of a demon in exultation at seizing the
soul death had flung upon his fiery shore! Could it
be mine? The thought roused the last slumbering
energy to resistance. I endeavored to rise, for the
rescue of my own soul, from the fiery hand about
to grasp it, when I fell to the ground. And now
in the distance I could discern a faint light, bright,
brighter—brighter yet. The scream was repeated;
a frantic one, but yet it had in it some note of joy.
It was uttered by the monk. Nearer, yet nearer still,
the light. Feeble though it was, I was compelled to
close my eyes: it blinded me. Philosophy says light
is the parent of life: with me it was so. That feeble
ray at once dispelled my dreamy state. I saw—I felt
—something whispered me I was still a living man!
With an energy I thought had passed forever, I rose
to my feet, and, supporting myself by the earthen
wall, looked in the direction of that light. It fell
upon the monk kneeling in the passage; his hands
were clasped and his head bowed in prayer. But,
alas, for my poor Saville! he was lying at the monk's

feet motionless, and apparently dead! With a desperate effort, I moved, or rather crawled, toward the
monk to raise Saville; but he was already in the
arms of the monk who bore the light in conducting a
party to the catacombs. A new spirit now possessed
me; the hideous torpor that had weighed down the
mind; the debility that had prostrated every energy,
passed away as under the influence of an overwhelming joy, that seemed, like electricity, to pervade my
whole being. I laughed—I cried—I prayed—I raved
—I admired the light, as an infant might be supposed
to stare at it for the first time; I thought the monk
who bore it had been sent to us from heaven, and I
remember distinctly, in my aberrations, falling down
and offering him worship. So intense and complicated
was this ineffable joy, that in itself it appeared to
absorb the sense of every thing, save that of my own
being and the unexpected preservation it had experienced. I forgot my wretched fellows. I knew but
that I lived. A wild and delirious joy, like an elixir,
ran through every vein, and its echoes rang in my
ear. The idiot laugh—the prayer—the mention of
God—the mockeries of Satan, rolled in fearful echoes
through the vault. I remember turning with a fearful shudder to see the hideous faces that were utter-
ing these unearthly sounds; but sank in the arms of
the monk, with the terrible conviction—*that I was
mad!* They were but the echoes of my own voice.

CHAPTER XII.

Now, by my soul, with all its depth and warmth
I greet thee ! Thou'rt the only ray that falls,
Amid the spectre ruins where I wander.

WHEN I awoke the next morning, I found myself
in my own chamber at the *Hôtel d'Allemagne*.
But when or how brought there, as difficult for me to
determine as for Mohammed to explain the process by
which he attained the seventh heaven. My bodily
and mental condition was such as to convince me
that I had passed through some terrible struggle, the
effects of which would require some time to remove.
Memory had entirely lost her seat, and the only rem-
nant of individuality that remained to me, was a consciousness of *something*, but of the what and the
whereabouts I was alike ignorant.

It was about noon, when my courier entered my
room, and presented me with a card, bearing, " ORSINO
SALVIATI, *Palazzo* ——."

" Who is this gentleman, Emilio?"

" He brought you here in his carriage, yesterday,
Signor."

K *

"Brought *me!* Where did he find me? How did he know—?"

"Your card directed him, Signor." This, then, was the *something* that I was striving to disentangle in my webbed and perplexed mind. Perhaps this Italian might be more successful. "Show him up, Emilio."

After a few minutes the stranger entered my chamber.

"Il Signor Salviati?" I said.

The stranger bowed gravely.

"Pray be seated, Signor. Your humanity, as I have learned from my courier, has saved me from something terrible; your courtesy will pardon me, I trust, in thus receiving you unceremoniously."

The stranger bowed again, but each time with an air of such gravity as the more strongly to rivet my attention on one I had regarded but as an ordinary visitor.

About forty years of age, the Signor Salviati was tall and handsomely proportioned. His manners, however, distant, perhaps repulsive, gave the stranger an impression that they were not the real exponents of his nature, but rather the result of circumstances that had chilled a heart whose feelings were originally warm, friendly, and, like most of his countrymen, partaking the enthusiastic. These observations I mad from our subsequent acquaintance. At times cold, repulsive, and silent, again, as by a violent struggle

with himself, he would wrestle with this absorbing
melancholy, and exhibit a mirthfulness so salient and
even boyish, that it appeared the true expression of a
nature that wore an habitual disguise. The subjects
that especially enabled him to throw off this yoke from
which he seemed to suffer so much, were the music
and the ruins of his country. These themes awakened
within him a fervor of enthusiasm and a power of language that left the hearer nothing to desire, save the
brilliant imagination that fell like sunshine, brightening and etherealizing every thing it touched. On such
occasions the Sibyl was ever before me, pouring forth
her prophetic fury in strains that mourned over the
ruins, or eulogized the minds that sought them as
shrines. His features were eminently handsome; possessing, however, rather the loftier pretensions of expression than classic symmetry. But no face have I
ever seen to which the line of Gray was more emi-
ninently applicable:

"Melancholy marked him for her own."

During our interview he informed me of the perils
from which the accidental visit of himself and daughter had happily rescued my friend and self. He proceeded to state that an acquaintance, commenced
under circumstances of such deep and solemn interest
should not, like an ordinary one, be abruptly terminated. I bowed in acknowledgment, not only of the
truth of his principle but the compliment it implied,

"But where is my friend?" I asked, impatiently, forgetting poor Saville in the Italian's narrative of the awful fate from which he had rescued us.

"In the same hotel with yourself," answered Salviati; "you have both, by my care, had the best medical aid that Rome can afford, and I shall take heed that your *maître d'hôtel* shall provide you with every thing your situation requires."

"A thousand, and a thousand thanks," I replied; "the blessing of the houseless and the wanderer be on you and yours!"

The Signor rose from his seat, saying, he was about to visit Saville, whom he would assure of my perfect convalescence. He bade me farewell with the same gravity and air of melancholy with which he had first struck me. The impression he left on me was that of the highest breeding, heightened by the noblest humanities.

In a day or two I was sufficiently recovered to seek the chamber of Saville, whom I found equally convalescent with myself, and on the point of dispatching his courier to me with tickets for the Opera that night, presented to us both, with the compliments of the Signor Salviati. It is of course needless to say that a favor so kindly tendered, was accepted in the same spirit. So to the Opera we went. By the way, the Opera in Rome commences about five o'clock in the afternoon. We were shown by the *custode* to the

Signor's stall, who had left with him orders to that effect. On our entrance we were received with that polish and courtesy our first interview had impressed me with. His daughter, the Signorina Amina, was under her father's protection, and his only companion save ourselves. To her we were presented. *Petite* but elegant in the extreme, we found her as highly cultivated in mind as *piquante* in conversation. Her features, like most Roman women I had seen, had no pretensions to classic regularity, but there is a charm about the full Italian eye, a majesty in the jetty hair that lends a beauty to features to which nature has denied it. So with Amina, not possessing a regular feature, still the eye was irresistibly attracted by a countenance that strayed on the confines of beauty, though not, perhaps, carrying a single impress of her touch. She spoke English with equal fluency and elegance as her father; which I learned from them was attributable to their frequent intercourse with foreigners. And of foreigners, when well educated, I have uniformly observed that they speak our language with a greater freedom from solecism, and choiceness of diction, than natives. I know not to what cause to impute this apparent paradox. It may be to the pride of foreign proficiency or a more *radical* study of the language. Be that as it may, Amina Salviati's English had a sound for me as sweet as ever fell from the lips of woman; the sweeter for the contrast be-

tween the perfect idiom and pronunciation, and the
Italian accent that gave grace to the one and sweetness to the other.   In words and tones as harmonious
as I have attempted to describe did we receive the
Italian's felicitations on our safety, and her self-con-
gratulations on the happy chance that had made her
father and self its instruments.

"Do you remain long in Italy?" she said.

"I can almost promise it," I replied, "if I may rely
on so true an Ariadné as yourself to guide me through
her classic labyrinth."

"Are you aware that this house is built on the
mausoleum of Mæcenas?"

"Is it possible?   The luxurious minister has but
exchanged the poetry to which he was so much af-
fected in life for her sister, music.   Well have the
Muses made his tomb their shrine!"

Our further conversation was interrupted by the
crash of the orchestra as the curtain rose.   The opera
was "Norma."   I know not how to describe the mingled sensations I experienced when I thought that I
was listening to Italian music on Italian ground.   The
very soil seemed to inspire the music with an individuality it had never conveyed to me before, often
though I had heard it.   Such is the force of association, and such the poetic talisman it can forge for
every soul that chooses to surrender itself to its influence.   Then the Roman costume of the *Dramatis*

Personæ! Truly was the illusion perfect. Imagination with her ready wand transported the scene from barbarous Britain to the city wherein I stood, and placed the Roman of the Cæsars before me. To this dreamy or poetic mood even the enjoyment of that exquisite opera was compelled to yield; and, much as I loved that music, and the memory of Bellini for writing it, its very performance was forgotten in the strange illusions that fancy had conjured from the scene.

But what was this to the deeper feelings about to absorb my whole nature? Can it be? Impossible—that figure—face—oh! yes, it must be—it must—Bianca Romano. Whose voice but hers? Oh! Bianca—Bianca—have we met again? Is this thy dream? This my reality? It is—it is Bianca—! I held my breath—I bit my lip, and had indeed to exert a violent effort of will to prevent the betrayal of the thousand emotions that voice, like something of the past, awakened to memory. From the time I had saved her life to the present, how brief; yet how many and fearful the incidents compressed within that brief space! When we first met I was a disinherited son, and now—an exile—it might be—no—no—not murderer; even though in a theatre, I felt my heart rise with gratitude to God, that I was not a murderer!

I had been standing as she entered, and, amid the torrent of applause that hailed her entrance, I took

my seat in the effort to compose the feelings her sudden appearance had so much agitated. But soon the
enchantress took captive ear and soul. Ah! who save
Bianca, had that faultless precision, that analysis of
execution, that let the ear linger with rapture on each
note, while the whole strain filled and inspired the
soul, like ocean heaved and swelled by the tempest?
Such execution as hers was (so to speak) a fine mosaic; we dwell with admiration on the entire theme,
but the eye brightens at every individual tone of color
the taste of the artist has called to his aid. And then
her acting; oh! it was the same Bianca; even still
more Italian than I had known her in Dublin for the
beautiful costume she wore as the Druidess. Her acting embodied that self-forgetfulness, that earnestness
that, in its extreme depth, defied the raptures of music
and the passion of poetry, and rose superior to both in
the supremacy of its own joy or misery.

The curtain had fallen for an act. "Why, Morven,
what's the matter with you? Has the Druidess enchanted you? What foul sorcery— ?"

"Nothing—nothing, Saville. I knew her in Dublin."

"Indeed!" joined in Amina, "she has not long been
here; but is now the idol of the Romans. They seem
to think she is the only Prima Donna they have had
for years, whose nature is truly inspired with their
national school of music. There is a romance, too,

connected with her, which, as it savors of mystery, lends her life the aspect of poetry."

" She narrated to me her history in Dublin, Signorina ; and it struck me as at once touching and mysterious. Has she been long in Rome ?"

" Not many nights ; but she came here heralded by the high praises she had won at Milan and Venice."

" I *must* renew my acquaintance with her," I said, with an enthusiasm that brought tears to my eyes.

" We know her ; and, having the *entrée* behind the scenes, shall be happy to accompany you at the close of the opera."

The curtain rose again, presenting Norma in that magnificent *scena* where, stung by the abandonment of her lover, she is about to extinguish the memory of her ill-fated passion in the murder of her wretched offspring. Her acting here was superb, while the alternate bursts of passion and melancholy, like the very wailings of Nature returning to haunt the soul she was on the eve of forsaking forever, called down such acclamations of applause and sympathy from the excitable Italians, as evidently wrought in Bianca a belief in the reality of her situation and the passions she was so greatly painting.

In the pauses of the act my familiarity with Italian made me privy to a conversation passing between two Italians in the adjoining box.

" Wonderful—wonderful !" exclaimed one.

"She is the greatest we have had," rejoined his companion; "others have sung the music only, but she sings from the heart and mind."

"They say," returned the first, "that Orsino Salviati worships her, and is willing to lay his splendid fortune at her feet. You know, he was always a passionate admirer of the Opera, and is unable to resist the fascinations of its best representative; uniting, as she does, the highest order of genius to surpassing beauty."

So occupied had been my mind with the events of the evening, that even the presence of Salviati had utterly escaped my memory. I fixed my eyes on him, however, attracted by the conversation of the Italians. His were riveted on the stage, or rather only when Norma was before him. When her *rôle* was played, there was a listlessness of manner, an abstractedness of eye that seemed to say, the heaven was dark now that the solitary star that illumined it was withdrawn. When Bianca filled the scene, the eye brightened, the whole face was informed by a fine intellectual sympathy with the being and the passion, that, for the time, completely overmastered the characteristic melancholy of his countenance. Strange, thought I, as my eyes were fixed musingly upon him, that my first meeting with Bianca, after so long a time, should be accompanied with the sense of rivalry !

The opera was concluded, and the curtain fell amid

the most triumphant tributes I had ever heard either
to vocal powers or dramatic genius. The musings
into which the opera and its heroine had thrown me
were now exchanged for the most ardent desire to
renew my acquaintance with Bianca, and express that
intense gratification I, in common with the rest, had
derived from her performance.

"In Dublin! Indeed—how strange!" said Orsino,
half musing, half ejaculating, as Amina communicated
my past intimacy with the *cantatrice*, and wish for
its renewal. I thought, I observed a flush upon the
Italian's brow, commonly pale and smooth as marble,
as he spoke. The thought that crossed him, however,
he soon mastered; and, with his characteristic courtesy, added; "my daughter tells me, your desire to
meet again the Signorina Teresa Carmonali."

The start of surprise I made at the name interrupted Salviati. I was not prepared for this; but the
noms de guerre (usually adopted by artists) dispelled
the momentary expression.

"Pardon, Signor—a lightness of the head I'm subject to. 'Tis over. I thank you for your kind offer;
and, in company with my friend, will avail myself of
it."

Under the guidance of Salviati we were soon initi-
ated into that dreariest and darkest of all labyrinths
(the vaults of San Sebastian of course excepted) ever
threaded by human foot, characteristically apostro-

phized by the stage struck Sylvester Daggerwood, as
odorous with oil and orange peel.   As we entered, what
with us is termed, the green-room, the first object that
met my eye was Bianca, her superb figure and queenly
bearing towering above her compeers with that conscious superiority that so frequently marks the exterior
of intellectual greatness.   She was reposing from the
exhaustion she had undergone, and conversing with
those around her with that extreme affability that real
genius employs toward its inferiors.

"In Rome—can it be.—The Signor—no—not the
Signor—my friend—my preserver—?" were the broken
words of the grateful, generous girl.   The conscious
pride and power that had sustained her in the artificial
world of characterization, now bent to the weakness
and the tears of woman, as we supported her to a
fauteuil.

"There is something melancholy—almost ominous
in meeting you in this most melancholy of all cities,
whose very dust and ashes apostrophize us in the language of all human hopes.   When first we met, Death
threatened us both, and now we meet in the very land
of Death!   But away with such thoughts!" she continued, after a pause; "Life is itself an epitaph, let
us leave it to those that come after to write it.   It
is not for us to change the Spring of Life into its
Autumn."

"My friend, the Signor Merton," I said, seeking to

change the subject, by presenting Saville; "Receive him, if not for himself at least for the sake of his country, Ireland, you so warmly praised when last we met."

"And still love," she answered, as she extended her hand to Saville, who raised and kissed it with all the befitting courtesy of a *cavallero andante*.

"I am happy of this opportunity," said Salviati, "afforded me by the presentation of your friend, to express the delight experienced from your Norma to-night. That delight, is, however, somewhat marred by the exhaustion your efforts seem to have left behind."

"That exhaustion," replied Bianca, "is the artist's best reward; it seems to tell us, the personation has been true, for the passion has been intense and sincere. It is in her hour of labor only, that the glow-worm sends forth her spark upon the night. Art is so exacting a goddess, that like old Saturn she sometimes even devours her own children. The life of the worshiper will sometimes mingle with the incense of the sacrifice."

We pleaded that exhaustion as our best apology for withdrawal; and, having once more exchanged a hearty salutation with Bianca, we were soon in Salviati's carriage, and dropped at the *Hôtel d' Allemagne*.

The following day Saville and I were by appointment at the *Hôtel de Londres*. The carriage of Salviati we observed at the door as we entered. So,

thought I, the siege is indeed pressed, and I fear the
fortress must capitulate.   I must confess that, at this
thought, I felt the fire of jealousy; for I will be equally
honest in avowing my passion for Bianca.   We inquired for the apartments of the Signorina Carmonali;
and, entering found Salviati and Bianca *tête-à-tête*.
She rose and welcomed us with her characteristic
warmth; "I greet you as my countrymen, for to your
beautiful country and its hospitable people I owe many
of the happiest hours of my life."

We acknowledged the compliment, if indeed that
which was uttered with so much sincerity might be
termed so.   Saville, on whom Amina, I found by his
conversation on our return from the Opera, had made
a strong impression, inquired after her with an interest
that could not escape Salviati's observation.

. "On my way hither I left her at the Vatican," continued Orsino, after answering Saville's inquiries,
"promising to rejoin her there in company with the
Signorina Carmonali.   We shall be happy if you take
a seat in my carriage."

We readily assented, and were soon on our way to
the Vatican.   We found Amina in the chamber that
contains the two masterpieces of the world—the
Transfiguration of Raphael and the Last Communion
of St. Jerome by Domenichino.   The gross flattery of
the artist has almost profaned the sanctity and subject of the former, by representing at the base of the

mountain one of the Medicis as witnessing the Saviour's
Transfiguration, in company with the apostles; a melancholy example of the self-profanation of genius by
the debasing means of interest and patronage.   Salviati, I observed, was unremitting in his attention to
Bianca, and unqualified in his admiration of her criticisms.   Saville never stirred from the side of Amina;
but seemed to hang with the mingled ardor of the
lover and enthusiasm of the antiquarian on every word
that fell from the lips of this fair cicerone.   As I listened to her glowing descriptions of art, history, or antiquity, given with all the becoming pride of a Roman
maiden, who read the lives and deeds of her godlike
ancestry in the monuments they had left, I could not
but lend my admiration to a mass of knowledge as sys-
tematically arranged as it seemed thoroughly digested:

"You would put to the blush some classics of our
Universities, Signorina Salviati," I said.   "Your range
from art to archæology astonishes me."

"And could I," returned the young Roman, with
an artlessness that purposely disregarded the compliment; "could I have studied in a nobler page?   Ignorance of the Roman and his history would have been
a disavowal of my own pedigree, an ignorance, as it
were, of my own language.   The pages of such a volume should not, like the Sibylline leaves, be scattered
to the winds, but laid in a shrine where antiquity
may teach them to her disciples and children."

On our return to the *Hôtel de Londres*, we learned from Bianca, that in a few days her engagement at Rome would terminate, whence she would immediately repair to Naples, being under contract to sing at the San Carlo. The announcement in itself was of an ordinary nature, apparently involving the interest of none save herself; yet it is almost impossible to depict the change that simple resolution wrought in the countenance of Salviati. He became deathly pale, the muscles around his mouth worked with such violence, as by the compression of his lips, utterly to expel the blood from them. Amina, too, partook of the fear or detestation that seemed associated with the name of that lovely city. The terrible emotions I have endeavored to describe in Salviati, did not appear original with her, but rather the reflex of what she observed in her father.

" When do you leave ?" at length said Salviati, with a languor that sought relief from the emotions that pressed on him, rather than from the indulgence of curiosity.

Bianca named the day on which the Opera closed in Rome with her engagement.

" Will you permit my daughter and self to accompany you ?" returned Salviati, " I have a beautiful villa in the suburbs to which none will be more welcome than she who will soon be the cynosure of every eye in that loveliest of cities."

"Father! father!" interposed Amina, "how can you go to Naples after what I have seen you suffer there—?" The words were interrupted by a stern glance of reproof from Salviati; but the deep tone of interest and affection with which they were uttered failed not to rivet the attention and awaken the curiosity of all.

"My daughter would make an ordinary accident a subject of anxious boding," said Salviati, endeavoring to smile away the suspicions kindled by Amina; "we will be a pleasant party, if the Signorina Carmonali suffer us to follow in her *suite;* gentlemen, you will accept seats with my daughter and self to Naples? You know the old proverb of the vain Neapolitan: ' *Vedi Napoli e poi mori!*' but, by Jupiter! we will essay to *live* there. Ha! what say you?" These words were uttered with a volubility and constrained gayety that contrasted fearfully with the expression of countenance the first allusions to Naples had produced. Saville and I bowed our acknowledgments to Salviati for his courtesy, professing ourselves at the service alike of the Signorina Amina and Bianca.

"I know of no part of Italy whose environs abound with localities more intensely interesting to the scholar than this same old city of the Greeks," resumed Salviati, determined to sustain the momentary rally of spirits he had so successfully made; "Virgil and Tacitus form our constant guides along the shores of

L

that unrivaled bay ; and imagination makes a magical transition from the history of the great Christian apos-. tle at Puteoli, to the horrors of the Sibyl's cave at Avernus, or the crimes of Nero at Baiæ. Rich in its intellectual harvest to the antiquarian, I know of no soil throughout Italy more pregnant with classic story than the suburbs of Naples and the shores of her bay. Ah! we must visit them all."

We could not but observe the change of Amina's countenance, as she listened to her father descant on the classic wealth of the city we were about to visit. A deep and thoughtful melancholy supplanted the characteristic sprightliness of the young Roman, as though even now she were realizing the danger, or distress, or whatever contingency she apprehended on her visit to Naples. But we were too much elated at the prospects of Paradise that city held out to us to dwell on any emotions but those of pleasure. The day was appointed for our departure, that night was fixed for our attendance at the Opera to witness Bianca's "Sonnambula," and we took our leave, promising to meet in the evening.

"Did you mark Amina?" said Saville, after a few moments' silence on the way to our hotel; "how, as she spoke to Salviati, the blood forsook her cheek, and the tears started, and—and—"

"That you are in love, my dear Saville," I interrupted, helping him out with his disjointed sentence;

" if I remember aright, at our first meeting, you challenged the Agrippinas and Messalinas to dance the cachucha, and lo! one of their posterity has arisen to avenge the insult by making the challenger her slave. *Ah, scélérat!* An you take not good heed, your men, I fear, will want their commander, and the epitaph of their late doughty Captain Merton will be, ' He fell a victim to an equivocal fever; something between Classics and Love.' "

" No, no, O'Moore; you know me better; I may plead guilty to the latter part of the epitaph, but hang it, man, those cursed vaults of San Sebastian have been quite enough to eradicate the very last feeling I had for those venerable old gentlemen, y'clept, the Classics. But what, in truth, think you of Amina?"

" That, were not my heart preoccupied, hers would be the image I should destine to fill it. Elegant in deportment, fascinating in manners, rich and cultivated in mind, such a one would be an ornament in the *salon*, a companion by the fireside."

" And who, returned Saville, " may be the preoccupant of your heart?"

" Who, but she whose beauty last night entranced every eye, and whose genius had a shaft for every ear and soul? But mine is a wayward fate, and—"

" What?"

I recounted to Saville the conversation I had overheard at the Opera.

"And does rivalry deter an Irishman?" said Saville. "If I know my own nature aright, it but stimulates resolution and nullifies every obstacle."

"It is not any outward obstacle I fear, nor any rivalry I care for," I continued; "my obstacles are in myself, and—but we are at home—we will talk of this again." We parted on the stairway, agreeing, after the *table d'hôte*, to adjourn to the Opera.

CHAPTER XIII.

Neapolis, thou fairest of earth's cities,
That callest rapture to the eye and cheek,
To this man thou'rt a talisman of evil,
And holdest, like the grave, some secret.

AND now we have passed the Porta San Giovanni,
and our carriages wake the echoes of the Appian
Way. The ruins of aqueduct and tomb that strew this
road are a fine proëm to the mighty sepulchre that lies
within old Rome herself. The mind is harmonized,
the soul solemnized, by these crumbled themes, for the
deeper and more epic strains that wake the air from
the Capitol to the Coliseum. Like a fine organ sweep
upon the soul, waking up the deep fountains of its
worship, rise those fine ruins on the Via Appia; a prelude, as it were, to the bended knee and the awe-
stricken soul that pours forth its adoration in Rome
herself, and weeps and worships in her Holy of Holies!

And now St. Peter's dwindles in the distance, and
the huge Pantheon that Michael Angelo said, "he
was about to raise in air," shrinks to the size of a
minaret. The mighty Queen looks down from her
seven-hilled throne, whence went forth her fiat against
the kings of the earth; and, as she weeps over the

ashes of her children, reads their eternal monument
in the works they have left behind, and their memories
in the pilgrimage and eulogy of the stranger.

And now we see the Latian hills in the distance;
the first germ of the mighty tree whose branches
covered the earth, sheltering some, but flinging over
others the deadly shadow of the Upas; the first nu-
cleus of that colossal power whose stride, like that of
the angel in the Apocalypse, was over continents. The
flight of her eagle was from the savage shores of Britain even to the last stronghold of the Jew, the glory
of his temple. That night we staid at Velletri, possessing no features of antiquarian interest but the
associations of its name. It is a modern town of the
Volsci, commanding a magnificent mountain range,
bathed in that soft and dreamy light that, in Italy,
converts the mountain into a pile of softest cloud.
Our next stopping-place was Tevvacina. Our hotel
here enjoyed a prospect of the finest and boldest surf,
up to its very walls, I have ever seen; while the
towering Apennine, like a fortress, flanked the very
road with its granite battlements. Our next *route*
was by far the most interesting. Midway, we passed
Caietæ, the scene of Cicero's assassination by Anthony.
It derives also a mythical memory from its having
been the birth-place of Æneas' nurse. As I looked
upon the lovely waters of this bay, the distant head-
lads seemed pre-eminently to borrow that visionary

character of the Italian sky. Indeed, the whole scene appeared touched into life by some angel hand with colors caught from Paradise ; while the mind hung in trembling balance between the ethereal beauties of the scene and classic reminiscences it awakened. Thence we halted for the night at Minturnæ, celebrated in Roman story for the flight of Marius from the advancing power of Sylla. The suburbs of this town present the peculiar characteristics of Italian scenery ; a deep and extensive valley, richly festooned with vines, and surrounded by lofty hills, whose beautiful verdure forms a natural bridal with the green creepers at their base. The next day we reached Capua, but one stage from Naples. Here we observed the absorbing melancholy of Orsino, against which he had successfully struggled during our journey hitherto, once more gain the ascendency. Our vicinity to Naples seemed to him as the evil spirit to the guilty king of Israel. The classical themes suggested by the road—the affection of his daughter—the conversation with which Saville and myself sought to divert this brooding, so far from soothing, but irritated the sufferer's sensibility ; and we were compelled to retire from the unsuccessful conflict, leaving the victim to his silence and melancholy.

"Naples !" I cried, with a child-like ecstasy, as we entered the city ; "Now, saith the Italian proverb, it is time to die !"

"Naples—!" mechanically echoed Salviati: he shook off the reverie in which he had been since we left Capua, and, looking around him on the beauties of the bay, as one by one they rose like golden exhalations from the water, breathed into being by the warm sunlight; "Signor, you now see the Italian's paradise. Well does he tell you to die when you look on Naples, as earth holds no lovelier scene for human eye!"

"You see there are *two* Vesuvii," observed Amina, following up the theme with animation, and all the self-confidence of a well-informed cicerone; "two Vesuvii. It was the old one that played that terrible prank with Pompeii, and threw up the modern one, which has, in grateful return for its birth, extinguished the old volcano. You see," she continued, to Merton, for whom her *penchant* seemed hourly to strengthen, "that all the representations of Vesuvius are exaggerated, and, like many stage scenes, done merely for effect. I have watched it at all seasons; have seldom seen fire emitted from it; and you must acknowledge the mere film of smoke that now rises from it is almost invisible."

"Very true," returned Merton, who appeared to watch the natural splendors of the scene with an interest greater than he had exhibited toward the classical remains.

"And yonder, you see," continued his fair cicerone,

with increasing interest; "yonder is Capri—that beautiful island, that seems rather like a sun-palace, dropped from heaven, than aught ever trodden by human foot. That is the paradise chosen by the tyrant Tiberius for his residence, and desecrated by the sanguinary decrees with which he decimated the Senate. And yonder (but you can not see it hence), at the base of that treacherous Vesuvius, lies Pompeii. It and Venice are my *enfants gâtés* of cities;" and, with the rapture of a child, she clapped her hands at the lovely visions both cities had conjured to her fancy.

We were now passing down that magnificent street called the *Strada del Gigante*, commanding Vesuvius in the distance, and the magnificent headlands that jut from its base into the bay. A sudden turn brought us in full prospect of the latter; and well might the poet exhaust his finest fancies, or the artist his richest colors, ere either could embody the glories that nature has given to that, the loveliest of her children. And yet, were I asked in what chiefly lay the unrivaled loveliness of that scene, I should say, not so much either in the forms of the land, or the land itself, of which she has been so prodigal here, but rather in that soft, voluptuous light resting on every object, like a haze—so thin as to leave every point and outline visible, yet so rich and warm as to impart to the whole thing an artistic light and coloring. That bay and these hills, I thought, were haunts meet for the

L*

light ,and fanciful Greek.   Not a hill-top but the superstitions of mythology might have tenanted with a god and a temple; not a wave in that bay but sparkled to the wheels of the sea-nymph and the Triton. Oh, Greece, we forgive thy fables for the sweet fancy that has framed them, and the grace that, like summer leaves, twines together the fair garland of thy myths

CHAPTER XIV.

Why, man, your cheek grows pale; your teeth they chatter;
Strangers would deem thee but a puling child,
Cowering o' winter nights by drowsy embers,
And trembling as he hears the witches' broom——
Stir up the sky to strife.
                    What hast thou done?

IN habits of daily communion and intimacy with
Bianca, it is not to be wondered at if, more susceptible to her fascinations of mind and soul, I found
myself at length in the situation of the gamester, who
forgets the magnitude of the stake in the mad excitement of the game.   Mad it certainly was to me; for,
though I found myself daily more entangled in the
snare, and daily more and more hemmed in the
magic circle of her genius and her high endowments
of heart, I dared still to brave the spell of the enchantress, mayhap too rashly, confident in my own strength.
Though beset by the attentions of the Signor Salviati
—attentions, that by the kindness of their *prévoyance*,
and the courtliness with which they were paid, partook the grace of chivalry—it seemed to me that she
was either indifferent to him, or that some other object had pre-occupied her affections.   On viewing her

relations to me with all that calmness the subject
would admit, I could not but be convinced that I was
the chief cause of her indifference to the enamored
Italian and his courtesies. But as I became the more
convinced of her partiality to me, how often have
I questioned myself as to the honor of encouraging
feelings I felt present circumstances precluded from a
happy issue. The accident of preserving her life had
bound the grateful Italian to me by feelings strong
as life itself: but since that event, circumstances had
transpired in my own life that, throwing me on my
own resources, and making me, as it were, I know
not for how long, an exile in the great highway of
life, would render my union with Bianca an act of
cowardice and humiliation in my own eyes. How
knew I the actual result of my *rencontre* with Desmond? To involve a woman in the terrible sympathies
with such a catastrophe were cowardice; and, in the
poverty that formed my father's only bequest to me,
would it be generous in me to encourage the attachment of one for whose moral qualities I entertained
such respect, and whose genius had kindled within me
such admiration? Whatever struggles of life might
hereafter await me, I felt within myself strength of
character and fertility of plan sufficient to encounter
and, mayhap, overcome; but I am free to say, however ardently I would have loved such a high-souled
companion in these struggles, the princely fortune

Bianca was already accumulating by her vocal and dramatic powers, placed a barrier insuperable between herself and me. The more dependent I felt myself, the stronger development of pride I felt : nor do I set forth these disinterested feelings of a galled and wounded sensibility to challenge an empty praise, but as the sincere expression of a pride legitimate and deep. Yet, though resolved on this course, upon a presumed preference for myself, how could I resist the attractions of one whose genius, acquirements, and heart created a magic circle around her, spellbinding all those who entered it. Art and Nature had in her divided the shrine for their worship ; and, as the devotee laid his oblations on the altar, he felt it an offering to the embellishments of the one and the purity of the other.

We had been but a few days at Naples, when Saville and myself, in company with Bianca, went to visit Salviati at his villa. It commanded one of those unrivaled sites in the vicinity of the city, on the road to Posilippo, where stands the tomb of Virgil. Placed on the eminence of an eagle's nest, it swept in one grand panorama not only the bay itself but the city below, opposite to which rose Vesuvius, placed there like a giant to watch, or, it might be, to destroy her, as her fair sister Pompeii. The grounds of the villa, in the exquisite taste of their cultivation, where the toil and ingenuity of Art were but rendered the hand-

maidens to their great mistress Nature, were in all
worthy of the almost unearthly prospect they commanded. Through them we wandered, in company with
Salviati, whose attentions were now so obvious to
Bianca as frequently induced her to enlist me in the
conversation.

"True, Signor," she said, in reply to some observation of the Italian; "but do you think, Signor Irland-
ese," she continued, addressing herself to me; "that
the artificial modes of life, with all their constraint of
conventionalities, the conversation that but displays
the treasures of the mind without satisfying the wants
of the heart, the overdone *politesse* that but counter-
feits sentiment to which the nature is utterly dead; do
you think that qualities like these can possibly repay
us for our temporary forgetfulness of Nature; or that
the false and artificial, however gilded to the eye or
flattering to the ear, can ever compensate us for that
which alone is true, because it bears the impress of
God? Believe me, society is but the golden bracelet
of the Egyptian queen wreathed by the serpent that
is drawing her very life."

"Somewhat strange a theory, Signorina," I replied, "for one whose sphere is not only an artificial
one, but whose orbit therein is so preëminently brilliant."

"Ah! like many inexperienced in art, you measure
brilliancy by applause, we by the inward satisfaction

we feel in approaching the ideal of art. A 'bravo' or
an 'encore' tells us we have done well, but the child
of art is not contented till from each succeeding triumph the heart whispers, that Nature can not trans-
cend the last and perfect embodiment. But to return,"
continued the *cantatrice*, with an animation that glowed in her dark eye and cheek, as she gazed on that
bay and seemed to transfer to her heart as a shrine
every object of her own beloved Nature; "it was not
my choice of artificial life that made me adopt the
stage; but the accidental possession of powers that
unfitted me for any other sphere; and even the very
Nature it is our province to portray, is but a finer, a
subtler expression of that mysterious power than those
material forms that on all sides surround us."

We were now entering the villa; a rich conserva-
tory, lading the air with its perfumes and gladdening
the eye with the bright colors of that heavenly climate,
led the way to the grand hall; that, like many of those
on the Lake of Como, the taste of the proprietor had
converted into a gallery of art. We had ascended the
staircase and entered the withdrawing-room, in which
we observed a man seated. The refined and costly
character of the furniture was somewhat at variance
with the dress and bearing of the stranger. He was
dressed in a jerkin clasped round his waist by a leath-
ern belt and large buckle, that gave him somewhat
the aspect of a public official, while the large slouched

sombrero (common in Italy) threw its shadow over a
brow, that required nothing to darken its jettiness or
give a daring to the resolution it expressed. There
was an air of authority about the man, bordering on
audacity, for he never raised his hat to the presence
in which he stood; the more remarkable in an Italian,
who is cringing and sycophantic to the last degree.
In the reservation of his hat, however, he seemed jealous to assert that air of authority before his superiors,
which they could not recognize in the rank or bearing
of the stranger. There was something so revolting
and obtrusive in his overbearing demeanor, that had
a demon suddenly appeared in a shrine consecrated to
deity, the devotee could not have wondered more than
we at such an apparition amid the taste and elegance
of the Villa Salviati.

"I have come by appointment, Signor—!" said the
man.

"Hush—I had forgotten—we will speak together,"
was the incoherent reply of Orsino; as with blanched
cheek and quivering hand he led the way to an adjoining apartment, followed by the stranger. "Pardon—pardon!" said the courtly Italian, with whom
even the excess of mental distress could not efface the
fine sense of breeding. We bowed in acknowledgment;
but observed that the words were almost inaudible
from the quivering lips that uttered them.

"Not dead—?" were the words of surprise we heard

from Salviati, as the door closed on himself and companion.

"How happy," said Amina, while the tears came rapidly, "would life be in lovely Naples, were it not for the presence of that man, and the feelings his presence uniformly awakes in my father."

"What can be the cause?" inquired Saville, with an interest greater than he had yet exhibited toward any thing in Italy; our misadventure at San Sebastian having completely extinguished the very last spark that lingered in him toward the Roman.

"I never could discover: communicative on all other subjects, his silence is marked and reserved on this alone. Affectionate to weakness, whenever I press him on this subject, there is a sternness in his manner so repulsive as to awe me, and render communication with him painful for the remainder of the day;" and, while she spoke, the tear she strove in vain to suppress bore witness to the truth of her words, and the pain with which they were uttered. Her short narrative, though directed in particular to Saville, seemed strongly to address the warm sympathies of Bianca; the generous nature she had aroused, betrayed itself in the shifting color of the cheek, and the breathless attention with which she heard her.

"Is this your constant residence?" asked Bianca.

"We divide the year between Rome and Naples," replied Amina; "else were our life, protracted here, insupportable. As far as I can judge, my father is bound by some obligation, whether of conscience or otherwise I know not, to be in Naples for a certain portion of the year; but that is to us the severest penance of our life. While here, there is a cloud that seems to exclude every cheerful image from his mind, and throw, as it were, a pall over his whole life."

" Have you a mother?" questioned Bianca, with that hesitancy that indicated the conscious delicacy of the question.

" My mother died when I was but six years of age; but, strange to say, I neither saw her remains, nor was I permitted to witness the funeral rites. They were conducted at night, as my father told me; and, oh! that night I shall never forget. My father told me to retire early, but it was not to sleep; for I listened and listened through its long watches; but all was silent—silent as the grave, to which they were hastening my poor mother."

" Did you witness her death?" inquired Bianca, in that affectionate tone, that sought the indulgence of a feeling rather than curiosity.

" No—my father suddenly acquainted me that my mother was so dangerously ill that the physicians enjoined extreme quietness—excluding especially the presence of her child, as too exciting for her enfeebled state."

Any further communications on the part of Amina

were interrupted by the opening of the door, and the
reëntrance of Salviati with his·mysterious visitor.
The *brusque* and overbearing manner of the fellow
had increased evidently from the interview, while the
trepidation of Orsino, so conspicuous on their first
meeting, now bordered on an obsequiousness approaching servility.   This was the more remarkable,
as between men of such different ranks and bearing;
the courtly and polished Italian exhibiting such deference to one whose whole aspect was that of a bravo.

"Pardon, once again," said Salviati; as, leading his
rough companion, with a marked courtesy, he led him
from the room to the staircase.   The fellow stalked
across the room, leaving it, as he had entered it, without raising his slouch, or recognizing any of the party.

In a few moments Salviati returned.   The cloud
that had rested on his brow with an almost visible
power, seemed now removed by the disappearance of
the man; his spirit resumed its buoyancy, and he extended a fresh welcome to his guests, by introducing
us to a collection of antiquities found in the vicinity
of Pompeii.

"You are aware," he said, addressing Bianca, "that
all the antiquities disinterred from that city belong to
the government, and are immediately removed to the
Muséo Borbonico."   While he was speaking, I accidentally observed his eye fall on Amina, whose countenance still retained the evident tokens of the tears

we had observed. The expression was stern and re-
proving. She seemed to understand it; and, turning
to Saville, she was, as usual, engaged in the office of
cicerone, for which her extensive and thorough information gave her a *penchant*.

"By the way," said Salviati, "if I remember aright,
I observed on our route hither, that Italy possesses no
city abounding in its suburbs with more treasure for
the antiquarian and the virtuoso than Naples. What
say you—shall we visit Puteoli and the Sibyl's cave,
and—?"

"Drink old Falernian at Baiæ?" chimed in Amina,
with a classical rapture that utterly exorcised the evil
spirit that had darkened the first moments of our interview.

"And see that most exquisite bay," followed Salviati, "where the Roman moored his galleys, and in
which Nero threatened to bury his mother during a
summer fête? Tacitus tells the story: he caused a
vessel to be constructed so artificially, that, at a given
signal, its timbers were to fall asunder."

"I remember," said Bianca; "and the reward of
the tyrant son was, to see his mother swim in safety
to shore.—*Andiamo.*"

"The most authentic likeness of the wretch," said
Amina—"for even magnificent criminals have a charm
for posterity—is to be seen at the *Muséo Borbonico.*
It is a broken equestrian statue found in Pompeii.

Physiognomy is not at fault in the features of the matricide—they are those of a sensualist and brute."

"My daughter partakes the classical mania incidental to so long a residence in Italy," remarked Salviati. "You will find her equally at home on the shores of Avernus as among the ruined temples of Baiæ. May we claim the company of the Signorina Carmonali?"

Bianca assented, and the morrow was appointed for our visit to these classical localities. We returned to Naples with Bianca, full of the intellectual repast we anticipated from a visit to these ruins, and Saville much more eloquent in his praises of Amina than of either Virgil or Tacitus, who were to be our guides on the ensuing day. The distresses of the young Roman had touched a new chord in his generous heart; and the sympathy he expressed for her, was but another element binding and strengthening the attachment whose roots, I found, had already deeply struck.

A lovely morning that morrow! One which memory loves to register with white, amid the woes and chances of the past that have blotted her fair page. The sun poured down that richest flood that seems native to the Italian sky alone. The distant islands, as they donned their bright mantle of haze, appeared but to have passed from the deep dreams of night to the waking slumbers of day. The waves danced and sparkled, like the very deities of the Greek, risen

from their palace of waters to hymn the jubilee of
morning; and far as the eye could stretch, from the
base of Vesuvius, where sleeps the voluptuous Pompeiian, to Capri, and still on to Cape Misenum, those
waters leaped and glinted in the sun as gladly as when
the adventurous Greek steered his bark to the paradise
shores of Neapolis. " Time wrote no furrow on their
azure brow."

The road to Puzzuoli (Puteoli) winds, by a lovely
and gradual ascent, along the bay. It was about a
mile or two on this road that our carriages were met
by another, containing the rough visitor we had encountered at the Villa Salviati. The carriage passed
us at an almost furious rate; but not sufficiently rap-
ly to prevent Saville and myself from identifying our
friend of the previous day, accompanied by a woman,
whose bedizened appearance, partaking the *bizarre*,
impeached her taste, if it did not the sanity of her
mind. Saville and myself were in the same carriage
together; but Bianca afterward informed us that this
unexpected meeting produced in Salviati the same
nervous and harrowing feelings we had witnessed at
the villa.—Such is life : misery and happiness travel
the same highway; and the bright eye and the glad
heart have neither a tear nor a sympathy for the fel-
low-pilgrim that may sink by the way. The circumstance elicited nothing more than a transient observation from Saville and myself; the former, perhaps,

dreaming of the sweet cicerone who was to con for him the classic page, of which my own heart and mind were full even to inspiration.

Our carriages, some few miles from Naples now, occupied the grandest eminence I ever beheld; doubly grand not only for the features with which Nature had stamped it, but the sublimity it borrowed from the memories of Roman story. Immediately below us lay a valley trailed with vines—that peculiar drapery (so to speak) of Italian scenery—but of so precipitous a character as almost to render the head dizzy while one looked down, yet, from its abrupt and rugged steepness, blending the wild and romantic with features of the most prodigal fertility. Never shall I forget the emotions of childish delight with which I looked down on that valley; I felt my breath checked, I could have wept for very joy, such deep and mysterious sympathies does Nature either in her grandeur or loveliness awaken within us. Before us lay a lovely crescent bay, whose hither side was skirted by old Puteoli, in its apex we descried the Lucrine Lake and Lake Avernus, while the opposite side was occupied by the ruins of Baiæ, the once celebrated watering-place of the Roman voluptuary and *noblesse;*—while at the farthest extremity of the crescent rose the huge form of Cape Misenum, like a tower of strength, where Pliny was stationed when he first witnessed the fatal eruption of Vesuvius. But even the rich and varied associations

that thronged the mind were lost in the one grand and
absorbing image of the Roman power, as the eye rested
on those waters, now sleeping in their eternal rest from
the cry of the Roman soldier and the sweep of the
Roman trireme. Descending, we rode along the mar-
gin of the bay, till a gentle ascent from the water's
edge brought us within the walls of old Puteoli, in
which we observed traces of the old Appian Way.
We visited Solfatara, the oldest extinguished crater
of Vesuvius, whose volcanic power issues now with
such violence, through so small an aperture, that the
visitor apprehends a momentary eruption. The extreme desolation of the huge area, and the great interval that had elapsed since its last eruption, were
more suggestive of antiquity than any of the remains
of human hand. We passed thence to the amphitheatre; and, as I looked on its massive columns, arches,
and buttresses, I was surprised so vast a structure (to
me rivaling the Coliseum in strength and durability,
if not in extent) is not more known to the world.
Above the roofless theatre rose the *Monte Barbara*,
the old mountain from which Horace and his Augustan clique drew many an *amphora* of their choice
Falernian. From the roadside the ruins of a magnificent temple, dedicated to Serapis, met our eyes at
some distance below us; while from it half-way to the
opposite shore of Baiæ stretches the broken bridge of
Caligula. We visited afterward the temple of Serapis,

where the peasants were dancing the *cachucha;* an assemblage of the ugliest men and women I ever beheld, but fully worthy of the hideous discord to which they were executing their graceless movements. Let not the devotee of Italian music seek for the favorite object of his worship, where most he should expect to find it, on Italian soil. Italy has no itinerant music; and the few stray voices I heard were rather screams than possessing any pretensions to harmony.

Every place, in travel, is inspired by its own peculiar *genius loci,* that seems to render the very "stones capable," and inform the inanimate ruin with a spirit that shall survive the wreck when it has crumbled away forever. As I walked through the ruins of the old town, the majestic form of the mighty Apostle of the Gentiles was before me; over the spot on which I stood might his shadow have passed, and the ancestry of the poor fishermen who surrounded me might have heard the voice of God Himself from the lips of that Christian hero!

We continued our route by the sea-shore for some few miles; where, leaving our carriages we diverged into a beautiful green by-way trellised with vines and creepers. To our left lay the Lucrine Lake; while, a little farther on, we stood on the shores of Avernus! There are some passages of travel of so utterly dreary a character, that their dwelling-place seems more proper to the fancy than the earth. The hell of Virgil

M

had been to me almost a myth; an assemblage of the
gloomiest images grouped together as a dwelling place
for the wretched; but here I found the reality; yet,
perhaps, the reader will be as much surprised as myself in meeting in Lake Avernus one of the loveliest
sheets of water that ever mirrored a summer sky. It
is situated in a valley, girded by high lands whose
garb of richest verdure stretches in summery slope to
the water's edge. We were informed that the bed of
the lake was probably in Virgil's time the crater of an
extinguished volcano (not at all improbable from the
sulphurous and volcanic character of the soil around
Naples, designated by Virgil "*Phlegræi Campi.*")
But the gloomy terrors of the poet's hell were soon to
be realized in all their imposing and fearful reality,
more especially when contrasted with the sunshine
and the bright silver sheet by whose banks we walked.
We were suddenly arrested in our progress by a door,
whose antiquity might certainly have dated back to
the era of Augustus, and there greeted by some three
or four stout fellows (each bearing a huge resinous
torch) who seemed to guard this entrance to the Sibyl's
cave, if not in the likeness, at least with the pertinacity
of Cerberus. But a trifling *buona mano* (piece of
money) is as all-powerful in winning over the modern
Italian, as the cake in bribing the vigilance of old
Cerberus. So, thought I, this is the "*descensus
Averni.*" We were now in a spacious and lofty vaulted

passage; so gloomy that we needed all the light the
smoky torches of our guides could afford us. The
passage itself is like the tunnel of a modern railroad;
by some supposed to have been a subterraneous communication between Baiæ and Cumæ on the opposite
shores of Avernus. But this is no place for the speculations of the archæologist; I merely record them as
I heard them on the spot. But we were soon to test
the "*ease*" of which the poet speaks as characteristic
of this "*descent*."[1] Whatever it may be morally, of
which I entertain not the least doubt, in a physical
sense I must pronounce it one of the most arduous
and, withal, ludicrous expeditions on which the traveler can possibly enter. At the extremity of the passage, we suddenly wound off into a very steep descent,
so narrow as to admit but one at a time; while the
stone walls on either side were so smutted and carbon-
ized by the torches, as to render the hands that came
in contact with them as black as the walls themselves.
In single file, thus, we marched; the occasional laugh
or grumble at any mishap sending its echo down deep
below us; while the torches of our guides, flaring high
above us, and sending out their heavy volumes of
smoke, must have lent a highly picturesque effect to
the group—if we could have enjoyed it! After a slow
but steep descent, in which the strong glare of the
torches served but to make the darkness visible of this
mythical hell, our infernal pilgrimage terminated in

what properly bears the name of the Sibyl's cave;
about as unpropitious a place for the poetic germina-
tions of oracles as could well be conceived. As intensely dark as the narrow passage that formed our
descent, and filled with a puddle of water, in which,
our enthusiastic guides informed us (each doling out
the classics of this hole with the voice of a Stentor),
it was the daily habit of this Cumæan lady to perform
her ablutions, while Nero amused himself, *à la Turc*,
by gazing on her faultless proportions through a huge
hole, at which one of our guides stood, at the same
time thrusting a smoky torch through it, for the purpose, I presume, of proving the practicability of the
imperial feat. We complied with the prevailing custom here not of *rowing* but *riding* over Styx; so each
of us (gentlemen) selected his biped steed, and in the
very ridiculous attitude of hugging the unfortunate
guide almost to suffocation, while with the utmost
difficulty we kept our feet free of the water, we crossed
this puddle (in my opinion better entitled to the name
of "Avernus" than that beautiful stream we had left
in upper air) and stood on the opposite bank. This
classical feat accomplished, we were not sorry to return to the glimpses of the moon, and exchange the
dark and suffocating horrors of Roman myths for the
bright and beautiful truths that beamed from that
azure sky, and glowed in the bosom of that lake, that
seemed the abode rather of angels than of fiends.

And now resuming our carriages, a short ride and a
gentle curve round the water's edge speed us on our
way to Baiæ. But a solitary wall by the wayside
marks the site of Nero's palace, doubtless in its time
rivaling in prodigal splendor his " Golden house" at
Rome. The former, a small board bearing the inscription " *Stufe di Nerone*," informs us has degenerated
into warm baths, while the latter has been almost over-
built by the baths of Titus. We passed the ruined
palaces of Cæsar and Sylla, standing like fortresses
above the water. The remains of the summer villas of
the Roman came down even to the roadside, while far
below us lay the lovely bay of Baiæ, its waters sleeping in that calmness as though an eternal summer had
rested on them since the light barque of the Roman
voluptuary had rippled them. Judging from the number of ruins here, it must have formed the most extensive summer *séjour* for the luxurious Roman. Independently of the rich natural features that formed the
attractions of Baiæ (the town itself forming a sweet
valley, backed by a high range of hills and fronted by
the water), art and luxury lent their aids to enrich it
with every thing that could invest this summer retreat
with the dreaminess of a Paradise. The temples of
Mercury and Venus stand almost by the roadside; and
the richly embellished marble baths, in which the
Roman diverted his *ennui*, or sought recreation from
the summer heat, lie now in utter neglect, overgrown

with vines and rank vegetation. We closed our day of classical explorations by drinking the genuine Falernian, of which there seemed no stint, judging from the number of amphoræ that crowded the apartment.

By night we reached Naples.

CHAPTER XV.

To say, I do not love thee, that were false ;
But that I dare not claim thee, it is true.—
Turn the dark page of my unworthiness,
And, in the blackness of each character,
Read thine own light !
       By heaven, she weeps !
Not Portia's self was dearer to her Brutus
Than thou to me.

THE professional exertions of Bianca rendered some
days' respite necessary ; and, it was one evening
after our return from visiting Pompeii and Hercula-
neum, while sitting in a beautiful arbor that commanded the bay of Naples, that Salviati announced his intention of giving an entertainment in compliment to
the *Prima Donna*, as well as for the purpose of affording many an opportunity of testifying in person that
admiration that had been lost amid the plaudits of a
theatre. It was evident that Salviati's whole soul was
absorbed by the Italian ; he had no ear save for her
voice, no tongue save for her praise, and no theme save
for her genius. At such moments of impassioned fervor would Bianca turn her beautiful eyes on me, as
asking a sympathy for the admiration she was receiving, or avowing incredulity, because it found no echo

from me. But there was neither the expression **nor**
the echo she sought. As sensitive to the influence of
her genius, as deeply penetrated with admiration as
Salviati, and bound to her by an earlier and stronger
tie, that of preserver, there was a power over me, from
the circumstances to which I have alluded, that made
me desirous if possible to place a wider barrier between
Bianca and myself. This resolution was the more
strongly confirmed from the very partiality she exhibited toward me over Salviati; a partiality, only the
more strongly commending to me her nobility of character, by the utter disinterestedness it displayed. Yet
to encourage where I could not reward, to build up
affections by the hopes, endearments, and favors of each
day, but to dissolve them in a dream, were unworthy
a man who had a heart himself or honored it in a
woman. It was thus that, loving Bianca almost to
idolatry, I was compelled from my own very silence to
hear the worship of another, while I even now knelt in
the deepest adoration of soul. My heart was bruised
and crushed within me. Bianca never should be mine
till I stood clear as in my own conscience I deserved,
and so free in means as to acquit me of all obligations
of dependence. The love I felt for the noble and ingenuous Italian was exalted by the very admiration I
entertained for genius that had passed unquestioned
so high an ordeal as Italy; it was this that, while,
feeling for her the passion that combines the strength

of soul and mind, I was compelled like the frantic
devotees in the vale of Hinnom to stand by the altar
and witness the destruction of my own offspring.
Thus, while really abandoning the ground of contention
to Salviati, and disavowing all claims of the rival,
while with a breaking heart and without a struggle I
resigned her who might perhaps have been mine, it
was evident, from the constrained manner of the
Italian, and the blood that flushed his cheek whenever .
Bianca manifested her preference to me, that he was
unwilling to acknowledge in myself any other character
save that of rival. And, strange to say, I experienced
that utter passiveness, that would not disavow the
rivalry I neither felt nor encouraged.

It was, then, with such feelings as I have attempted
to describe, that we all approached the Villa Salviati,
on the night appointed for the fête in compliment to
the *Prima Donna* of San Carlo. The assemblage was
great, yet select, comprising all the *élite* either of the
Neapolitans or travelers. Salviati had, on the present
occasion, lavished all the resources of taste, elegance
and design in welcome of his *inamorata;* for so my
own despair compelled me to regard her. His superb
galleries of statuary and painting were thrown open;
and, brilliantly illuminated, formed a promenade for
loungers and *conoscenti.* But it was chiefly in the
beautiful grounds of the villa that the rich and cultivated taste of the host was displayed. The beautiful

M*

parterres of flowers, now in the high bloom of a Neapolitan summer, threw out their bright and varied tints
even amid the shades of twilight from rows of small
lamps so dexterously wreathed above them as to sym-
bolize the language of flowers.   Thus the iris hues of
orange, crimson, and purple that rose like an exhala-
tion of light from these flowers, deluded the fancy with
the rich play of the rainbow even during the sombre
.light of evening.   Fountains too were there, flinging
up their jetty sparkles; and in their brief airy play
catching the rich light from around, and falling back
to their parent fount like a train of stars on the dark
robe of night.   Arbors had been constructed of the
vine, the rose and jasmine, the odors breathing out an
Eden on the sense, and their exquisite forms receiving
a bold and rich relief from the colored lamps whose
hues melted and blended with those of the flowers they
enwreathed.   The *coup d'œil* of the gardens was, on
that lovely night, a dream of the Orient; needing but
the pictorial costume of the East to transform the
reality into a dream of Bagdad and the Caliphs.   Here
and there through the grounds were scattered groups
of singers, each relieving the pauses of the other; and
whether the air had the amatory and passionate tone
of Italy or the chivalrous rapture of old Spain, the
"prisoned soul" willingly yielded itself captive to
sounds that, as they wandered like spirits through the
arbors, or lost themselves in echo in the distant hills,

seemed. for the moment like harmonies of heaven
hallowing this Elysium. Anon the tale of song would
be relieved by a rich burst of martial music from a
band screened from view by a small wood; and the
clashing cymbal and the drum would rouse those
energies once again that had been lulled by the languor
of song.

"You have dreamed of the Orient, Signor; for nothing but such a dream could call so magic a scene
from dull earth," said Bianca, as, between Salviati
and myself, she was walking through the enchanted
scene.

"The fancy that has a talisman can create as well
as dream," returned Salviati, "and where it has found
a Houri it will not be long in discovering a Paradise."
As he spake, his pale brow was suddenly flushed, and,
as he cast on me rather a hasty and impatient glance,
I was not slow in divining the cause.

"Yet," continued Bianca, with dexterity evading
the compliment, "constituted as man is, with energies of mind and body to develop, an intellect to
satisfy and elevate, a heart whose kindly feelings
must be fed by sympathies with the wretched, and
generosity for the distressed, no one could say that the
state of the visionary was that of happiness. In a
negative sense it may be, because it is passive amid
the wretchedness and wants of others, but not in that
true sense for which we were created—that of alle-

viating the one and ministering to the other. One
moment of real good that springs from the higher
cravings of our nature, transcends all the opiate
dreams of Mohammedan happiness the Impostor ever
promised to his Paradise."

Salviati paused: he had touched a new chord in
Bianca's character; he had viewed her merely through
the artificial medium of the stage, and the dreamy,
haze-like charm it flings around its luminaries; but
he had never deemed the pure, the natural, the holy,
could dwell in a soul that Art seemed to have peculiarly consecrated for her own.

."Look at these lamps," resumed Bianca, with an
animation that showed the subject had awakened
every kindred feeling of her heart; "their bright va-
riegation rivals the rich hues of the flowers that clus-
ter round them. Break the lamp, the hue is gone, but
that of the flower lives through its season to delight
the sense. Such is the difference between the dream
and reality: the one passes away with the brief hour
it brightened and adorned; but the other, like a firm
and unchanging friend, walks hand-in-hand with us
through life, and continues its fellowship with us even
beyond the passage of the final bourne."

"How can you impart such vitality and eloquence
to an art which, in its best acceptation, is but a
dream; expressing the lineaments of character that
but for a moment fill the mind's eye, and giving the

terrible energy of truth to passions you are conscious to yourself of only counterfeiting?" said Salviati.

"When I first entered upon the stage, the character and the passion had both the impress of nature within me. I *felt* them then—they are a *habit* now. And this is, perhaps, the most painful penalty the artist must pay for that sacred initiation into the very depths of his art, that crowns him with final triumph —the utter disenchanting of every attribute that once made her a deity."

"You must not breathe this to the many," said our host, "else will you disenchant the temple in which they have shrined your-genius."

"The wand is almost broken; what companionship can art have for one who is lone and friendless in the world? My father buried in a foreign soil, and my mother—" The melancholy and abstracted tone in which these words were uttered was lost in the tears that followed. In a moment the strong will of the Italian mastered the weakness: "Art has had her sacrifices; nature must have her tears."

"We are waited for," said Salviati impatiently, as the crash of the band announced the dance ready; and, offering his arm to Bianca, he hurried her from my side, but not before she had said, in a tone that seemed wormwood to the Italian, "Addio, Signor O'Moore, we shall meet again."

I lingered on the words till they seemed a very

echo. Like the leaves of the Sibyl, scattered to the wind, they seemed susceptible of whatever interpretation fancy or passion might attach to them. What if we *should* meet again? It was but to place myself within an influence to which, though I resolved not to yield, yet, paradoxical as it may appear, I made no effort to resist. The spell was weaving around me, the incantation of the enchantress herself but provoked my entrance into her mystic circle; the voice of the siren was in my ear, the sweeter, perhaps, for the certain shipwreck to which it charmed me; for that rock was her home! Yes, we should meet again, but it would be to rouse myself from the apathy, or rather the dream, into which her genius, her beauty, and her goodness had plunged me; to sting myself to a sense of the precipice on which I stood, and, like a madman dared; to tear from my heart the shaft that rankled there, resign her to another, and bid her—no, not farewell—but blessing!

I loitered into the *salon de danse*, to witness the amusement in others I had no heart to participate myself. At the head of the room stood the queenly Bianca, with whom Orsino was evidently engaged in topics of interest deeper than those usually suggested by the mirth and levity of the dance. I watched him narrowly. The expression of his countenance, while earnest, was that also of the deepest tenderness; and the fine intellectual melancholy that was its leading character was lost in that tenderness, that spoke the theme of their intercourse was rather that of heart than mind. My eyes wandered to Bianca : her manner was rather abstracted than cold; rather that of one whose heart is with the absent, than indifferent to the voice or subject of the speaker. Their *vis-à-vis* were Saville and (of course) Amina ; the former, day by day, more importunate in attentions which were gaining a fast ascendency over the latter.

The dance was concluded ; and, recurring to the words of Bianca (the superiority of nature over all the triumphs and multiform designs of art), I retired to the grounds. The bright lamps were now fast paling before the moon, just climbing the dusky cone of Vesuvius. But this one feature was needed—but this last dash of Nature's mighty pencil—to complete the paradise that lay below, around, and above me. The lamps paled, like stars whose watch had expired, as their brighter sister burst from her silver shrine to awaken the glories of night, and set their vigils to her attendant stars. That rich and holy light, that makes the lover a worshiper, rested on the unrivaled bay, like a shroud dropped from heaven over the departed glories of the day ; while the deep stillness that brooded over this Sabbath of the night, was the more strongly marked by the pauses of mirth and song and dance that burst from the merry revelers. I wandered amid the grounds, drinking in at every sense the magic of the hour and the scene; thoughts that seemed winged messengers from heaven took captive soul and mind, again laden with the dull weight of earth, by every sense of sorrow connected with the past and uncertainty of the future; I felt myself but an Adam, wandering in a paradise, while the trail of the serpent was over every flower that wooed the senses with its treasures. Now I thought of my father, then of my fatal meeting with Desmond; anon the image of Bianca would, like a ray of moonlight, lighten up the dark wilderness of turbid thought and undefined feeling; but even there, the cloud stood by the side of that fair thought, ready to obscure it, and leave me in darkness. As the mind wandered from the eternal glories of heaven to the sad associations of earth; as the dead, the parted, the estranged rose before me in the cold and stern lineaments of truth; and the heart drifted like a wreck from wave to wave, seeking rest but finding none, and drawing from the unchangeable types of heaven those hopes of eternity that gladden and strengthen us on earth, that beautiful verse of Moore came to my memory, cheering with its certainty of a final rest and undecaying affections :

"Oh! well may we hope when this world is gone,
To meet in a realm of more permanent bliss;
For a smile or a shake of the hand, hastening on,
Is all we can hope or look for in this !"

Abstracted from every thing earthly by the feelings

I have essayed to describe, I was standing a few steps removed from an arbor, whence I heard a violent sob. I turned—Bianca was before me! Her face was buried in her hand, and the quick heaving of the bosom betokened no slight conflict of emotion.

"Bianca! Bianca! how is it I find you thus? What hath chanced? Has Salviati—?"

"My mother! my mother!" was the only disjointed reply that followed my anxious question.

"What of your mother?" I said, gently taking her hand in mine. "When we first met, and you spoke of her, you were not thus moved. Look on that sky, Bianca; its holiness betokening the bright presence of a God; its stillness yielding a foretaste of that quiet He has appointed there for the wrecked and storm-beaten souls here! Look, Bianca, on the cloudless glories of that sky, bright and inextinguishable as the spirits of the blest, and the loved that have at last found their dwelling-place above! Had you the power, would you recall a single soul of the great troop that made your heart's life in this world? or ask them to resign one moment of heaven and their Father's presence for a lifetime of earth, sated with its perishing joys and pleasures? Oh, Bianca! that great Book that operates like a magnet on every thought and sensibility of our complex nature, has sentiments that go to its very roots, from the power of their truth and the exquisite diction that clothes them. When we would weep for the dead, our tears should turn to joy for their happiness; the greater, for that they can not return to us, though we must go to them."

The words I had spoken, and as deeply felt, carried with them the small freight of comfort they were intended to convey. Bianca was soothed; and, fixing on me those full eyes in which tears struggled with emotions of gratitude, she pressed my hand in hers, and thanked me. "Foolish—weak!" she said; "the thought rose on me as I thought of my solitude in life, amid all the tributes of success that can gladden it; and I have been unable to master it. I thought of my mother, and that thought revived her guilt and shame; and I wept with bitterness that I had wronged my mother in the presence of a stranger."

"Do you count *me* a stranger, Bianca?" I inquired, rather desirous, it might be, for the last time to analyze our relations, than interested in the answer.

"You?"

"Yes, me!"—and, as I spoke, I fixed my eyes on her in the full light of the moon—that, did they utter the thousand complex feelings that flowed and boiled, like a mighty tide, within me, would doubtless have awakened some awe in the Italian. "I know," I continued, "that you will allude to that schoolboy feat of saving your life, for which you have so frequently and liberally repaid me by your acknowledgments, and for which, I doubt not, this moment you are deeply grateful: but that is not the point. Strangers we can not be, in the social acceptation of the word;—but are we strangers to each other in the deep and subtle world of the soul? Is there a feeling of love. or despair experienced by one that is not participated by the other? Have our souls an echo?"

There was a pause: our eyes met, and in them seemed fixed all the powers of speech. I felt myself dumb for the moment, as under the resistless charm of Bianca's gaze.

"You are not happy here, Bianca," I resumed; "here, where the fadeless natural glories of Campania feed every sense, and the dreamy beauties of a Caliphate are gathered to receive and welcome you;—still you are not happy. Methinks, in your upturned eye, as it glows and expands to that heavenly light, that I can read a yearning of the soul after something more permanent and solid than has yet been awarded you by the empty praises of the world. Is it not so? Do you not look on the various objects of life, however tangible success and applause may render them, but as so many mutes in a funeral procession, the more melancholy for the embroidered splendor of their trappings? I have felt it so, Bianca—"

"And I," interrupted the Italian.

"And yet," I resumed, "to have secured the truth —the adoration of one amid all that is false—would not that repay you for the toils you have endured,

and the restless watchings of mind and body through
which you have passed ?"

" Of whom speak you ?" said Bianca

" Salviati! No theme, save yourself, on his tongue;
no ██████ on earth, no star in heaven for him, save
yourself. We speak of the madness of love ; his passion has not yet reached that triumphant stage ██████
may we judge from its incipient symptoms, ██████-
choly, and jealousy—"

"Jealousy!" iterated the Italian.

"Yes, Bianca; and of me—of me—poor—wanderer
—outcast, he is not far from it."

I felt, as I uttered them, there was a bitter wildness in my words, a self-irony in my manner, to which
I was forced to yield, as the best commentary on my
own position in life.

" Have I not seen the fire flash, and the hot blood
mount, and the thin, irascible lip gnawed, because,
forsooth, you listed better an observation that fell
from me than him ?"

"Who told you, Signor Oracle, that I preferred you
to Salviati ?"

" The oracle that never fails the questioner—my
own heart. The heart is to the lover what conscience
is to the sinner ; and never fails the confidence we
repose in the unspotted clearness of its mirror. Bianca !" I cried, flinging off the disguise of periphrasis
and delusion I had worn so long ; " Bianca, he was

jealous of me; not because you loved me, but, with
the quick eye of an Italian, he observed my love for
you. Did your eye wander to me, his followed, watching your heart in the light or shade of your glance;
had you an ear for any word of mine, his ▓▓▓▓▓
▓▓▓▓ to rest on the breathless attention with which
▓▓▓▓arded us both. Yet, why was this? He saw
I loved you—loved you more strongly, deeply, for
that I sought to hide my own heart from myself,
and made an assumed indifference the interpreter of
a passion I felt was hourly wasting me. Oh! who
can speak the tortures of such a passion, when the
heart, like a smothered volcano, becomes a holocaust
from the wasting of its own fiery bosom? Bianca!
pardon—pardon! I have told you all—yet not all. I
have told you but of my passion, but not of the
suffering it has left in the wild and desolate path it
has wasted—the suffering of despair. Our loves are
unblest: you never can be mine!"

While I was speaking, Bianca's head was reclined
upon her bosom; but when I alluded to the despair
of my own passion, she raised her eyes and fixed them
on me. The tenderness, almost to tears, that suffused
them, banished the half-frantic spirit that hovered in
my words; and, though despair was strong as ever, I
felt more calm and re-assured.

"You have read the oracle aright," she said, "when
you are present I have neither ear nor eye for my

own countryman. Morven, for so I must call you,"
she continued, clasping her hands with violence on
her bosom, "in your hand lies the spell of my life; on
your lips the word that must either doom or save."

"Then 'doom' be the word!" I cried, "for wretch
like me shall never drag down the one he professes to
love to the same perdition with himself."

My words had struck more deeply than I intended;
Bianca's cheek was flushed rather by the fear awakened by my words than any pride she might have felt
in my refusal to unite our fates. Her manner was
agitated, and her voice choked with the emotions I
had raised.

"Were it another thus branded you," she said, "woman though I be— But what—what can you mean
by words like these? Your face, your manner, alike
belie the word with which you slander yourself. Gentle, generous, and brave; Morven, can it be that a
heart, tenanted by such as these, should send its current through the veins of a wretch?"

"When first we met this language would not have
been misapplied; but since then, a cloud, darker even
than that cast on me by disinheritance, hath flung its
deep shadow over my path, withering every flower I
might have found there. Then I was only penniless,
but now, perhaps—a murderer—!"

A shriek from the sensitive Italian told me too
plainly the abruptness of my communication. She

sank on my breast, while her hands were clasped with horror to her eyes.

"It is false, false!" she cried, "by that moonlit heaven, it is a trick you work on me to thrust from you the soul that loves you. Were it not better to disown me forever, deny that we had ever met, and call down even a curse upon our parting, than thus break a heart that loves you, by a tale that blots out every tie of truth and honor that has ever bound it to you. Morven, Morven, unsay that word, and I will bless you for a gift dearer to me than the life you gave me back; oh! dearer far: for is not your name dearer to me than my own life?"

"Would to God I could unsay it! Hear me," and with blanched cheek, and parted lips of agonized attention, she leaned upon my breast while I related to her my *rencontre* with Desmond, and the awful issue that had compelled my self-banishment from Ireland.

"It is false! still false!" she cried, starting from my breast on which she had lain during my recital. "If Desmond be dead; he must blame his own rashness or revenge. You never sought his life; your soul is as pure to me as that moon that has witnessed your confession."

"I trust I am—I trust so; for that one thought, Bianca, dashes away a full cup in this sweet land from my lips, turning its nectar to poison. And, oh!

when to appearance intent in mind and soul on the
thrilling ruins Time has spared us, and the brief epitaphs of mind and soul and action she has written on
them, who knows the demon shadow that walks at
my side, the agonized heart whose promptings exiled
me from my own land but to haunt me in that of a
stranger ?"

I had confessed all, disowned the treasure of which
I felt myself unworthy, and passed from the paradise,
without the companionship of an Eve to beguile the
rough and solitary path on which I was entering.   I
felt the tie was forever parted.   Bianca, as though
reading my thoughts, said :

"Are we, then, to part?   Is it thus you requite my
love ?"

"Part we must, as lovers, Bianca, but, oh! not as
friends.   Still let me sojourn at your side, be it but
to hear you, be it but to feel I am not alone.   And,
though another's you may be—to stand by you at the
moment of sacrifice, hear the words that call down a
blessing on another invoke a curse on me—see the
form that might have been mine clasped and claimed
by another; though in such an hour it may be like
rending the very heart-strings, yet, Bianca, shall I rejoice in the constancy that has enabled me to resign
you for your own happiness."

"You have fulfilled your terrible promise," answered the Italian; "your word has been that of '*doom ;*'"

and, as she spoke, all the fires of her intense nature kindled an expression I could not interpret.

"What has *doom* to do with a scene like this?" uttered a voice, with such a freezing emphasis on the word, that both Bianca and myself started at what we deemed was the worst realization of its worst import. We turned, and the eyes of both met those of Salviati; not as before we had seen them, beaming with the blandness and amenity of the host, and the pride he felt at the pageant with which he had welcomed his countrywoman, but fierce, fiery, and wandering; lighted with that wasting passion to which I had alluded, and which I myself had unconsciously kindled. With the skill of a practiced actor, however, a moment witnessed a change. The passion was either mastered or in abeyance; his countenance resumed its habitual melancholy, and his manner its wonted courtesy.

"You are bidden to the feast," he said, "but make excuse—"

"We were admiring the grounds—the bay, and—the moon," said Bianca, almost stunned at the sudden appearance of Salviati, and the strong passion she observed at work in him.

"Very beautiful, very beautiful, no doubt," returned the Italian, testily; "but *Il Signor Irlandése* finds before him a star brighter than any he can see in yonder heaven;" these words were spoken with a keen and sidelong glance at myself.

N

"Every nation, Signor," I returned, "has its own *Keblah ;* the Moslem has Mecca, the Italian, Rome, and an Irishman may be pardoned for selecting genius and goodness for his."

"No doubt, no doubt, Signor," responded Salviati ; "I have ever heard of your nation as generous even to a vice; you will not be an exception by monopolizing to yourself the high qualities of which you speak."

"I resign all, but with your own Italian Jew, I add :

> "'You take my life
> When you do take the means whereby I live.'"

I stood rooted to the spot. What was life to me now, when that night I had resigned, nay, flung from me, all that could turn what was now endurance into pleasure? I could scarcely realize all that had transpired between Bianca and myself. My mind was wildered as in a dream, from which I started but to find the realities far worse than the tortures to which my thoughts exposed me in that visionary state. My eyes were still fixed on her till I saw her enter the villa, and the moonlight fling its last flash on the diamonds that enwreathed her hair.

CHAPTER XVI.

. 'Twas gold betray'd
Him whom mankind acknowledge as their King;
Its curse remains, like serpent's trail on Eden,
And brands its stigma on the gambler's brow.

"WHY, what's the matter, Saville? Has the circle been squared, or have you disentombed a relic that will startle the *savans?* Or—or—?" This question was addressed to my friend some few days after the events of the previous chapter, as he was pacing his chamber with incoherent mutterings and extravagant gestures.

"Neither—neither. Now, my dear fellow, don't bother me so; you can't sympathize, so you had better be silent."

."Sympathize! with what? Your feat at San Sebastian?" this allusion was always a sore subject to Saville, and never failed to call down his mightiest malediction on classic scenes and memories.

"Oh! curse San Sebastian!" retorted my military friend. "Truly ought my classical tour to be written out in full for the benefit of all neophyte pilgrims, with notes, illustrations, etc. It would serve as a most excellent *vade-mecum*, a chastener to the frantic enthusiasm of these classic wanderers; I commence by running the chance of mingling my bones with the canonized martyrs . in Sebastian's catacombs, and I wind up—"

" By falling, like the merest neophyte pilgrim (to use your own words), madly in love."

" Worse than that, O'Moore; by wrecking myself on that most iron of all coasts—a father's heart."

" Ah! the old story of rejected lovers. Your woes, however, derive some dignity from finding their prototype in poetry. You remember what Octavian says: 'Fathers have flinty hearts.' But jest aside, my dear fellow, what is the cause of this unexpected turn in the tide? When last I saw your bark, it was before a smacking breeze; all sails spread—"

" My dear O'Moore, the present is no exigency for the beauties of metaphor. The fact is, as you may have observed, there was nothing in all this land of wonder attracted me half so much as that artless, *naïve* little Roman, Amina. Well, not to flatter myself, my attentions seemed as captivating to her as she to me; and, with the usual precipitancy of our countrymen, I was pondering the conclusion before the premises were clearly adjusted in my mind. In short, my dream of domestic happiness was well-nigh realized. I had made up my mind ' to sell out,' purchase part of my brother's large estate in Ireland, naturalize this young

Roman by transplanting her to the Emerald Isle, and devote myself to the doméstic and agricultural."

"And what's the obstacle?"

"To be brief, Salviati has destined his daughter to a convent."

"Why, it was but the other night that every sense of the intended novice was bewildered by the arts and embellishments of life."

"That splendid gala, at least to judge from results, was meant to celebrate her retirement from the world. Salviati made the announcement but yesterday; and the strangest thing of all is, that this horrible incarceration seems in some way connected with that infernal strappado of a fellow, with the slouch and the swagger, we met at the villa."

"Something rotten in Denmark there, Saville! But how can the fate of one like Amina be connected with a fellow like this?"

"She can not divine that herself," returned my companion. "All she can tell me in reference to it is, that immediately upon another interview with this fellow, that demon melancholy, to which we have observed her father so subject in Naples, seized on him with a power more relentless than ever, and that it was during the presence of the fit, he made the announcement to Amina."

"Well, there was certainly nothing monastic in the appearance of the Gasparoni, to associate the adoption of such a step with his presence," I replied; "but what says the novice herself?"

"That she would rather die than take a step, repugnant at once to every feeling of her nature as to every sincere interest of religion. I spoke of flight, and promised her a shelter in my own country from what I deemed a tyrannical exercise of parental authority. But she was dissuaded either by fear or affection for her father."

"Have a care, Saville; to rouse the passions of an Italian, and that in their most aggravated form, by interference with the authority or economy of home, is but to play with a naked stiletto. Heaven save me from the enemy, who dares not brave the sun of day, but husbands his blow for the blanket of the dark."

"I defy him, and all his cowardly vengeance," retorted Saville, with a true Hibernian impetuosity; I could not but sympathize with; "it is the part of society to interfere, when the relations of life become a burden, from the tyranny with which they are exercised."

"That's a question for ethical writers; nor, do I assure you, am I willing to test the soundness of that principle here in Italy, and, least of all, in a matter connected with their religion."

Our conversation was interrupted by the servant handing in Salviati's card; and forthwith the Italian was ushered in. A glance passed from myself to Sa-

ville, as to the necessity of preserving silence on the
topic of which we had been speaking. We received
Salviati as his noble hospitality deserved; but I could
not fail observing a cordiality, an *empressement* of
manner to us both, the more surprising as he had
never exhibited it before. Indeed, his habitual manner was that of *bon ton;* what fashionists term "*good
breeding*" (heaven save the mark!) a manner*ism* that
sacrifices every fine impulse of our nature to stoicism
and formality. The change was still the more surprising to me from my recurrence to our last meeting
in presence of Bianca, and recollection of the circumstance with which Saville had just acquainted me.

"Well, has Naples disappointed you?" inquired
Salviati; leading the conversation with more ease and
bonhommie than I had ever witnessed in him before.

"Exceeds every thing I had imagined myself or
read in story, Signor," I replied, "and the princely
hospitality of her son is worthy the city he adorns.
Have you seen the Signorina Carmonali since?"

"No—not since. Ah! *Signor Irlandése*, what is
the talisman your countrymen possess that secures so
many favors and triumphs with women? Where an
Irlandése enters the lists, knighthood flees from competition, leaving spurs, sighs, sentiment, and all to his
invincible rival."

"You flatter my country, Signor; but I am not
aware of possessing, much less claiming, any preëmi-

nence in the esteem of the lady in question. Indeed, were 'preference' the word, one would naturally impute the strongest chance of that to her own countryman."

A shadow passed over the face of Salviati; for I have never seen one more indicative of every passing emotion than his;—expressive to transparency.

"How fares the Signor's fair daughter, Amina?" interposed Saville, opportunely.

"She has left Naples," returned Salviati, with a laconic air that seemed anxious to waive any further inquiry. Poor Saville's expression indicated all he felt at the reply.

"Her departure was sudden: it is not long since she honored me with an interview, in which no mention was made of her purpose."

"The purpose was mine, not hers," returned Salviati, as briefly as before. "Are you engaged this evening?" he resumed, after a pause, addressing us both.

"No," I replied; "strangers here both, we gladly hold ourselves at your service, and, with thanks, receive your attentions."

"La Signorina Carmonali does not sing to-night," he answered, "and you may probably find yourselves *ennuyeux* in quest of amusement in a strange city. So, with your permission, I will undertake the office of cicerone, and probably render the evening more agreeable to you both than it otherwise would be."

We both assented ; for, indeed, a stranger in a foreign land is but a tabernacling Israelite. "You play, dc you ?" he said, with some hesitation.

"Oh, any thing for excitement!" said Saville, with that habitual, dare-devil manner, that the classic atmosphere of Italy could neither remove nor refine. "The fact is, *mio caro Signor* (a wonderful effort for poor Saville, who had no affinity for languages, either ancient or modern, and whose constant interpreter I was compelled to be)—the fact is, one becomes cursedly tired of Homer, and Virgil, and Horace, and all those 'Trojan Greeks,' as—who is it?—somebody calls them."

"Shakspeare," said I.

"Oh, ay ; you are up to all these ancients, you know."

"Why, Saville, Shakspeare was a modern!"

"Thank you, my dear boy—a thousand thanks ! 'I owe you one!' as the man in the play says. My friend, O'Moore, Signor, would give you the impression that Irishmen enrolled Shakspeare among the Greek authors."

"Not as long as he furnished in himself the best evidence to the contrary," returned Salviati, with a graceful bow.

"*Revenons à nos moutons !*" resumed Saville, like a well-trained hound, whose scent was not to be diverted. "I was remarking that this constant patter-

N*

ing of the classics in Italy reminds us somewhat of
the '*toujours perdrix*' of the French king: we want
change; it is only taking a prolonged draught of the
Trojan war in manhood, of which we have drunk to
repletion in boyhood. Any thing for excitement, dear
Signor. *Andiamo!*"

"I will most willingly accompany my friend," I
said, "though not a player myself." The fact was,
I feared for Saville: it was one of his vices in college;
and, with his impetuous temperament—sanguine to
an extreme when gaining, and desperate in loss—I
thought it but the part of a friend to accompany him.

Salviati was true to his appointment; and, wend-
ing our way along the splendid Corso, we entered a
building of such large dimensions and costly structure, that elsewhere it might well have borne the
appellation of palace, though in Italy but an ordinary
residence. Through a small court we were conducted to a spacious staircase, the walls of which were
enriched with copies of the *chef-d'œuvres* of the
old masters, and the landings with specimens of the
finest statuary. Knocking at a false door, formed
by a sliding-pannel, the existence of which would
have baffled any save the experienced eye of our
conductor, it opened within, as from the touch of a
spring: a word passed between Salviati and the *custode*, and we stood within an apartment possessing all
the usual features of taste and splendor with which

this passion allures her votaries. One magnificent lustre served to illuminate the whole, and bring out into broad relief the varied expression of the tenants of that chamber. There were the loungers, looking listlessly on; their callous apathy contrasting strongly with the haggard cheek, the sunken eye, the deep and furrowing interest awakened by the turn of a card, to be removed, perhaps, by the fairer chances of the next. There stood the *habitué* gambler of years, disguising, under the assumed smile and bland manner, the passion whose first intoxications had flung a dreamy delirium on his after-life; but, in the keen and anxious glance that passed from the card to the competitor, it was not difficult to discern the fire wasting and smouldering within, though the lips were smiling and the brow unruffled. And there was the novice, with hopes high and ardent as the soldier in his first battle; the cheek flushed, the eye dilated, the breath suspended—all bespeaking a something between hope and fear that the next turn of a card would seal with certainty. The magnificent sideboard was laden with the costliest vintages; in which some were burying the memory of their losses, and others, from the stimulating draught, acquiring fresh courage for the next encounter.

Salviati was greeted on all sides, as a veteran in the ranks, by his comrades. Salutations were promptly made, and invitations extended to our conductor to

join in games then deep in progress. But all he de-
clined, on the plea that his visit was solely to introduce his friends, *I Signores Irlandesi.* This announcement, of course, drew on us the courtesies and attentions of the parties present; and, at the suggestion of Salviati, Saville and myself were soon seated, and launched on the exciting stream of the game.

The individual with whom we played (for we were but a party of three) was a man of the most winning manner and polished exterior I had met in Italy. His features were of that school termed classical, and borrowed their attraction more from their regularity than any intellectual expression which seldom accompanies that perfect conformation. Indeed, there was a strong contrast between a countenance strictly Roman, in contour, and calm to melancholy, and a manner enlivened by the mercurial vivacity of the Frenchman. There seemed an antagonism between the face and temperament. As we entered, he was lounging at the sideboard, engaged in conversation with some guests; but, when he saw Salviati, the presence of others seemed perfectly forgotten in the cordial welcome he extended to him. It was, while exchanging greetings with Salviati, that I observed a peculiarity apparently inconsistent with a countenance otherwise perfect. It resulted from a habit I never yet met in persons of high or ingenuous character—that of not looking *at* the person they address. We were soon seated, and all preliminaries arranged with eminent courtesy on the part of our opponent; it was not long ere I participated the mania that my friend Saville exhibited from the first. Salviati, meanwhile, left us in charge of our new friend, and wandered from table to table, conversing or looking on, as the humor suited him.

As is usual—and what I anticipated and feared on occasions like the present (for, as the reader knows, my finances were rather limited)—commencing merely *pour passer le temps* the stakes were increased with the interest and success of the game, which latter was wholly on our side—more, however, on Saville's than mine, owing to his superior dexterity and experience.

"How goes the game?" said Salviati, reaching our table, after loitering from one to another.

"Il Signor Merton is very successful," replied our antagonist, in Italian, with a blandness that disarmed the sting of defeat.

"His countrymen are generally successful," returned Salviati, glancing at me with a smile, whose allusion I perfectly understood.

"Here we serve Fortune, Signor," I said.

"And *there*," returned Salviati, promptly, "a goddess whose favor is won more frequently by the honey-tongued flatterer than the worshiper."

"Were her favors granted on those conditions," I

answered, " few could compete with the Signor Salviati."

" Except—"

" Five to one on the next !" interrupted Saville.

" I wish you success !" was the reply of Salviati,
as the turn of the card verified his wish ; and he
passed on.

Salviati parted from us at the steps of our hotel.
The night had been eminently successful for Saville ;
so much so as to produce the result I feared—the
revival of a passion the stronger from the absence of
any more refined or intellectual tastes to counteract
it. For myself, I found my purse considerably re-
plenished ; but, without cant, I would much have
preferred remaining in my original condition, to the
receipt of this accession.   In this respect, I acknowledge myself much more culpable than my companion,
in whom the passion was much stronger, therefore
the more irresistible, without any of those mental pre-
ventives that, perhaps, existed in my own case.   As
with many, with me also—the table was a matter of
pure expediency.   Cut off from any other pecuniary
resource (except that which pride forbade—a union
with Bianca), the table, while it presented a prospect
of recruiting my finances, afforded also an excitement
that I found not altogether disagreeable. Thus, I first
entered this *salon* as a Mentor, but, unfortunately,
remained as a snare : and the passion I sought to

moderate by timely counsel, I but aggravated by example.

"It was your particular friends, the classics," said Saville, as at breakfast, on the following morning, we were recapitulating the events of the previous evening, "who first taught me the practical question, ' *cui bono ?* ' a satisfactory solution to which we both found in the rational manner in which we spent last evening. *You* would have us exorcise antiquity herself from broken stones, and religion from ruined temples—drink apocryphal Falernian or Cœcuban from vines that, perhaps, have not numbered twenty summers, and take a Stygian row on men's backs over that infernal Sibyl's puddle ;—all wrong, my dear boy, depend on it—all wrong !—last night was your true *nox ambrosiana ;* the *ambrosia* all travelers require— money !"

Saville's position was entirely too strong to admit of controversy—more especially in my situation, so much needing the *ambrosia* of which he spoke ; so I even left the tree where it fell.

"Will you go again to-night ?" I said.

"We must maintain our country's honor, in a foreign land," answered Saville : "you know we promised."

"And Amina—?"

"And Bianca—?" interrupted Saville. I felt the retort, and held my peace.

"Drive out Nature with a fork," saith Horace,
"and still she will return." Whatever changes we
may have undergone since that period in our external
modes and social habits, nature still holds the same
lease on our hearts in unaltered language. The passion had in Saville but acquired fresh stimulus from
success ; and, I regret to add, the same motive exercised on myself a similar influence. The following
evening saw us both re-enter the Palazzo. The same
company, with some few variations, the same attraction and brilliancy of object to lure the unwary
and rivet the chain of the devotee. How strange to
analyze the feeling which we know has power to
drag us on to ruin, and to which, nevertheless, we
yield with all the impotence and resistlessness of beings without will or reason ! In such cases we but
resemble those standing on a precipice whose dizzy
height, producing a temporary frenzy, impels them
finally to the fatal leap. Is there, may there not be, a
principle in our nature called fascination ? On what
other grounds can we account for this passive con-
cession to habits and feelings that reason condemns,
though will is too impotent to resist?

It was not long before Saville was deep in a *tête-à-
tête* game with our *quondam* competitor. I lounged
and talked with the rest ; beginning to enjoy my
intercourse with the Italians, from the daily mastery I
was gaining in the language. I was enjoying a choi

glass of *Lachrymæ Christi*, when the conversation accidentally turned on Salviati, in the group standing near me.

" He is not here to-night," said one.

." His tastes for the *salon*," rejoined his friend, " seem to have declined since the arrival of this new Prima Donna. Indeed, I hear it is only the hope of obtaining her hand that renders life supportable to him here in Naples."

" No wonder," was the laconic reply.

· " Have you heard his new purpose ?" continued the second, gathering round him a small knot of *confidants*, to indulge them in the last *morceau* of Neapolitan gossip. " They say" (here a shrug of the shoulder accompanied the Italian's ' *si dice,*' as much as to leave to the hearer's discretion the exact complement of credulity he might place in the communication)—" they say that he has determined on his daughter's taking the vail. He gives out (for she is not to be seen) that La Signorina has left Naples ; but I have it from good authority (and here the speaker demolished a pinch of snuff he had long been threatening)—that she is immured in the Palazzo with a priest, for the purpose of bending her contumacy, and commending more to her affections the spiritual life for which she entertains a strong aversion." .

" *Povera donzella !*" was the unanimous murmur

of sympathy from the gossips, who were devouring up his discourse.

At that moment the father of the "Povera donzella" entered; the gossips were instantly hushed—and Salviati advanced to me with the most cordial greeting.

"Happy exceedingly," he said, "that my suggestions have been so successful. Travelers always require a lounge; and, as your friend observed, the classics may, in their own language, to a sated appetite, become the '*bis crambe cocta.*' But why are you not playing? Lost last evening, eh?"

"No, Signor, I was successful; but—"

"Let's join your friend," interrupted Salviati; so to Saville's table we went.

"What luck, Saville?" said I.

"Splendid, my dear boy, splendid. Fortune favors the adventurous as well as the brave. My last stake was a high one. 'Tis won. Some wine there!" The wine was brought and drained at a draught. I saw the blood was firing with the interest and magnitude of the stakes; so I joined the party, in hopes that by reducing the latter I might in some degree lessen the excitement I saw fast gaining the ascendency.

"Pshaw!" said Saville; "we'll have no reduction—*aut Cæsar aut*—what? Curse that Greek. I could never get on with it at Trinity!"

"That's Latin, Saville," I interposed as calmly as the blunder would permit.

"And this is Fortune," was the reply; as, with the turn of the next card, he claimed the stakes.

"You should swear now by Venus," said Salviati, in allusion to the highest throw upon the dice among the ancients; but Saville was deep in the mysteries of the next deal, and utterly ignorant of the classical information conveyed.

'Twere needless as tedious to weary the reader with the chances of a gaming-table; suffice it to say that Saville and myself experienced the same good fortune on that night as on the previous, and returned home winners to a large amount. In the increasing appetite with which success kindled me I could not but find an ample justification for a passion I had but too often condemned in my friend; indeed I felt the hunter was spreading his net; and, that to avoid the toils would require more resolution and self-command than I could muster. Like the ancient Saxon I was called in as auxiliary and remained a spoiler.

"All is not right with Salviati," said Saville, in reply to the communication I made him respecting Amina; "there is something more than that melancholy, had we but skill to probe more deeply and find it. Then this unnatural constraint upon his daughter to adopt a life as repulsive to her nature as to every principle of conscience and religious duty. *Mehercle!* (come O'Moore there's a classical oath for Italy) I begin now to suspect even his courtesies; they are too

obsequious ·by half, and then that Jesuitical, deep,
meaning smile of his; I never see it, but I think on
Cæsar's murderers, presenting a petition with one
hand, while the other clutched the dagger."

" Why, Saville, who can say there is nothing in-
fectious in atmosphere?   Italy is certainly to you a
Pierian spring, a very Castalia; during your whole
sojourn at old Trinity I never heard so many classic
allusions as you clustered together in that one speech.
You really make me extend Pythagoras's doctrine, by
showing that metempsychosis may take place this side
of Styx."

" You are facetious.   But is it not time to pay our
vist to the Signorina Teresa? Ah! you grow pale.
Come—come; you can not deny that you love her
passionately.   Weep a little, my dear fellow, and then
you draw to the full the portrait of old Middleton:

> ' Why should those tears be fetched forth? can not Love
> Be even as well expressed in a good luck,
> But she must see her face still in a fountain?
> It shows like a country maid dressing her head
> By a dish of water; come 'tis an old custom
> To weep for love.'

" Ah! Morven you extol the classics, but take up our
old dramatists and compare them with our-moderns,
and you will find the latter but tinsel, swagger, and
trope when laid side by side with their genuine ore of
language and sentiment. · For quaintness of language,
depth of image, and pithy morality, they distance

to nothing your vaunted classics and our moderns.
You are welcome to your Augustan, if you only leave
me my Elizabethan era."

"Well done for Saville! By Jupiter an you were
not so much a man of pleasure, I would have some
hopes yet that the world might receive a wandering ray
from your torch. But I fear—"

"Oh! for yourself as well as me," interrupted
Saville. "To the full you enjoyed last night's bout as
much as myself. The difference between us is, that I
carry the voluptuary on the surface and you bury him
under the refinements and amenities of Letters. But
to the point from which we have digressed, like the

metaque fervidis
Evitata rotis

Of your favorite Horace, in whom by the way I never
could recognize any claims higher than those of the
Epicurean, cunning, selfish, and flattering. Do you
wed or not? However, Morven, it is ungenerous to
trifle and base to abandon where you are certain of
success. Thamyris or Mæonides, both of whom Mil-
ton has kindly left on record were blind, could almost
see the passion Teresa entertains for you; so marked
and unreserved is every preference she shows toward
you."

"I have told you, Saville, I never will wed, though
to give her to another will be like tearing very life
from the heart."

"And why?"

"You have asked me a question in confidence. I feel
myself bound as honestly to answer. I am poor, and
she rich. I am obscure, and she eminent; and what
must be the result of a union under these circumstances, save the most abject dependence and sacrifice
of every marital right, except what was conceded to
me by the liberality of my wife. I know my' blood
too well; it has a dash of command in it; but I never
yet met an O'Moore who knew much about obedience.
No, Saville, Teresa may stand before the altar with
another; nay, call on me to kindle the sacrifice by
placing that hand in another's I should love so dearly
to claim as my own; but I have resolved that nothing
under circumstances at least equal to her own, should
induce me to wed her."

"You are not the first of your blood I have met (by
the way, strange mixture that blood of the old Irish
chieftain), and I do assure you I would not withhold
from it one jot of that pride and obstinacy you are so
punctilious in exacting for it."

"Saville," I said, springing from my seat, stung
with bitter feelings I could not control for the moment;
"you know not the deep humiliation that poverty
strikes to the very soul of him in whose nature the
pride and delicacy of the gentleman are enhanced by
the refinements of education. May you never live to
feel them as I! His mendicant garb is scouted and

jeered at by the crowd of brainless popinjays and
gaudy fools, to whom mind and soul are unwrought
mines, indicated to the vacant eye only by the few
sparkling particles they see upon the surface. But, in
Bianca have I met one, whose eye has searched deeper
than the poor and thriftless exterior I present. Is this,
then, to be my appreciation of a soul that can sympathize with mine, and a mind with which I never hold
communion but to feel how ineffably superior it is to
mine? No, let Bianca wed; ay, an if she please, the
wealthy, proud Salviati; I see he adores her; I shall
be there, even at the altar; yet, it will be but to look
on the last flame that leaves in ashes the only true joy
and deep love I ever felt in life."

"As for your poverty (pardon the word, you applied
it to yourself), you know my purse—"

"I thank you, Saville, a thousand times, not more
for the generosity of your offer than the delicacy of
language with which none save a gentleman could
have offered it. A thousand—thousand thanks; I
don't need it yet; and, should I accept it, it will be
but on the condition of my note of hand, payable
whenever Fortune blesses me with the power."

"You need not be so cursedly strict with a friend."

"Honor, Saville, should always be the current coin
of gratitude. Will you join me in my visit? 'Sdeath!
there's a fascination for me around Bianca, that
makes me cling to her very image, like the foolish

moth to the flame, though I know ruin must be the
issue."

"Well, we are both mariners launched on the same
sea. Heaven forefend shipwreck. For myself I will
not rest satisfied till I have untied this Gordian knot
that wraps the destiny of Amina. For mine she shall
be, bating all power save death. *So, au plaisir !*"

We were soon on our way to the *Hôtel de Russie*,
the residence of Bianca. She was at home. We had
not met since the night of Salviati's fête. That short
period had, however, sufficed to produce a manifest
change in her feelings toward me. Her manner, before ardent almost to affection and unreserved to freedom, was now more constrained and distant. It was
not, perhaps, that her affections were blunted but that
her pride was wounded. I was not aware, at the
moment that I felt myself impelled to speak from
deeply rooted principles and convictions I found as
impossible to crush as to transform my whole nature,
that in repelling the sensibility and discouraging the
passion of a woman, I was engendering a hostility
deeper, stronger than the passion itself. Nor is the
feeling so awakened an object of either wonder or
blame. Our nature in strength and endurance does
not extend beyond one object; on that she lavishes all
her depth, her intensity and hope; in the light of that
single object, as in her only sunshine, blooms every
flower that can wreathe the heart's bridal, while its

absence flings a blight and darkness that withers every leaf but to scatter on her bier. We love but once; and that love is the deep and holy worship of the heart to the first dawn that gilds its morning; we may love afterward, but it is only with the desultory feeling of the pilgrim, whose momentary joy is awakened by a bright but straggling beam that lights up the stormy sky. This deep and despotic passion, then, I had slighted. The shrine had been opened and I had disdained to enter; all the untold treasure of the heart, that makes up the sum of woman's wealth and happiness on earth, had been laid before me; her hope or despair, her bright voyage or her dark wreck, her home or her pilgrimage, and I had not even stooped to count the treasure; should I, then, wonder at the change? Yet, cost what it might—joy or despair to her, friendship or hate to me—I was resolved.

"You have been eating of the lotus," at length said Bianca, addressing me; with difficulty shaking off a melancholy I had never observed before in her buoyant spirit; "Like those who forget their country, you seem to forget your friends. How comes it we have not met since Salviati's fête?"

"My friend and I were so busy in exploring the classic environs of Naples that—"

"Antiquity," she interrupted, "has a greater charm for you than friendship."

"The fact is," interposed Saville with timely aid;

O

"we have both been so busy; O'Moore, as usual, burying himself alive in these old stones and striving to inoculate me with his own enthusiasm; that—that—"

"I can easily account for the manner in which *you*, Signor, have spent your time," returned Bianca, playfully: "I understand *La nina Amina* has fled her father's house to avoid the imposition of a revolting vow."

"It is but recently," said Saville, "that I have received this intelligence; and I do assure you any apprehensions of a selfish kind that so rash a step may create are lost in sympathy with the maiden, who has doubtless been driven to this by her father's cruelty."

"Poor Salviati!" said Bianca, "I never look on that noble, manly face of his, clouded as it is by melancholy, but I long to look into the heart, and crush the worm that's gnawing away its very health and life. It is not crime that so works upon him; his is not that wandering eye that fears the steadfast regard of any because it may glance suspicion, nor his the anxious and trembling manner of the criminal, that fears intercourse from the inward demon that may goad it to self-betrayal; but rather that of the calm and meditative man, suffering in silence and patience the wrongs he has rather endured than inflicted. Poor Salviati!"

"Your sympathy seems deep," I said; while I felt

strongly the burnings of jealousy, the stranger for that
I had resolved to resist and conquer the passion. My
manner was not unobserved by the quick Italian.
Her eyes sparkled, and a rich flush mantled her cheek,
as she replied :

"You are almost now in sight of Virgil's tomb.
You remember the fine lesson he has embodied in the
character of Dido, whom even the despair and madness of abandonment could not divest of that highest
prerogative of woman—sympathy. She had loved and
been repulsed—forsaken ; the poisoned barb rankled
in her heart even as the huntsman's shaft in the side
of the wounded deer of which she speaks ; yet though
she vainly waved her perfidious lover back as she looked on his white sails lessening in the distance, and on
returning to her palace saw the pile blazing—the last
resource that despair and madness had left her—her
misfortunes had but the more strongly roused the
woman within her, and gentleness was the spirit that
winged her soul from the funeral pile to the stars."

I almost trembled as I listened to this unexpected
analogy (too plain to be mistaken) between Dido and
the speaker. The parallel, from the intense emotion
of Bianca, had not been hammered, as it were, by
fancy, but forged in the very fires of her own heart.
Her eyes flashed and dilated, as she recounted wrongs
which found an echo in her own heart, and which I
had unwittingly inflicted.

"And is not your sympathy as strong for the daughter as the father?" I asked.

"It is for both," returned Bianca; "for him, for the wrong he seeks to atone, and for her as the victim. Yet, it is for me to postpone a sacrifice," she continued, turning to Saville, "involving such dreadful conditions to the sufferer."

"For you?" was the rejoinder of both.

"For me. Look here!" Saying, she rose from the *fauteuil;* and, drawing aside a crimson curtain that covered a small alcove, what was our astonishment to see Amina stretched in sleep on a couch within! We were standing in mute surprise at the picture thus unexpectedly revealed to us, and looking with incredulity alternately from Amina to Bianca, when the door of the apartment was suddenly opened, and Salviati stood at the entrance.

"Thank God! thank God! I have found her, my child!" were the ejaculations uttered by Salviati, as, with unsteady step, he advanced into the chamber, and sank upon a chair. He was much paler than usual; his brow was moist, and his whole person trembling with excitement. It must have been a picture to any one who entered—the attitudes and motives of the different actors alike incomprehensible. Bianca still held the half-drawn curtain in her hand, like some magician, himself fascinated by the spell he had conjured to appall another; while the eyes of all were turned now on Salviati, who bent forward on his chair, his head buried in his hands. While we thus stood, we heard a groan from the Italian ; then, starting from his seat with violent impulse, in a moment he was at Bianca's feet, her hand clasped to his heart. " How shall I reward thee, benefactress ? By saving her, my vow is yet unforfeited to heaven !"

" Signor !" said Bianca, raising Salviati, " not to me, but her own fears of this terrible vow, you owe your daughter's safety. It was but last night that, weak in body and soul from the struggles and terrors of this vow you would force upon Amina, she sought shelter here, and with it implored my intercession with you to rescind a purpose so fatal."

A shudder ran through Salviati's frame as he heard this narrative of Amina's resolution, in defiance alike of his own authority, as the holy life to which he would bind her. He strove to speak ; but, unable to command utterance, could do no more than raise his hand reverentially to heaven in token of the registry of that vow and the fulfillment of it exacted above.

" Rash girl !" he at length said, " would she make her father perjurer ?—add one other stain to those that already pollute my conscience, and blot out those hopes that alone lend light to the future ? Lady, it can not be ! The entreaty thou hast offered, though it may not be heard by a mortal on earth, from the straitness of a promise guilt has extorted, will plead for thee

above, where Mercy was never yet deaf to the prayer
of Humanity and Love!"

" Yet," interposed Bianca, " what virtue can there
be in sight of heaven from the fulfillment of an obligation imposed by no will of the devotee, nor fulfilled
by any religious convictions ?"

" None to her; but—for me—question me no more,
I pray thee! She wakes—my child! my child—!"
Saying, he was in a moment by the side of Amina,
and strained her to his heart with a fondness almost
irreconcilable with the rigidness that marked his resolution.

" Ah! my child, Amina!" he cried, alternately fond-
ling her, and parting the thick tresses that lay in disorder on her brow—" why wouldst make thy father
wretched, and, worse—false to heaven! Thou may-
est deem thy fate hard, to change the gay livery of
life and youth for the vail and weeds of holiness, and
fling from thy hands those flowery links that bind
thee to both ere thy senses have been wooed by their
freshness. Yet, wouldst thou not blame me, didst
thou know the stain thou cleansest, the whiteness thou
givest to my soul, the peace to my conscience—"

There was a pause, filled only by the sobs of Amina.
The strong appeal of Salviati had evidently sunk
deeply in the daughter's heart; her resistance to his
wishes wrought compunction in her; and, with a
passiveness that spoke penitence for the past and

submission to the future, she bowed her head on his neck in tears.

" My child—my own Amina—!" faltered Salviati ; " I am but parting thee from a world where folly, mayhap crime, might have beset thee, as me. The toils of the hunter are spread for youth and innocence like thine. I would not have thine unwary foot ensnared while thy father's hand could save thee from destruction."

Saying, he folded his arm tenderly around Amina ; and, without a word, saluting those present, led her from the apartment. We hastened to the window: the carriage stood without ; the poor girl sank back in the seat ; the blinds were drawn, and, in a second, they passed from us at a rapid pace down the Corso.

CHAPTER XVII.

The ship ne'er struggles with the central wave
Of the huge Maelstrom, more than with his fate
The gambler. Strange ! an idiot monarch's toy
Should start the sweat upon a strong man's brow,
And antedate old age !

"AND this is the man," said Saville, interrupting a long silence which was, doubtless, occupied by the events we had witnessed ; "this is the man to whom you would surrender the woman you profess to love, and whose passion for yourself is as unreserved as either word or token can make it ! 'Sdeath ! did I make the same avowals as yourself, there is no weapon I would fear to face against such an opponent !"

"I feel as deeply as yourself, my dear Saville, the truth of every word you utter. I see, too, the necessary result of my last interview with Bianca. The words I then uttered have left an impression too deep for the forgiveness even of one so gentle-souled as herself. I have roused in her the woman, and must abide the issue. But the principles by which we propose to regulate our actions must be ever superior to

the antipathies we create in others. Her heart is forever estranged from me. Did you remark the passion
that glowed in every feature when she spoke of the
despised, the forsaken Dido? It is now too late—I
resign all. Let the dream pass : it was but the twilight that foreruns the setting sun, and not the steadfast ray that warms the heart and brightens our path.
Henceforth, I will tear from my heart the flower,
stem and leaf, that twined itself with every fibre of
my being. Mine is a wayward fate ; let my way be
strewn with the withered leaves !"

The interview we had so unexpectedly witnessed, in which the rigid resolution of the father but
borrowed fresh strength from the submission of the
daughter, cast a gloom over Saville to which I thought
his elastic spirit must ever be a stranger. The determination he had made to resist the parental authority of Salviati seemed now relaxed, and he began
to regard his passion for Amina as hopeless and chi-
merical. His extreme depression demanded a corre-
sponding excitement ; and, with the desperation of
one who has staked his all and lost, he turned for
relief to the first stimulus in which, as the inebriate
in the wine-bowl, he might drown the memory of
sense and suffering.

"Life, O'Moore—!" he exclaimed, starting from
the sofa, on which he had been lying for some time
in silence and reverie ; "Sardanapalus and our own

countryman, Swift, were not far from the right in
their estimate of its triflingness. 'Eat, drink, and
love,' said one, '*Vive la bagatelle!*' exclaims the
other; to which, as we say in phrase parliamentary,
I beg leave to add an amendment—'the game!' Its
chances and excitement are the best medicine that I
know of. So come along, win or lose—I am reckless
which! As long as my banker holds out, they are
welcome to it all, if they only teach me to forget
myself!"

In such a mood it was as vain to resist Saville as
to curb the ravings of the maniac, whose fury is but
lashed by the clankings of his chain and the echoes
of his cell. The ill-success that darkened his passion
for Amina, by tending to wean his feelings from the
object, only diverted them to another with greater
force and concentration. His early passion for the
table remained with an absorbing and earnest force
that made me tremble for the result, even though the
strength of friendship compelled me to lend him the
example of companionship.

He did not wait long for the indulgence of his
wishes; our competitor was, as usual, true to time
and place. Indeed there was a punctuality about the
attendance of this man, that presented him to me as
a sort of official connected with the establishment, an
impression the more confirmed in my mind from the
obsequious attentions bestowed on the guests in gen-

eral, but especially on Saville and myself. I never
looked on that cringing bow and sycophantic smile,
without suspecting the integrity and honor of the
heart of which they appeared the true exponents. I
entertained the suspicion alone myself, without communicating it to my friend, as I feared his purpose,
aggravated as it was by recent circumstances, would
but be strengthened by the opposition presented by the
superior skill and practice of our opponent. So down
we sate, each in a different mood; he reckless for the
result, and I trembling, as failure would but render
me pensioner to the proffered generosity of my friend.

Our previous successes tended to inspire Saville with
a pride, as it were, to maintain the character we had
both acquired. I know not whether it was my own
suspicions of the character of our opponent that made
me observe, if possible, a more servile politeness of
manner, a something of a sneer in his smile, on this
night, I had not perceived on any former occasion. It
might have been that he was a *decoy*, and we the unwary victims he was about to snare in his toils; and
that this peculiar smile, of which I speak, might have
but expressed his contempt for those with whom, as a
skillful angler, he might have *played* for a time, to
net us only with the more certainty in the end.

The game progressed with an increased and suspi-
cious courtesy on the part of the Italian; while I felt
myself partaking momentarily of the deep and fearful

earnestness that marked my companion, at every stake. From the successes of the previous night, we commenced with a slight increase in the amount; but fortune seemed adverse, and we both lost. It is a mixture of pride that will not brook defeat and desperation, that makes the unfortunate more anxious to increase their wager than the successful. Even trifles carry with them a pride and resolution of character, the more determined, perhaps, from the invisible enemy against whom we contend in the person of Fortune. It was so with me; and I willingly consented to prop up our threatening luck by acquiescence in Saville's proposal. The stakes were doubled, and—lost again! I felt it the more incumbent to retain my coolness and self-possession, as I observed our bad fortune threatened the balance of Saville's temper.

"Curse the jade!" he cried, flinging down the last card that decided the game; "she has forsaken us entirely to-night."

"You won the last night," interposed the Italian, with that subtle smile that was meant to oil the wound, but only tended the more deeply to irritate my suspicions; "if you will take the trouble to count, you will find yourself my debtor to a large amount."

"I did not come to lose," grumbled Saville sulkily. I saw his brow was lowering and his blood warming, not so much, perhaps, for the adverse chances, as the despair that had driven him to the excitement.

"My dear fellow," I said, seeking to propitiate this wayward mood, "you must remember Fortune is like Janus, or the mask of the old Greek plays—she has two faces; and we must only abide our chance for her turning toward us the fairer one."

"Or rather," returned Saville, humoring the allusion for a moment with which I sought to divert him, "like the temple in her own street in Pompeii, she seems to have abandoned her shrine, and left but ruins to her worshiper!"

"Do not despair," rejoined the subtle Italian; "double the stakes: that, perhaps, may induce her return."

By this time all my winnings of the past nights were exhausted. I was obliged, for the next stake, to borrow of the *bank*.

"Lost again!" cried Saville, dashing down his card with a violence that presented a powerful contrast to the habitual coolness and equanimity of our competitor.

"You have but to try again," said the Italian; "it was defeat that first taught Frederick of Prussia how to conquer." This was spoken with a leer that was not lost on Saville, bespeaking as it did the conscious irony of the Italian in the comparison he had made.

"We are not fighting battles," said Saville.

"*Temper*," retorted the Italian, with a weighty emphasis, "is not more necessary in the field than at its mimic representative, the table."

"The fiery Italian is the last to give us so important a lesson," returned Saville, petulantly.

"Signor," rejoined the Italian, with a courtesy irresistible to the most ruffled temper, "if you please to continue, command my services."

"I am a borrower of the *bank*," I interposed, "and can not therefore continue the high amount for which we have played." .

"You need not trouble yourself about loss or gain," said Saville; "it is for my accommodation, not your own pleasure, I know, you are here; my purse is, therefore, in common—we will continue for the same stakes."

The sum was "put up" for both. I began now to merge all interest I had previously taken in the game in anxiety for Saville. He was fast losing all self-control, which made it the more obligatory on me to retain my own. I watched him narrowly; his brow was gloomy, his lips compressed, and the whole expression of the man denoted that fearful combination of anger and will with which we determine to bait and dare the very chances we can not propitiate. Should this game prove unsuccessful, I resolved steadfastly with myself to play no more; and, though I might not be successful by the influence of example, at least to be no longer accessory to a course that might not only involve him deeply, but leave myself proportionately his debtor. I began to suspect now,

that our antagonist was a skillful proficient, and that
our incipient successes were but golden baits that
cunning had thrown to the unwary.

"Signores, Fortune *is* against you to-night," said
the Italian, with a mock sympathy, as he swept "the
bank" to his own side.

"I'll play no more, Saville," I said, rising quietly
from my seat; "honor forbids me from contracting
any further debts, as I am unable to liquidate present
obligations."

"O'Moore," he returned, with an angry flash of the
eye I had never before observed, and could now easily
pardon; "if you stir from my side, you forfeit my
friendship."

"It is unjust," I answered, "under such an obligation, to bind a man to that his conscience condemns
You compel me to stand here; and quietly by my
presence to sanction your ruin by play with a competitor your superior at once in skill and temper. I
see from your manner you are serious in your threat.
I remain, but absolve myself from all responsibility
in the issue I see as plainly as though it had come
already!"

"You will not play?" he returned, pushing forward
his purse to my side of the table; "then, I hold you
bound by your promise to stay with your friend."

With as much patience as I could command under
the painful obligation thus imposed, I returned the

purse; but, alas! only to see its weighty contents
dashed on the table with that reckless violence that
bespoke the utter hopelessness of the stake.. My fears
and patience were not long taxed. The Italian won
all. Saville started - from his seat. His brow was
crimsoned; his eyes literally glared.

"I told you so," I said. "You should have been
more prudent than to have staked so fearfully in the
face of such superior skill."

"Signor," said Saville, fixing on the Italian an
expression of such mingled passion and defiance as
made the winner's hand tremble with the purse it
held, "we meet again. The chances have been yours
to-night; but the next—"

"Signor," returned the Italian, with a courtesy of
tone and manner that curbed Saville's passion for the
moment, "you heard no complaint from me when the
chances were yours."

"True," said Saville; "I entreat your pardon!—
we meet again!"

CHAPTER XVIII.

She will not see me!   Then is it dark, indeed!
Dark as his heaven to the Gheber's soul
When clouds shut out his sun!

"HER last night at the San Carlo!" I said, as I laid down the morning's paper; "Carmonali's last appearance to-night!"

"Why, what's in the stars?" said Saville. "What can induce her to cut short an engagement that opened with such triumph and promised so prosperously? By Jupiter! I have it—Salviati—!"

"Salviati!" I interrupted, half-yielding to the impression I disavowed by my exclamation of surprise.

"Ay, and yourself! *You* have played with a passion that has devoured her. You have kindled a flame, and have not stretched a finger to extinguish it!" I scarcely noted the words of the speaker, so wholly absorbed was I in the paragraph that concluded the notice of her appearance. It notified the public, that the present was her farewell to the stage.

"Now, you believe me, O'Moore! I'll wager my losses last night that Salviati has something to do with this farewell!"

"And my own heart," I involuntarily added.

"You will not trust yourself there?" said Saville.

"I will, though Death barred the entrance," I answered; "I'll hear her—see her, for the last time—and then—"

"What, then?"

"Plunge with you, perhaps, into the gulf on which we are both hovering. And, though I may not find fortune, I may forgetfulness."

"I'll draw another draft on my banker to-day; so you will excuse me. I am not contented without some revenge on Fortune's spite last night."

"If you were playing for the opiate of mere excitement and forgetfulness, Saville, with my present feelings, I should not blame you. But, remember, failure is a stimulus, as well as success; and we are as anxious to retrieve the one as maintain the other. Depend on it, this is a practiced player—one to the manner born—whose habits may, for aught I know, make him a proficient in the backs as well as the faces of cards. What chance can you stand with him? Add to this, you are a traveler. Your generosity has made me last night your debtor. What present avails have I to exonerate myself? And, should your reckless precipitancy lose all—"

"I have a touch of the O'Moore blood about me, I believe," was the indifferent reply; "that has, unfortunately, always rendered me deaf to advice that would prevent the prosecution of any determined plan."

"You profess love for Amina," I said, seeking, if possible, to avert his purpose by the gentler feelings connected with her name.

"I do, most ardently! But what can be done in the face of that superstitious driveling of Salviati, who cants about heaven, his soul, and all that; with one hand burying an inoffensive child in a convent, while with the other he seeks to lead your inamorata to the altar! Resolve me a plan for her liberation, and I promise you to abandon the table forever; in which, perhaps, I am but seeking the delirious opiate of which you speak."

We parted for the day—Saville to his banker's, to recruit his finances for the enemy's onslaught, and I —to ramble, in my efforts to forget Bianca.

The house was (in theatrical phrase) a jam. All Naples seemed to have rallied her beauty and intellect, as a parting tribute to her whose meteor rise in her world of music, had flung around so rich an illumination only to leave it in as sudden a darkness. The opera was, "Sonnambula." Her first entrance was greeted with the tumultuous applause that usually welcomes the "star" of the evening; but the greeting, that seemed to come from hands with hearts in them—that spontaneous burst of joy, and pride, and welcome, that seems to say the whole treasure of the heart is inadequate to our admiration of the object, and unworthy of its acceptance; all seemed incapable of rousing Bianca from a melancholy that seemed to rest like a lethargy on the heroine of the night. I could see the warm expressions of the audience moved her to tears; but there was an absence, a wandering-ness (so to speak) of tone and manner, that told us there was a current of soul and pain far deeper than the mimic and garish scene, in which she appeared, had power to awaken. It so happened the stall I occupied was rather close to the stage. In return-ing her acknowledgments for the greetings of the audience, our eyes met; hers rested on me for some moments. That glance seemed to rekindle every dor-mant energy, every slumbering power of soul, and body, and eye. She trod with a firmer step; there was the light of a new spirit in her eye; and she seemed no longer to tread the boards as one who feels her talents tributary to the pleasure or intellect of others, but as one who felt suddenly inspired with the command of every power that could exact triumph or assert supremacy. I *felt* it was her last appearance to me!

The opera proceeded; but the full powers of the actress and vocalist did not reach their acmé till the scene in which her lover's rejection calls forth the agony, the tenderness, the wild and passionate pro-testations of the abandoned Amina. She flung her-

self at his feet, wept, implored, and clung to him
with that vital force, as though the strong clasp of
the hand expressed the last energies of a true but
breaking heart. Flung from the hand of her insulted
lover with the repelling convictions of her guilt, she
sank into the arms of the attendants with such an
utter collapse of every power, as to convey the impression that the abandonment of her lover had shot,
like the very ice of death, to her heart. The curtain
fell amid plaudits that attested the fearful *vraisem-
blance* of the *scena* and the vivid powers of the artist.
As for me, I felt this burning expression of grief and
passion was not the empty symbol, usually presented
on the stage, of counterfeit nature, and emotions that
lie no deeper than the words that utter them. It was
real—it had a fearful reality for me : it was but a
last fearful apostrophe to a passion on which she
flung all the light, the warmth, the truth, and depth
of her soul, as on a pile, ere she crushed it to darkness forever !

The curtain, at length, fell upon the "*vivas*" and
"*bravos*" of the audience ; but, as it was falling, I
felt the full light of her eyes fixed on me. Their expression, amid all that was calculated to exhilarate
and brighten, was not that of gladness and triumph,
but rather of sadness and abstraction, that seemed to
say the soul was far away from the gay scene that
wildered and dazzled the eye. When that curtain fell,

amid the buzz of admiration and excitement that filled
the house as with one voice, I felt myself indeed alone;
and, perhaps, there is no solitude more oppressive than
that which isolates us in the very midst of our fellows.
Tersely and truly has Tacitus expressed this withering
feeling in the words of the old Caledonian, Galgacus—
"*Faciunt solitudinum et pacem appellant.*"

My heart was, in sooth, the *waste* of which the his-
torian speaks; but where was the *peace?* I had lost
it not only myself, but robbed it from another!
Through what an ordeal of pain and humiliation must
Bianca have passed, as to have so fearfully translated
into art the dark language she had studied in nature!
I was the guilty one. It was I who had commended
the chalice of poison to her lips, the dreary volume of
wretchedness to her eye! The scene she had enacted
was but the burning reflex of those feelings I had
partially kindled at our interview in the garden. Like
the Ephesian youth, I had fired the shrine; and the
meed of my temerity was to stand upon the ashes of
the idol before which I had wept and worshiped!

Yet, though in the *abandon* of the actress I could
read the insulted pride and desperation of the woman,
the circumstances that impelled me, and the principles
on which they operated, I felt must remain unchangeable. Though, like the Spartan boy, I carried next my
heart what was draining its very blood and gnawing
away my life, yet still must I bear it, rather than

sacrifice to the hateful circumstances that surrounded me, the woman for whom my passion and admiration were but the deeper and more sincere, from my refusal to involve her in the net in whose meshes I was but a struggler myself.

It was, then, that like the bird that hovered over the waters of Avernus, the very dip of whose wings in its waters was certain death, that I felt myself still irresistibly attracted to the presence of Bianca, though I knew our intercourse, however transient it might be, but involved despair and misery for both. Life has but few pleasures equal to being in the atmosphere of a heart instinct with a pure and noble nature, even though we know it has not a sentiment to bestow on ourselves. The curtain down, I resolved to go round to the stage door, and send up my card, were it but to express my hopes that the arduous exertions of the night had not been attended by any injurious influence. I went round. There was a carriage at the door. It was Salviati's. With a heavy heart I handed my card to the janitor. He went and returned with the few following words in pencil :

"La Signorina Carmonali trusts that the extreme exhaustion under which she labors, will excuse her from complying with the request of the Signor O'Moore."

"As I deserve," I murmured bitterly to myself; "I have lost—lost her—forever."

I folded up the billet with care, and placed it next

my heart. It had touched her hand; that very touch was to me the invisible presence of the spirit in the shrine. Trifles, as with an oak root, twine themselves with the world of memory; a withered leaf may rebuild for the lover his Paradise, and a single strain of the exile's song recall the green fields and the fireside of his childhood. I have that relic still.

There was a fascination in the very stones she must tread to reach her carriage that bound me as powerfully, as the faith of the martyr makes him cling to his stake; for it is a strange anomaly in our nature to love the more ardently in proportion to the obstacles that beset and the barrier that divides us from the object. I lingered about the door, resolved on seeing her; and cared not if it were daybreak before I should realize my wishes. The announcement of her "last appearance" had created a *furore* among her devotees; and the entrance was thronged with Neapolitans of rank, assembled there to render their parting homage to the star that now lingered on the horizon ere it sank, and forever. I felt myself the more stung, and convinced that the billet I had received was but a feint, as not many minutes elapsed before there was a general buzz in the assemblage. "*Eccolá*"—"*Ecco*" —"*Viva*"—"*Viva Carmonali!*" And, while I was elbowing my way toward the carriage, the murmur rose into one concentrated shout of "*Viva—Viva!*" as we saw her approach the entrance, leaning on the arm of Salviati. The crowd, on the instant, made way. The steps were lowered. As she was ascending, supported by Salviati, I could not restrain the impulse; but, with starting tears, I bent forward and pronounced " Bianca !" She turned, fixed her eyes on me. " So, no longer !" were the words she uttered. The steps were raised, and, in a moment, the fiery horses had whirled her from my sight !

A reverie must have succeeded this meeting; for, when I awoke to consciousness I stood alone. The crowd had dispersed to a man. I looked for a moment earnestly on the spot she had trodden. It was but a dream. But the voice and form had made it tangible. " So, no longer !" These words were simple. But were they not to the ear as the sword of flame to the rebel that had lost his Paradise? Despair hung around me with the weight of a felon's chain. Life was all despair. I was reckless, and cared not how soon or where it would end. There was but one ray on my path ;—the honor that forbade me from dragging down Bianca to the gulf in which I had sunk myself. I rushed from the spot, that now harbored a serpent, where late I saw a shrine ! I wandered, I know not whither, till, as by insensible agency, I found myself entering the gaming saloon. It was late ; the sultriness of the room, the haggard and wan features of the players, the waning lights, all sank with a depressing power on my spirits. I swallowed a draught of wine.

P

The stimulus soon heated my blood, and kindled appetite for excitement. Yet, that door was closed against me. My own finances were gone; and I was already Saville's debtor. So lost had I been in my own feelings, that I scarcely, for some moments, thought of looking round for Saville. I, at length, looked in the direction of the table at which we had been in the habit of sitting. The lights were fast waning in their sockets, the cards were scattered in confusion, and the table was deserted, save by one. The desperate resolve of my companion with which we had parted rushed to my mind with the force of prophecy. Its very worst form was realized as I approached nearer, and saw Saville still sitting at the disordered table, his head, bent in his hands, resting on it.

"My God! what's the matter? Is this the end? Have you lost—"

"All—all—all!" was the incoherent answer, uttered in a tone that spoke the despair and ruin of the speaker.

"Where is the Italian?"

"In hell! where all gamblers should be," thundered Saville, starting from his seat, and fixing on me eyes that glared with all the fires of rage and vengeance: "Ay, in hell! where, if he is not already, I'll send him, and that ere long."

"Be calm—be calm, Saville. Come home. Sleep will refresh you, and in the morning—"

"I care not to see it! What has ruin to do with sunshine and day? Night—night!"

I saw his mind was rapidly losing its balance, and, taking his arm, I was about to lead him from the scene, whose associations were but ministering to his disordered state.

"O'Moore!" he cried, dashing me from him with violence, "lay not a hand on me, or, by heaven! I'll send you to keep company with that Italian. Ha! ha! You will not thank me for the change, though; you can not *spend* your gold *there*, though you may count it with Judas. Not a carline left—not a carline—ruined—not a bajoccho at the banker's—gone —beggared!" The rapid change, from the tone of desperate defiance to the bitter lament of ruin, stung me to tears, as I saw the poor fellow totter, and, from very weakness, sinking in his chair, bury his head again in his hands.

"What is to be done? You can not stay here all night; as it is, it is not far from morning. Come, come, Saville. You'll feel refreshed after sleep, and then—"

"What then?" was the answer, as he raised his pale and working face, every line of which wrought with the terrible conflict that was passing within; " where can the tree better fall than on the spot where it has been stripped of every leaf? Where—? My God —my God! and is this the end? Beggared, penniless, and in a strange land!"

I saw that calmness and reflection to the real sense of his situation were resuming their sway; so, seeking to confirm, if possible, this gentle mood, I seated myself by his side, and took his hand in mine.

"Things are not so bad as they seem," I said. "I know a means of extricating both. I have resources within myself that can not fail me even though among strangers. Do not despair—all will be well." While I was speaking, I could scarcely muster confidence for the effort. I was but inspiring another with hopes I did not feel myself; for, at the moment, I was destitute of plan or expedient "Where is the Italian?" I resumed, after a pause. My only and last hope was to throw ourselves on his generosity, for the present merely, until we could arrange some definite plans for the future.

"*Borrow*, I suppose," was the ironical reply; "I'd see him *dead* first!" The word was emphasized with such a terrible blow on the table as made the room ring again.

"*Dead!*" was the echo. We both turned, as though the fearful denunciation conjured amid the spectral chimeras of the apartment (now growing dimmer and dimmer) the very embodiment of the word. "You would see him *dead* first?" continued a voice in Italian. We looked in the direction, and observed a figure approaching: "Your prayer is answered—he *is* dead!"

"Merciful God!" cried Saville; "pardon—pardon!" His face grew to the ashiness of death, his hands trembled, and, as he attempted to rise, his knees knocked together, and he sank back in his chair. "Speak—speak!" he said; "what is this riddle?"

"Antonio Sebastiani, the most, noted gambler in all Naples, with whom I saw you play to-night, and whom I saw rise from the table, had not passed a street from the *salon* before he was murdered!" continued the speaker, with a coolness of detail that removed every doubt of the catastrophe.

"Murder and ruin—ruin and murder!" groaned Saville; "which is worse? The beggar. He lives —lives—"

"Come and see," returned the Italian.

"I *will* go," said Saville, with that emphasis that implied a doubt in his own power, so overpowered was he with weakness and excitement.—He sank in his seat, powerless as an infant.

"Your hand, Signor," I said; and with the help of the Italian we assisted him from his seat. With some delay—so very debilitated was he—we at length reached the street, and, by the light of some torches, were guided to the spot where lay the body of the murdered gambler. The crowd that surrounded him presented the usual anomaly of a mass of people on similar occasions: some were ejaculating, some jesting, some offering up a prayer for the soul of the dead, some

wishing for at least a small share of the money he had
won in his lifetime; some would pop their heads over
the shoulders of others, cry " *Uomo povero !*" ("poor
fellow!") and pass on; while the censors of the crowd
(in the minority) would shake their heads with phar-
isaical sanctimony, as much as to say, he had met his
reward.

"Let me see him!" said Saville. The crowd made
instant way for us, when it was bruited that the man
we were leading had been his victim. Oh! what a
strange and humiliating sight was that! · The man,
whose actions, but a few moments before, had been
strong enough to call down blasphemy and impreca-
tion from a fellow-worm—strong enough to light up
even a momentary madness in the mind, and wring
from the heart a prayer that death might come, freeze
up every pulse, and eclipse every object that but now
was joy and light to the eye—lay dead at his victim's
feet!

"My God! and is this thy judgment upon us
both?" said Saville, as, stooping over the body, he
looked on those pale and rigid features, over which
played the sickly flicker of the torchlight, like the
very shadows of the grave itself.

"He has been robbed of every thing," said one;
"see, his pockets have been rifled."

"Not all," said another; "that breast-pocket has
not been touched."

" They knew well enough," I said, " where the
money lay, and doubtless tracked him from the door.
Have they escaped ?"

" San Pietro !" said a burly fellow, turning over the
body on its side, with the insensibility of a butcher in
the shambles, " they knew their business, and did it
well. See! here's the wound."

The poor wretch had been struck on the back of the
head. The skull was actually caved in. While this
burly fellow was inspecting the wound with the nicety
of an *amateur*, another was engaged in rifling the
empty pockets of the man—like one of those human
vultures that follow an army for the purpose of spoil-
ing the dead. His exertions were at last rewarded ;
but not as he expected. There was not a carline of
poor Saville's losses that the murderers had not appropriated, with the exception of a paper, folded in the
form of a letter, which this harpy drew from the
breast-pocket of the dead. The paper was unanimously
handed to me, I presume from the incapacity of any
of the crowd to read. It bore the superscription—"IL
SIGNOR ANTONIO SEBASTIANI, Strada di Toledo." I
opened and read the contents, translated as follows :

" I hold myself bound to Antonio Sebastiani in the
sum of one thousand piastres, together with the total
amount of his gains, provided he employs his *usual*
skill" (this evidently applied to some trick of the gam-

bler) "in winning the very last bajoccho from the strangers I introduce to him for that purpose—I Signores
Merton and O'Moore.   ORSINO SALVIATI."

My eyes swam, a sickening dizziness whirled through
my brain; the staring, senseless mob, the torchlight,
the dead man, all seemed blended into a mass so vague
and indistinct as to elude my touch, like some momentary vision fancy had conjured from the earth. The
paper dropped from my hand. At such a moment,
when every vital energy seems to have forsaken us,
and Nature to have abandoned her stronghold of life
and strength—when the soul, as by supernatural abstraction, becomes an inmate of another world, familiar
with its forms and penetrated, as it were, with its
subtle essences, it is strange how even a single tone
has power to recall consciousness to the scene it had
left forever. I heard the rush of a human body, as
that of a maniac, and the grasp of the paper I had
dropped with a force that crushed it. Then followed
a groan and a curse, that concentrated all the vengeance the human heart was capable of imprecating
on an enemy. The violence, though but of a moment,
was sufficient to dispel the trance supervening my
weakness. The whole scene was again vivid before
me; but painted now in colors of such strength as imparted a hideousness of truth to the scene. The man
was paler and more like death, if possible; the crowd

more revolting, from their stupid gaze and senseless
curiosity; the torches had that whitish and sickly
glimmer that fancy associates with the vigils of the
grave. But it was in Saville that my waking moments
recognized the change. He, on whom when last I
looked, was pale, shivering and nerveless, stood now
before me, bold, upright and firm. Resolution fired
his eye, a violent suffusion flushed the bloodless cheek,
and the whole man was informed by a new spirit that
asserted and craved retribution for wrong.

"By heaven! this quarrel is mine, and me he
shall answer!" said Saville, calmly unrolling the letter
that in his passion he had crushed, and placing it in
his breast. I saw that this was no place, and the
present no time, to arrange or expostulate. Availing
myself of the resolute spirit that had given Saville a
rational calmness, I withdrew him gently from the
crowd; but not before the public authorities had reached the spot, and removed the body of the murdered
man, whose guilty career had met so sanguinary a
fate.

CHAPTER XIX.

This is our parting hour!   The mystic voice—
" *Let us go hence !* "—that rang through Judah's Temple,
When the proud Roman trod its blazing ruins,
Sank not with drearier omen on the Jew
Than this " Farewell" on me.   We met in darkness,
The cloud still rests upon our gathering-day.;
See how our sun hath set !

EQUAL partner in the wrong which had been inflicted on both, I of course sought a participation
in the accountability of the offender.   Saville was bent
on assuming the whole *onus* of the quarrel for both.   I
remonstrated with him on his recent relations with
Amina; only to prove, however, the utter insufficiency
of any passion to countervail that of revenge.   What
had either done?   Why this hypocrisy of attention
and hospitality?   Why this mask that, like that of the
old Athenian actor, presented a twofold profile, love
and hatred?   But we were both weary of asking
questions, whose intricacy reminded us of enigmas,
and seeking solutions by answers that, like the ancient
oracles, but left the questioners in deeper doubt and
obscurity.   Of one thing we were certain; a machina-
tion had been formed against us, artfully contrived,
sufficiently important in its consequences to be paid

for, successfully carried out by our ruin, and alas! by
the death of the poor wretch who had hired himself as
instrument. Saville would hear nothing to exculpate
Salviati, or allow me to supplant him in the demand for
reparation. The blood was up; and early next morning he was on his way to the Villa Salviati.

The period of Saville's absence was long and weary
to me. I returned to our hotel several times, but he
had not returned. I lounged from one restaurant to
another, spelled the papers, and heard criticisms on last
night's opera. I then came down the *Strada del
Gigante,* and gazed on Vesuvius, till imagination saw
the fiery flames and the molten tufa and lava pour
down in boiling torrents on the doomed Pompeii. But
there are some moods of so practical and matter-of-fact
a nature, that the abstractions of fancy and dreamy
musings are too insubstantial for their requisitions.
Such was the mood I then experienced. My mind
was on the rack to solve the mysterious villainy of this
" supersubtle Venetian," that threatened to enmesh my
friend and self in the same terrible and undeserved
fate. As the deep craft and foul stratagem of Salviati
borrowed a stronger coloring and aggravation from our
entire inoffensiveness, I was on the point of going to
Bianca and narrating the whole transaction, to deter
her from a connection so fatal alike to her honor and
future happiness. Yet, I could not believe that so
pure and lofty a being would link her fate with one so

utterly depraved as this transaction represented him.
Though I felt my own union with her impossible, I
could not contemplate for a moment the possibility of
a union which, the more it forced itself on my attention, "looked like truth." Her last words were to me
the final rupture of any tie that might hitherto have
bound us; the knell of the last hope, over which I
could scarcely weep, for I had buried it myself. I
looked in upon my own heart; it was indeed, dark,
blank and desolate, for it was myself, or rather the
melancholy contingencies of my life, that had turned
it to a grave!

I returned to the hotel. Saville was there; but not
the dark and moody being I had left him, brooding on
revenge; but rather presenting the satisfaction of one,
whose stern exactions had been paid to the last letter
and washed out in the last drop.

"Have you seen Salviati?"

"No!"

"No!" I iterated. "Your manner would indicate
that, like Shylock, you had your bond."

"He was not there. But I saw Amina; and, therefore, did not dare to broach the subject. The poor
girl was in tears. Would you believe, O'Moore, he is
pledged to Bianca, and the day appointed for their
union?"

"I not only believe, but expected it. That is—"

"And will you—can you—see her wed Salviati?"

"What can I do? Even did my pride allow me to sue for the heart I might have had, I doubt if she would restore the affections I have lost. You know that circumstances compel me to resign all interest in Bianca. Pray, let us change the subject. Men can not control their fate, and mine has been forced on me. It is that has separated us."

"Then it must be left to Amina and myself. I see your situation prevents any interference. She has made me privy to a plan, that must defeat the villain's hopes, and liberate Bianca from so fatal a vow."

"Thank God! thank God!" I said; "but what—?"

"She has implored me to keep the secret; and honor, therefore, binds me to silence. Poor Amina!— I seldom witnessed a more terrible struggle than that resulting in the resolution to betray her own father. She needed a confidant to aid her, and, as by chance, I stepped in at the moment. So, aû revoir for the present. What's lost, is lost. The snare laid for us both has, so far, succeeded. But we enter it not again. Had it not been for the murder of that poor wretch, gambling might have heightened its passion to madness. I have some arrangements to make for us both at my banker's in drawing fresh remittances from Ireland—"

"For both!" I iterated, while I bit my lip with pride and self-scorn, that a new folly had but deepened my dependence.

" Yes, O'Moore, for us *both !*" returned Saville, in
that determined tone of his that forbade contradic-
tion; "for us both; so that ends all twaddle about
your dependence. In sooth, a true-hearted man would
Saville Merton be to plunge his friend in the water,
and not stretch one friendly hand, or fling out one
plank to rescue him! Not many more days ere I shall
hear from my estate in Ireland, and have enough for
both—ay, enough to taunt this Italian traitor with
his abortive attempt to beggar us. So, *aû revoir !*"

Poor Saville, like most of our countrymen, was as
rapid in utterance as movement; and before I could
open my lips to express the gratitude that glowed and
trembled on them, the generous fellow was gone. I
sauntered to my window that overlooked the bay. As
I looked on that blue sky of Campania, that in its
quiet and purity seemed an emanation from the cloudless glories of the Invisible Throne beyond, and thence
to the waters that, in their motionless beauty, dreamed of that heaven they were permitted to mirror on
earth—a calmness, imbuing me with the holiness of
all I saw and felt, entered into my heart, and, like a
visitant from a better world, dwelt there! It is this
communion with nature, with the type in place of
the substance, that, next to the worship of God himself, raises us above our own humanity, its cares and
littlenesses and sorrows, teaching us that they, like
the body they agitate, are but of the moment, and

turning our hearts to those outward symbols, the
rock, the wave, and the sky, that, like their Maker,
are eternal! The lessons they teach raise us from
the grave to the stars, from the mortal to the arch-
angel; the hopes they inspire, are an ark to the drift-
ing soul; and the end to which they point, that haven
of light and peace, where the voyager of life longs
to furl his sail, and strand his shattered barque forever!

Oh, it was a lovely sight! and, as at every sense,
I absorbed its every form into my soul, I could have
lingered on that matchless prospect, and dreamed myself into the existence of that other world that lay
spread before me in the brightest raiment of a summer's heaven. All—all were forgotten, save one—
Bianca. I had flung the flower from my hand, and
thought to steel my senses to its perfume and its
beauty; but it had left a canker behind, that first
had withered its leaves, and now stung the heart of
him that had scattered them! Impossible as was my
union before, it was rendered doubly so now from the
involuntary dependence in which my parting interview with Saville had left me. His generous soul
would cancel that favor, but, alas, my own pride kept
it in legible characters before me. That name, Bianca, dissolved the Paradise a few happy moments had
conjured around me: I was back on earth again, and
the wing that had borne me to the eternal blue—ay,

and to the splendors that it vails from mortal eye—
was now trailing, broken in the dust! I would see
Bianca, and forever break the chain whose iron was
entering my soul.

A few moments sufficed to bring me to her hotel
and presence. As I entered, she was seated at the
harp: and the notes I heard were those of Moore's
Melody:

"Hath sorrow thy young days clouded?"

The words had for the minstrel a meaning beyond
the imaginary one of the bard. They were the em-
balmment of her own griefs; and, like the bird of
night, the solitude in which she sang but deepened
them by its echoes. The tears were in her eyes; and,
as I entered, an abrupt and impatient chord closed
the verse she was singing.

"A melody of old Ireland—and in Italy!" I said;
"surely, there is more than memory in this. You
must love that country, or you would not thus recall
her in that holiest form of song, in a land rife with
the affections of the child and the pride of the woman."

"I do love it, Morven," she replied, with more
tenderness than I had anticipated from her parting
words; "but with that undefined, unearthly love of
the living for the dead! The eye is beamless, the
heart pulseless, senseless, and the lip silent; and,
though we feel the spirit is gone forever, and but a

clod lies before us, yet do we cling to it, as though life, and speech, and love would breathe on it again."

"Can you thus love a land not your own ?"

"Whether country or man, it is human to love the agent that has touched the inmost spring of the soul, and taught its waters to flow in freshness and in strength. It was Ireland first gave the Italian girl a home, and, with it, friends ; and she who first taught me that—"

"You hesitate—your lip trembles—"

"It is with old memories the name of that country stirs within me. Happy in my recollections of it— still happier had I been, had I never entered it."

"Why, what wrong has she done you, Bianca ?"

"Oh ! Morven, Morven ! let us no longer play in masks, or speak in riddles. You know as well as I the fatuity of a passion that has proved but a dream, the fatality of a hope that, like the Pillar of old, while it guides the pilgrim with its light, can also turn his path to clouds and darkness. In that light I walked ; in its gladness I rejoiced ;—it was to me as a moving sun whose ray had no tinge of setting. But it has sunk from the eye, and left behind but the memory of its image."

"Bianca ! Bianca ! why will you madden me thus, in making me traitor to affections I cherished too much to blast, to hopes I dared not strengthen, from the dark fate I knew must extinguish them forever ?

You brand me as false, and yourself as miserable, for the very humility that would not dare to woo you for its own, though it might worship at a distance; and make me perfidious, for the truth and depth of that passion which would award you a higher and a happier fate!"

"Fate!" iterated Bianca, with more sadness than irony; "truly, mine is Fate! Disowned where I loved, I am reckless where I wed. Salviati—"

"I foresaw—I guess—I know it all! Oh, Bianca! by that bright, undying sky that looks down on us, like the immortal love that reigns above us; by all my despair—and what deeper vow can I make to attest my sincerity?—wed not Salviati! There is a mystery around him that belongs not to truth—a gloom overshadows him that never yet went hand-in-hand with honor and innocence. Wed him, Bianca! and I may be at the altar; but it will be as though I stood by your coffin; the blessing of priest will be but a knell to bury, or a spell to curse, and—"

'I care—I care not," returned Bianca, with a passionate wildness that discarded all hope of happiness in the union that threatened her—"I care not though the moment that saw me wedded wife beheld me a corse at the altar steps, where I had pledged my faith. Oh! why should I seek to survive a vow to which but the despair of rejection has driven me! You, Morven, were the first I loved; you were also the first to tell me

my love was vain.. You crushed the affections of the
woman, but you could not extinguish the pride of her
soul. Next to love—the life and soul of woman—a passion for admiration possessed me, which derived an
unhealthy stimulus from the profession I so ardently
pursued. In refusing the heart that beat but for you,
you wounded my pride, by showing that we may seek
without deserving admiration. From that moment I
resolved to wed Salviati. Morven—Morven—you will
be there, to bless—oh! what do I say?—to weep at a
fate you might have blest with your smiles; to look on
a heart you found in its purity and strength, yet left in
ruin; stained with a perjured vow, and broken by a
hand whose touch might have borne balm and healing!"

Every word she uttered went like a poisoned shaft
to my heart, and in my very soul I felt the brand of
traitor, that had turned purity and truth to perjury.
Yes, every word was true; coined in those unsearchable depths of the heart that none but God seeth, and
sealed with those witnesses that falsehood could never
summon to her cause. Bianca was in tears. Every
tear she shed fell on my heart like fire. I felt the
truth; I saw her wretchedness; I was the cause; yet
the fate to which I would have bound her would have
been scarcely less dark or miserable than that she was
about to entail on herself.

"Bianca, you would make me a wretch in my own
eyes: one who has won the affections of a heart but to

blast and betray it; who has woven a garland of
flowers, as bright and beautiful as ever summer smiled
on, but to place it on a victim's brow! Where you
have reproved, you should have spoken kindly; and
for bitterness I should have received gratitude.
Heaven knows what fate awaits you with Salviati;
but I know the fate would have set its dark seal on
your union with me. I love you this moment as few
have ever loved—can ever love; that very love was
deepened by admiration for the genius, that, while it
commanded every mind, touched and softened every
heart. Few privations I would not have undergone for
you. For you, where is the sacrifice I would not have
made, the prayer with which your name would not
have mingled, the blessing and the praise which would
not have singled you for their object?"

"Then let your prayer be offered now; for I feel a
boding weight upon my heart, that tells me 'twere
better I stood coffined on my grave brink than robed
for the bridal at the altar. I tell you, Morven, in this
act of pride, or despair—however you may please to
name it—I feel as though my mind were not my own;
as though I had lost all moral agency. The wounded
deer, can it but wrench the shaft or escape the hunter,
recks not whether it bury itself in the woods or plunge
in the wave."

"Bianca, this is but madness—but self-revenge—
to wed where the heart has no share."

"I have no heart now, Morven; no wish to warm and dwell within it, save one."

"And that?"

"To die! that I may meet my mother."

This was a theme that, like a talisman, always roused her most painful emotions. Unable to command herself, she clasped her hands with violence, and sank on the *fauteuil*.

"So young, so beautiful, to wish to die," I murmured gently, as, kneeling by her side, I clasped her hand in mine. Sobs were the only reply I heard; till, in the silent pauses of her paroxysms, I heard her distinctly whisper, "My God! my God! give me death!"

"Oh! yes," she said, raising her head, her words but the continuance of the solemn whisper; "it is for the young to die; for them the crown is brighter, and the song of angels sweeter, for they are more akin to the spirits that welcome them. The meteor that has tracked a tedious path loses, ere it reaches earth, all the splendor it brought from heaven; and the pilgrim of years has less of God's own image than the young, whom Time and Earth have not yet all polluted. Morven, I would die."

"Bianca, if I wrong you," I cried, kneeling at her feet, "before bridal or death—for the altar seems but the grave to you—I would have your pardon."

"And where can pardon dwell in a broken heart, or

what avails the forgiveness of a woman as gu
he she pretends to pardon? Oh! let us not
each other; for the last wrong I shall ever suf
earth my pardon is too weak to cancel. Seek it
—ay, there, Morven, where I shall shortly be
may God, when he gives it, give with it als
blessing, where I could only speak the reproach
a bruised and erring soul."

" I am too recreant, Bianca, to ask pardon eve
my own heart, much less of heaven; and yet, in j
ing, I would entreat you to fling your reproache
Necessity, that has goaded and pursued me as with
iron whip of Fate. Wretched, because I have made
so ; unloved, because despair and poverty and cri
have stripped the young tree of its branches, t
might have drunk in the sweet breath of Life's su
mer, and left it broken and blackened by the waysi
Oh! Bianca, you would not, dare not, wed with a fa
like mine. Farewell! farewell! The lips that dar
not share with thine the marriage vow, may yet l
heard in prayer for you ; and the heart that woul
this moment gladly lay down life for you, though
may not beat in the harmony of the bridal with you
own, still may be the shrine of Bianca's image!"

I tore myself from the chamber. On fire with emo
tions I deemed I had stifled forever, but which now
resumed their mastery, it was not till now I discovered
the depth of my passion, and the sacrifice of all I was

called on to make to my pride. Saville was right.
The day was appointed; the barb had yet to send its
last rankle home; the chain had yet to bind me with
its last link. Religion has had her martyrs; so has
love. The stake has been welcomed, and the pincers
of the torture braved to seal the constancy of faith;
but the legends of ill-fated passion present an ordeal
as fiery and a torture more lingering. It is not life
we surrender to the torments of a moment that destroy it, but all that makes the sum of its happiness
and hopes. The heart pines from day to day beneath
a wasting atrophy; and, flower by flower, it sees its
paradise turned to a wilderness. * * * *

That was a mournful and tedious week that pre-
ceded the bridal of Bianca. " Like a foul and ugly
witch" limped every hour along, but in the end to
reveal a sight more hideous to me than my fancy had
conjured during its lapse. · Scarcely a moment that-
Bianca was not before me; her intellect, like some
heavenly light, irradiating my mind; her voice, as
from a being of another world, thrilling the soul to
impulses ·that seemed not to belong to this. Like
the Indian, I had felled the tree, but not to pluck the
fruit; no, but to look on that fruit, beautiful enough
to have tempted and robbed our first father of his
paradise, withered and untasted at my feet! The
strings that had wakened the sweetest notes of my
wayward and jarring life, I had confided to the touch

of another; the mind, the soul, the whole nature, one with my own, I had rent from me rudely, and left them to wither and die in a cold and ungenial soil. And now I was to feel that last fearful struggle between passion and pride, to which all I had before felt were but as rites preparatory to the sacrifice. Hitherto it was a joy—perhaps a sad one—to speak with her, to hear her, to drink in with her, as 'twere, the same dreamy beauty of every object beneath that heaven-born sky of Campania ; to stand, like the mourner by the dead, still to touch the hand we can never again call our own, and *feel* that presence, that, like the statue in the desert, ushered in every dawn with music ;—but even that was lost to me now : her hand was soon to be clasped in another's— her voice to sound for him alone ; for him alone her mind to dispense its treasures, her heart its wealth. Henceforth I must be alone. At the altar would I bid her farewell, and leave Italy forever !

Saville had left me to keep his appointment with Amina, informing me the hour designated for the bridal at the *Chiesa di San* ——. I was there for some time before the hour, loitering from aisle to aisle, admiring the *chef d'œuvres* of art that Romanism has so cunningly called in aid to the solemnities of religion. Here was a kneeling suppliant, and yonder in the niche kneels another, pouring into the ear of the priest, at his side, the sins and levities of his life.

Here is a group of stragglers, some of them *cono-scenti*, investigating and analyzing the different paintings with the eye of criticism, perfectly unheeded in this secular amusement by those who have entered the *duomo* for prayer, who, with the abstraction of the Moslemin, still pursue their spiritual communings ; others, loungers, amuse themselves with examining the richly-carved ceiling, that dazzles the eye like one unbroken surface of gold ; while the soul is now and then diverted from the *materialism* of religion, that absolutely realizes the gorgeousness of Zion, by strains from the organ so distant and so soft, that the heart deems them wings for the descent of the Spirit to hallow and dwell in this shrine of his glory.

I was but a saunterer among the many, who, in the above description, constitute mainly the frequenters of an Italian church. A lounger among the idle, I scarcely noticed the artistic and architectural grandeur of the church, from the one absorbing thought that continually diverted my attention to the altar, and the sad spectacle my fancy already painted there. At length I saw a movement in that direction among the ecclesiastics ; some three or four ascended the altar, followed by acolytes with lighted tapers. I stood transfixed, as 'twere, to the spot—it was the rising of the curtain for the last scene of a painful drama. Soon entered the bridal party, embracing mostly Neapolitans, connections of Salviati. But all

Q

was as a dream; an indistinguishable mist rested on
every object, only lending the stronger relief to one
object—Bianca. Oh! did she look like a bride? was
the question I involuntarily asked myself. Was she
like one who, in the present, was treading the flowers
and breathing the odors of an Eden, and whose future
she would scarcely barter for the visions a saint has
of heaven in his dreams? Where was the bright eye,
the light and joyous step, the high beating heart, that
flashed in the eye and flushed in the cheek—the joy
that has found a heaven on earth, and the hope that
would not exchange that earth for heaven? Where
was all this? Not in the joyless eye—not in the
heavy and life-lacking tread that expressed the very
burden was weighing down the heart—not in the
colorless cheek, that wooed Death rather than man
for a bridegroom! Oh, no!—this was not the Bianca
I had once known; it was her image—her automa-
ton;—not a being moved by the will and the conscious impulses of life! Her long vail, thrown back
from her face, was borne as a train by a troop of
young girls, whose laughing joyousness presented the
stronger contrast to the living mockery whose happiness they had assembled to commemorate. It was a
bridal wreath on the brow of the dead! an epithalamium chanted at the grave! Brightly sparkled the
rich *aigrette* of diamonds in her hair, but to mock the
dimness of that eye, that how often had I seen quick

with the light of intellect and the fires of passion!
That eye, whose glances I had seen, meteor-like, dart
from soul to soul in the theatre, lighting or withering
at choice with its power, was now turned inward,
and the broken heart it looked on lay like her own
dead child at the feet of Niobé. Her hand was in
that of Salviati;—but lay it there with the sentiency
of life, or reciprocity of touch? No: cold and dead;
its owner had scarcely consciousness but that it lay
inertly at her own side. Salviati was pale as his
bride;—but, while she seemed like one supporting an
utterly unconscious part in a pageant, there was in
him an uneasiness of manner and wandering restless-
ness of eye, that told the utter abstraction of mind
from the scene on which he was about to enter.
Amina was not there.

All that I had hitherto endured was a dream—
a vague sense of pain, that left behind a numbness,
compared with that I was now called on to witness and to suffer. Had Bianca sunk dead at the
altar, I believe I should have thanked my Maker, and
left Italy without a tear. It was not jealousy that
rankled through me with her fiery shafts, but rending
to fragments the heart she has not the mercy to con-
sume; but grief—despair—a wilderness of emotions,
that spread its dark and blighting barrenness over
my soul, like the subtle Kamsin of the desert, penetrating and poisoning every pore. But why thus

torture myself? She would have been miserable in her union to me. I turned to the cold marble against which I leaned, and wept in bitterness and solitude.

The ceremony proceeded. I heard the words—I heard a sob—I raised my head—it was she, from the convulsive heavings of her bosom. The priest still went on, with that mechanical *sang froid* to which professional routine frequently degrades the nature. I closed my eyes—I listened on. There was a pause, in consequence of the arrival of strangers who had now joined the bridal party. I looked up—Amina and Saville were advancing to the altar, followed by that blunt, burly fellow we had met on our first visit to the Villa Salviati, and a female. She was the same I had seen pass our carriage on our visit to Puteoli. Her appearance was as *bizarre* and peculiar as before. Her hair was twined with flowers and straw, and the tawdriness of her appearance partook the spangled character and ridiculous pomp of tragedy queen. Saville pointed in triumph to the ludicrous object, by whose side still stood the ma with the vigilance of a keeper to a lunatic; Amu was kneeling at Salviati's feet, as though implori her father's pardon; Salviati had dropped the hand the bride, and, with open mouth and dilated eye, sto gazing on the apparition with such incredulous ter that one from the dead could not have inspired great

"Devils—Devils—!" groaned Salviati from betwe

his teeth, as his eyes shot rapidly from Saville to the woman's companion.

But an instant passed. A scream that seemed to rend the very heart that uttered it, rang from floor to roof of the dome.

"My mother—my God—my God—my mother!" were the words I heard. Bianca had torn from her bosom the portrait she had shown me in Dublin; and, in the tawdry maniac before her, recognized the original—her own mother!

There are moments in life that concentrate the experience of years, and events of so rare a nature as to tax all that experience to verify them, even though submitted to our senses. The maniac stood in stupid wilderment, looking with unconsciousness and apathy at the child who knelt at her feet;—that child;—oh! how soon had the marriage bell lost its music, the blossoms of the bridal wreath turned to grave-flowers, even on the brow of the bride;—that child still knelt by her, her face upturned and fixed on eyes that had no reciprocal glance for the feelings that spoke and gushed from her own; her hands clasped around that mother's knees, who, like the idol of the heathen, had ears but heard not, eyes but saw not; deep was the ecstasy that spoke from her quivering voice, but it was that of despair.

"My mother—my mother—oh God—! have I found thee, and not to know thine own child—!"

"My child—my child—what child—?" were the
broken words of the maniac; as, bending over Bianca,
she threw back the clustering hair that had tangled
with the vail, and gazing intently on those features
that long estrangement and present aberration could
no longer recognize, pushed Bianca from her.

"No—no—no child of mine. Husband and child
both are gone—no child of mine—!"

This revulsive shock—this sending back the waters
in all their strength to their parent source, this denial
of Nature pleading for her own immunities with the
earnestness and affection of a child, were too overpowering for the tension of mind and soul that Bianca
had brought to the altar. She sank back in the arms
of Saville, who, with myself, bore her from the scene.

Leaving her in charge of some of those who had accompanied her to the church, we returned in haste.

"Father—father—forgive me," were the first words
we heard from Amina; her arms twined round her
father's neck, who was sitting on the altar steps, his
face buried in his hands. He sate there, as apparently
unconscious as the maniac who could not recognize
her own child in Bianca, nor the affections of a daughter in her prayers. Amina's voice seemed the link
that bound him to the scene on which he had sought
to close his eyes—the association that linked him with
the guilt of the mother, and the still deeper guilt into
which he would have betrayed her child.

"Guilty—guilty—oh God—well have I deserved this!" groaned the wretched man, as with folded arms on his breast, he bowed his head in deep and agonized repentance:—"Take her hence—take her hence," he continued, waving his hand, but not daring to look in the direction of the wretched maniac;—"Take her hence—her presence has for me the murderer's curse; he but sheds blood—I have killed a soul—hence—hence—!"

That voice had a spell for the long slumbering nature of a heart that the tears and prayers of a child could not wake from its trance. Her eyes, on the instant, lost their wandering and unmeaningness;—a light, like the presence of a returning spirit to illuminate the shrine it had so long abandoned, shot through and brightened them, as, in violent deprecation raising her hands at the betrayer that cowered at her glance:

"Take me hence—take me hence—! It was not thus you spake, when you blasted the wife and murdered the husband." There was a long pause; the effort necessary for these few connected words, seemed too much for a mind broken and prostrate like hers. Clasping her hands to her head, she seemed striving to disentangle memory and association that had so long lain there like a web. It was vain;—the hand had lost the helm, and no Divinity was there to touch that chaos to order; but there was one string that, though when touched by the child, it gave no sound,

yet vibrated now with faint echo **through her** .
soul. She looked round as in search of some ‹
The gleam of momentary intelligence had **passed**
from her eyes, that now grew dim with **the tears**
filled them.

"My child—Bianca—where is she gone ? *Alon*
alone—and mad—!"

"Hence—hence with her—!" shouted *Salviati.*

"Traitor—betrayer—I have another left," was *t*
answer of the maniac, who now received the *tears an*
caresses of Amina, kneeling to the mother she had s‹
long deemed dead.

"Mother—mother," cried Amina, "oh! they have
wronged us both. Nothing till death shall part *us*
now."

Salviati rushed down the altar steps, about *to tear*
Amina from the maniac's embrace; but, as he approached, his step was stayed by the terrible impreca-
tion of the maniac that darkened in her eye *before it*
broke from her lip;—it was but the flash of a *moment*,
and all was dark again:

"Salviati! we part at the altar of God. Tremble!
Vengeance is His!"

Nature was exhausted by the stormy scene *through*
which the sufferer had passed. She *tottered back*
from her child, still following on her knees *the*
mother so newly found, and fell in *the arms of the*
keeper.

Salviati, pale and trembling, was borne by Saville and myself to his carriage.

There was something that made me happy in the release of Bianca from this union, even though under circumstances of so painful a nature. The mystery was solved, and Bianca was free.

"I told you," said Saville, "she would never be bride of Salviati. Amina had overheard an interview with this fellow; in which her father bribed him to silence as to the existence of her own mother. It was then she learned for the first time that her mother was still living; living dishonored as a mistress, and with the desperate atonement of madness for the guilt of the wife. Aware that this would be no bar to the marriage, she yet resolved to make a last appeal to her father in the person of that mother he had once loved, and whose child she was. The benevolence of the keeper forgot the bribe in the sufferings of the child. You know the rest. Bianca is saved—"

"From marriage. I fear the result," I said, "yet better death than such a degraded union."

That evening we went to the Villa Salviati. What a kaleidoscope is life, and how great the change a few brief moments may work in ourselves not only, but in the various scenes that joys or sorrows made, as 'twere, part of ourselves. As changeable as the sky, as calm or stormy as the ocean, we have but to look within, and find in the emotions and circumstances of our own

Q*

heart and life a reflex of the mighty changes
form or beautify Nature.   From the flower, a1
and dance of the bridal we had passed as in a 1
to the melancholy ravings of the maniac, the
of a long buried and a long silent heart, the rev(
of crime, and the imprecations of the guilty ;—ε
and in a moment, had transpired at a place cons(
to the presence of Him to whom the prayer oɟ
tence and the vow of the bridal are but as inće
the altar.   The last time we were at the Villa
ati, it was in the hour of feasting, song, and d
mirth was on the lip, light in the eye, and the
spirit of the soul had in it the gladness of the ma1
bell ; the cup sparkled like a ruby mine, and the
were as quick with their stream of life and joy a
nectar that went to gladden them ;—but now—

As we entered, Salviati was seated in a small cʰ
ber leading to the garden ; beside him sate Am:
her head bent on his shoulder and her hand claspe(
his.   Before them on the ground stood a portrait ʋ
its back to the wall.   The crape that had once cove
it was now thrown back; and, from its strong rese
blance to Bianca I recognized her mother—the unɟ
tunate maniac.   Salviati's countenance had chanɡ
much, even in the few hours that had elapsed sin
the fearful discovery he had made.   The brow w
tensely knit, indicating the terrible anguish and i
ward struggle of the sufferer.   His brow was mois

his eye haggard and wandering; his long black hair hung down in thick disorder. Humiliation and shame had now usurped a countenance, whose birthright seemed to have been that of pride. A cold and almost motionless salute, that recognized our presence instinctively without raising his eyes, was all that wel comed us.

" *I Signores*, father," said Amina.

His daughter's voice broke the reverie; he looked at us, sank back in his chair, covering his face with his hands. There was a long pause; when, still holding his daughter's hand, he said:

"Signores! I will not burden you with the recapitulation of a tale, which you already anticipate from the terrible disclosures of this day, and the fearful penalty which God has inflicted on me in the fearfullest form—the madness of my victim. Little did I deem the madness of the mother was also about to betray the daughter. Some five or six years after my seduction of this wretched woman, repentance for the crime to which I had betrayed her, wrought so strongly as to threaten and finally destroy her sanity. Observing this, I was bound in kindness to conceal from this, the only child of that guilty union, the preparations requisite for the peace and comfort of the sufferer. To this end, I informed Amina that her mother had died suddenly, and that the physicians pronounced immediate removal of her remains necessary. The child believed the cruel lie I forged on her; and the wretched mother was removed from a home of shame and guilt to that hardly worse one of suffering and madness. Left thus alone without home or companion (though I can not say that in the sense of honor previously I had either) I was thrown on society, for that deleterious excitement in which men seek to bury the memory of grief, or snatch even a single ray that flutters from the wing of hope. I saw La Signorina Teresa Carmonali, whom now I recognize as Bianca Romano, the daughter of that outraged husband who, on the night I betrayed him, laid me bleeding at his feet. Would to God! it had been my death, for then this crime and shame and remorse would not have been mine!"

His tears interrupted Salviati for some moments, when he resumed:

"I need hardly tell you, the highest aim of my life was to accomplish my union with her, who was the theme of every tongue, the delight of every eye, the entrancer of every ear that heard her. It is useless to analyze the motive that prompted to this purpose; it might have been affection; I fear it was—pride! To call her mine, was the ingot to the gold-searcher, the presence of his deity to the worshiper. My addresses were received, encouraged; and life promised henceforth, in the sun that was about to light my wilderness, a happiness, almost within my grasp, yet so in-

tangible, as to make me fear it the dream it has proved.
About this time my accidental appearance at the
Chiesa di San Sebastian rescued you both from an
appalling fate. The memory of that fact, though but
a contingency, is the only thing that can palliate the
part of the villain I was induced subsequently to play
to both. Bianca's affections I observed were already
plighted to you, Signor, before we had ever met. I am
Italian, and this fired my blood to jealousy and revenge.
For the wrongs I had dealt the wretched husband, and
now perpetuated in the madness of the wife, conscience
goaded and lashed me with tortures that only the
guilty can suffer. My heart spoke within me, there
was but one reparation I could make to God for the
injury I had done to man. That was to devote this
child of guilt to His service in the cloister. This intention was, however, interfered with by the attachment I observed gaining daily fresh strength between
you, Signor Merton, and my daughter. Resolved to
remove at a blow two, thus antagonistic to my purposes, I hired the most notorious gambler in Naples to
play with both till both were ruined. By acting thus
to you, Signor O'Moore, I sought to wreak revenge on
one my jealousy had taught me to regard as a hated
rival; and by entailing on you, Signor Merton, poverty
and ruin, the more entirely to deter my daughter from
a union, which to my conscience, interposed between
myself and the pardon of Heaven. I have no more to

add but to anticipate, Signor (he continued, turning to Merton, as he drew forth the bond that had been found on the body of Antonio) the bitter reproof and humiliation I read in that document you hold. Foiled and degraded as I am in the eyes of those I would have betrayed, there remains but one course to obliterate the wrongs I have done you both, by whatever of justice yet remains in my power."

Saying, he advanced leading Amina, and with strong emotion taking the bond from Saville and tearing it to atoms, he placed Amina's hand in his.

"Take her, Signor Merton; may the child be happier than the father; and her home as sacred to the wife and mother as the cloister I had destined for the novice. In this paper, you will find my ill-gotten and accursed gains returned with the maiden's dower, and in this, Signor (turning to me) you will, I trust, find ample reparation for all the injuries I have occasioned to you."

Our presence seemed as painful to the speaker as the subject that had demanded it; and bowing to us both, he retired quickly from the chamber. I saw that, by remaining, I would be but an intruder; so I retreated, leaving Saville and Amina to hold sweet converse together on bridal, priest, and ring.

CHAPTER XX.

Words are but symbols; yet are words like these
The sad and holy images the heart
Coins in its secret depths. The Athenian law
Was writ in blood, but this in tears!

ON my return to my hotel, the extreme anxiety I
felt for Bianca, and which I purposed relieving by
calling on her next day, was anticipated by the following, which I found on my table. It was Bianca's
hand; but there was a tremor and indecision about
the characters that bore witness to the agitation of the
writer. After recalling our first meeting, the omen
and shadow that rested on it from the death that threatened us both, and the feelings it had insensibly inspired
us with, it proceeded:

"Ah! Morven, I would have thanked God if that
hour had ended an existence, protracted now to shame
and bitterness! I have lived to feel that the love of
a child may gall and wound even like the arrow of an
enemy. That mother, how I loved her;—and oh!
may God pardon the imperfect prayers, in which the
eye was oftener turned to the image of my mother
than the heart to Him! In a foreign land, where the

eye of the stranger was cold, or his lip silent, or his language strange to me, I had but to look inward for that warmth and light that the very thought of mother awoke within my heart;—and thus to find her;—a wanton and a maniac! Oh! that the earth had opened; that where I stood branded as bride I might have sunk as corse, without epitaph, memory, or even name!

"The struggle has past with me, Morven, but the end, though it soon must be, is not yet. The bow has been too much stretched ever to have vigor again for the shaft. Even while I write, and look on those unmeaning eyes, and feel the hand that once fondled me, whose very touch was denial, and hear that voice that once hushed the babe now thrill and crush the heart of the woman;—oh God! Morven, when all these thoughts gather, as it were, into that one image of my mother, I pray that death may not be far.

"And for myself, what shall I say? The shame and madness of the mother have descended on the child! Could fate have borrowed from the very sables of the pall colors darker than those that rest on me? Think not that, because talent was triumphant, and while success glowed in my footsteps, and praise made the very atmosphere I breathed, I did not regard it as a dream, the more delirious for connecting a human heart with a state wholly transient and artificial. Think not that I did not look far below the surface;

or was betrayed into the false creed of him who be-
lieves that the momentary flash of the firefly is the
permanent reign of starlight upon earth. Oh! no,
Morven; it has proved a dream, and I knew it would.
You, too, loaded the air with praise, and where I might
have sought a higher and tenderer feeling—the only
one that assures man he is kindred to the angels, and
has not *all* lost the image of God—I found admiration.
Admiration, and for a heart that loved. Where, in
that which I claimed and received from the lips of the
thousand, was that for which the heart pined, which
could alone fill its solitude; alone tell it, like the dove,
that amid the waves and storms that had tossed it,
there was one spot where it might anchor and be at
rest forever? , Morven! It was not from you I sought
what I met with from all else. It was, perhaps, my
misfortune to be endowed with powers that placed me
before the public eye; but I was not less the woman;
and while mind or genius, if you please, sickened at
the trophies and tributes of public applause; the heart
sate lonely and musing in her own deserted chamber;
and, like Rachel, refused to be comforted. There was
no fireside to brighten, for my gods were shivered while
yet a child, and ere I could propitiate their protective
power, no still small voice whose music might hush
the thunders of the multitude, no hand, whose pressure or even touch could tell me that, though mother-
less and a wanderer, still was I human! When wo-

man turns and looks in on a heart like this, it is a ruin
and forever; Time, so far from repairing, but wastes
l crumbles the shattered fragments more.

"There needed but one more shaft to fill the relentless quiver of my life. Fate spared me not even at
the altar, and the iron has entered my soul. That
circumstance falls like omen on me. It is as though
God Himself had spurned me. It fell on me like a
cloud swallowing up the incense that might else have
found its way to Heaven. Exile in life, where could
I better seek shelter than at the altar of Him, whose
care is as a mighty wing to cover all? But the shadow it flung on me was to curse, not protect!

"I write not this to upbraid; what force could reproof have from one broken and humiliated as I? I
went to the altar not with the dreaminess of the girl,
for girlhood was past, nor yet with the pride of the
woman who hears in the bridal vow the seal of souls
to a happiness invincible to all save death! I went
there humbled even in the very face of the triumphs I
had achieved, for what could *they* avail in the new
life to which I was about to pledge myself? No! I
went there with a heart still bleeding from the wrongs
dealt it by a hand, that had no mercy to kill but only
wound; the hand to which I commended the bright
cup of my life, and yet dashed it at my feet!

"The struggle can not last much longer. Not many
days, and I shall have past away forever. Mind and

soul were both unstrung, as I looked on that wild and
senseless mockery of a mother, who looked on but
knew not her own child! You have stood by the altar
to see me wedded; there is but one more trial—to bear
me to the grave. Death, like a mighty conqueror, is
yet merciful;—he sends his messenger to warn of his
approach. I have received that warning, and bowed
to it. There is a prophecy of the heart, uttered by
Truth herself, that but strengthens the convictions of
the mind. Oh! Morven, when the last page is turned,
I pray you close the volume, and let the name 'Bianca'
be unto you, like the Evil Genius of the Persian, a
thing unnamed! Come, then, and see me, it will be
for the last time;—the vail has been lifted from my
eyes, and already I hear the thunders of the ocean
against the precipice on whose edge I stand. These
are facts; facts which, though they may not give happiness, will yet shed sincerity on our parting. We
have, hitherto, met in mist and twilight; but we part
in that full and fearful sunshine that the approach of
eternity flings on the dark path of the pilgrim. We
can not deceive each other now, and dare not if we
could. Life is detaching her ties one by one from a
heart that, like a steward, is hastening to give account
to its master. It is, even now, forgetting the language
of the world, and familiar only with that of prayer.
The last of this world's language that it utters shall
be a blessing on your name, Morven; and oh; forget

not my last wish, when standing on my grave, you
should never turn from it without offering a prayer
for—BIANCA."

This letter (every word of which received the self-
condemning endorsement of my own conscience) revived feelings and memories I had hoped to have
buried forever in the bridal of Bianca to another. But
all thoughts of self were extinguished in those painful
allusions the writer made to her own approaching end.
Bianca die! "All men think all men mortal but
themselves," says Young; and do we not extend this
assumption of immortality from ourselves to those we
love? How hard to associate with the heart's idol
graduated decay, the emaciated cheek, the palsied
hand, the cold and paralyzing routine of the burial!
How hard to turn from the bright summer that life
has painted and wreathed around the form of the loved
one to that last dread season of departure, that, like
winter's touch, has frozen the heart and nipped the
last flower on the cheek of the dying! Bianca die!
oh! she must have felt the prophet-power upon her;
for the truthfulness was earnest, and heart-born that
spoke in every line.

That day I found it impossible to comply with
Bianca's request. I feared, under the influence of
past and present feelings awakened by her letter, to
trust myself in the presence of her whose farewell
would be the blotting out of the last star that had

hitherto lighted my pilgrim way. On the following day I felt more strengthened for the bitter conflict of parting. On ascending the staircase, I encountered the physician, who, the servant informed me, had just left her chamber. My name sent in, I was admitted not to the presence of her I had once known ;—it was not *Bianca* as first I had met her : the bright and laughing lustre of the eye that seemed to deride grief, and recognize in joy alone the birthright of the heart— the youth that had taken a bond of Fate, and sealed it with the gay and bueyant spirit that Life was circling through every vein—the dark, olive cheek, suffused with the bloom of health and youth, that seemed proof to the cold kiss of Death—where were all these ? Not in the pale, and wasted, and wasting being before me, on whom hours had done the work of years, and with whom grief, and terror, and passion, those subtle enemies that mine the very walls of life even to the brink of the grave, had wrought like disease. Her voice was feeble, almost inaudible ; and, as I entered, she closed a book—it was the Scripture.

" My friend," she said, placing her trembling hand in mine—" for now, undeceiving and undeceived, I may call you so—this visit shows more truth than all the past. They were to blend tributes and flatteries with those of others, but this to see, for the last time, a dying woman. Nay, I know what kindness would say, even in the face of hope. I tell you, Morven, I

have lost all; I can not—I know I can not long survive the terrible shock—that, like the hand of God
himself, shook body and soul at that fatal altar.   Oh!
would I had been borne a corse to the burial, rather
than have been the witness of my mother's shame,
and jeopardized my own honor with the very man that
had caused it!   But the world is passing fast from
me; let me not dwell on its pains and trials, but
rather fix my eyes on that which is beyond.   In that
I have buried forever the memory of the world and
the depth into which I was about to plunge."

She pointed to a small heap covered with crape.
Below it I saw the faint sparkle of her diamonds and
the neglected finery of the bride.

" Do you know," she resumed, " what I was reading as you entered ?"

" That greatest of all books," I replied—" our
companion through Time, our guide to Eternity !"

" You are right, Morven; and were we asked for
one of the strongest proofs of inspiration, I would say
it lay in its grand distinctiveness of style—simple,
without poverty or puerility, sublime without effort—
it claims our acknowledgment of its truth, and re-
ceives all it claims.   Oh! did we, amid all that
distracts the soul on earth and profanes its purity—
did we ever keep before us the great and only fact
of Death it so broadly asserts, and for which it would
prepare us, how could we feed on the vile husks of

earth, when in almost every word of the Saviour we taste the manna of Heaven! The world guided me through its wilderness with smiles that have long since been forgotten, and adulations that are now as silent as though they were eulogies spoken over the Dead—to the eye and ear that willingly yielded to the spell they have proved delusive ;—oh! if I had turned from these idolatries that beset my path, like that of the Israelite of old, to this shrine of all that's supporting here and true hereafter, Death would be, perhaps, more welcomely greeted than now !"

"Bianca, you speak too calmly to regard Death with terror. But why speak of that which may be but the creation of your own fears ?"

"*Here* is an oracle that never erred," returned Bianca, laying her hand on her heart, while she raised to heaven her eyes that, though they had lost the light of this world, borrowed from their spiritual communion that holier light from above ; " and *there* the altar that never refuses the incense of a broken and contrite heart. I feel the sentence has gone forth, though I hear not the voice of the great Judge. Oh! let me not weep, but rather praise and rejoice for the strength and hope that, like a staff, in every word of this great Book, supports the steps of the wanderer. Hear the words I was reading as you entered." And, opening the volume, she read as follows, but in a voice so inarticulate from emotion and suffering, that

I could not restrain the tears, as I thought of the ruin before which I stood :

"Let not your heart be troubled!—Ye believe in God; believe also in me!"

"Morven," she continued, closing the book as she finished, "let not *your* heart be troubled when I am gone ; for I trust I have that faith which removes all trouble from mine."

"Oh ! Bianca, should this dark prediction of yours be verified, why assume this apathy, more galling than silence itself, by telling me to feel no trouble at your death ? I owned a passion for you ; and it was the very strength with which I loved, that doomed you to so luckless a bridal, and the awful spectacle it revealed to you at the altar. Oh ! it is cruel thus to taunt me ; more cruel when, as you say, the hand of Death is on you, whose touch lays bare the inmost secrets of the heart, and lends the lip a sincerity and truth it never knew before. Is it just, Bianca, thus to reward a passion that, however fatal it may have been to both, you know to be true ?—is it kind thus to reproach with coldness a heart that is this moment wasting with the strength of its own fires ? In wed- lock, I could have offered you a soul as fervent and as faithful as ever gave its vow to God, and received in return the benison of priest ; but you know I was proud, and dared not wed with the brand of poverty, perchance of murder—"

"Well—well—it is past!" returned Biánca; "and let it be *here*, as it must soon be hereafter with me—a dream. You have assured me of your love; *that* flings a passing ray over what else would have been all darkness in the closing hour of my life;—for strong though our faith be in the joys and mercies of that better world, the heart still seeks to part from this with some pleasing memory that, like the Patriarch's ladder, may link the loved below with the angels that hover above."

She rose with so feeble an effort that I sought to support her.

"I thank you," she said, gently refusing my proffer; "there *was* a time I would have received your support, Morven; but now, for the few remaining steps of the pilgrim, it matters not for my feebleness, for the shrine is not far distant."

She raised the crape that covered her bridal array; and, taking thence a diamond ring, she placed it on my finger.

"With this ring I seal a vow, whose truth I must soon register above. My life, you know, has been a lonely one—let my death have the sweet thought of fellowship;—that thought, Morven, will blend your name with my last prayer. Think not that, though of the earth, earthy, in our parting-hour we have no power to link the loved on earth with the blest in heaven. Nature, as she is ever eloquent in her types,

R

so is she as true and infallible as the Great Intelligence she represents. There's not a flower that dies
but sends up the odors of earth to mingle with the
airs of heaven. From the footstool to the throne—from
the atom to the Seraph, there is one bright and in-
dissoluble chain—Prayer;—and, as the name of the
wanderer we leave behind passes from link to link,
it is the theme of the bright chorus of angels as they
lay it before the throne of the Judge. Morven, you
shall not be forgotten. Wedded on earth, we shall
not be divorced in heaven !"

My eyes were filled; my heart was bursting; my
brain was a-fire with despair, self-reproach, and every
ingredient that madness distills into the cup of her
wretched victim. I was speechless, and stood before
Bianca, *the living guilt* of which she had been too
generous to accuse me. The shining bauble that glittered on my finger was another thorn in the heart now
pierced with many. It was the symbol of separation
to me, to others of union. Oh! curst beyond all I
could endure or fate inflict, I sank on my knees. I
forget the words I muttered. I remember the blasphemy, for it was not prayer. I asked for death;
death where I knelt; death, that I might be spared
the agony of standing on a grave I myself had dug for
her, who even in her wretchedness, could pray for me.
But while I knelt, my eyes were overdrawn by a thick
and palpable cloud that barred out the bright glories

of the Presence to which the soul was struggling upward—but in vain! I felt the heart still throb, the
maddening pulses still run with a torrent force through
every vein, and a voice rang as with a trumpet peal,
the curse of Cain upon me, that I must *live* and be a
wanderer. There was a gentle touch upon my shoulder, that seemed to say. "Peace—be still!" I rose
to my feet. Our eyes met. We had no words for a
Farewell. It was in our tears, our silence. The door
opened. In a moment the fainting form of Bianca was
clasped in the arms of Amina. I had but time to hear
Amina utter. "Dear—dear sister!" and rushed from
the chamber.

CHAPTER XXI.

The coil is shuffled and the drama ended—
Dagger and bowl have done their deadly work;
" *Vale !*" the actor cries; pray, raise the thumb,
And tell him—" *Plaudite !*"

I HURRY to a close—

"Ne'er erred the prophet heart that Grief inspires,
Though Joy's illusions mock their votarists."—*Bertram.*

The Poet was right.   The heart of Bianca had spoken
with an infallibility soon alas ! to be verified by the
event.   I did not dare to trust myself again in her
presence.   I did not dare to hear again that involuntary blasphemy of prayer that presence called down
upon my soul.   I was ceaseless in my inquiries; and
to every one the same monotonous, hopeless reply.
" Worse—worse—worse !"   Oh ! that sickening prostration of mind and soul, when despair presses on both,
and we feel that a giant's force is incapable of flinging
off the load.   When we are conscious of energy but to
mock us, of will but to defy us.   When the earth has
turned to a joyless wilderness, and the heaven spreads
above us like a sea of lead, sun, stars, very light itself
swallowed up in the blackness of our own souls!
When we offer up a prayer, and it returns back to our

own hearts, like the dove to her ark; but no olive leaf
to tell us that the waters have subsided, that the sun
is in the heavens again, the mountain tops are bare
and the trees once again have put forth their leaves!

The crisis had come—a violent fever had supervened, and Bianca's case was pronounced hopeless.
The next day I called; Bianca was—no more! * * *.

The last solemn duty, to which Bianca had so touch-
ingly alluded in her letter, now awaited me; a duty
the more painful for that it was self-imposed. How
short a space between the bridal and the death; yet
how varied and bitter, the emotions that had been
crowded into that brief interval, numberless as the
stars that fill the void between heaven and earth!

The rituals of the Romish church, so gorgeous and
dramatic every where, are still more enhanced in Italy
by all that is spiritual in music or splendid in art;
and it is this very dramatic character that imparts to
the funeral an imposing melancholy that, while it lulls
the sense, penetrates the heart with awe and mystery.
The dramatic vestments of the monks, the masks, the
low and stifled chant, blending the praise of God with
grief for the dead, the deep and flickering shadows,
making the very air a pall, that rise from the torches
borne by the long train of monks; all these tinge the
mind with feudalism, and heighten the common character of a funeral to that of a mournful pageant.

It was in the chamber in which we parted, that the

remains of Bianca lay. I scarcely dared to trust
myself in ascending the stairs; but there was a heart-
spell in her memory that lent itself to her ashes. I
ascended and entered the chamber. I looked on the
spot where last I had seen her stand, and thence to the
coffin. Oh! how I wished that I were alone with the
dead; that, with no eye save that of God to witness
and pity my agony, no ear save His to hear my
prayers, I might have flung myself on that coffin, and
dreamed myself into a revived communion with her I
had loved and lost. But I folded my arms on my
breast; the scalding tear was checked, the heart-groan
suppressed; and, with a soul on which the very forces
of Life smote with a power akin to death, I stood with
the apparent apathy of one who came to look and not
to mourn.

The chamber was hung in black, and the dim tapers
that burned around the dead flung around that funereal
light, recalling to my mind that sweet apostrophe of
Massinger:

> "How, like a silent stream shaded with night
> And gliding softly with our windy sighs,
> Moves the whole frame of this solemnity!"

At the head of the coffin stood a cross; twined with
flowers; those emblems and graces of sentiment, with
which Romanism invests the naked *matériel* of our
Faith. Around the coffin also were strewn heaps of
flowers, wreathed into symbolic forms. Monks and

nuns knelt and prayed with so deep yet still a murmur; that it resembled rather a communion with the dead than with God. Then slowly, sweetly, and mournfully above all, rose the following Hymn. The words can make upon the reader an impression but slight compared with that, which so saddened and subdued me, that the soul seemed to borrow wings from the melody, that rapt it to the very harmonies of Heaven—

HYMN.

" Hark, that sweet, celestial song !
. Flowing like the crystal stream
'Mid the bright, angelic throng
In th' Apocalyptic dream.

Sweeter yet and sweeter falling
From that bright and mystic land;
Angels, each their sister calling;
'Come, and join our spirit band !'

'Come, and look upon I Am
Crowned with stars that, ere creation,
Sang the glories of the Lamb
And the mercies of Salvation !'

" Come, see Him was crucified
Sitting on the burning throne;
Come, see Him on earth that died,
King—God—Father;—all in one !

"Sister, tune thine harp of gold
To the airs that swell in Heaven;
When the penitents behold
Him by whom they are forgiven.

" Take thou, then, thy sparkling crown
'Stead of that by Jesus worn;—
Wear it, sister; 'tis thine own;
Thine of gold, but His of thorn !"

With the last line of this simple hymn, that spake with such fervor and encouragement the hopes of the living for her that was gone, the monks raised the coffin. The solemn movement of the hymn; the muffled tread and whispers of the servitors, the dim tapers, the mask, the vestment, all rapt me to a sphere above reality, and I seemed to myself to regard a pageant, painted and moved by invisible hands in the air. When I awoke, Bianca had passed forever from my presence. I was alone. * * * *

Having left Saville and Amina to enjoy their honeymoon at Naples, behold me, reader, once again in Ireland; the charms of Italy having passed with the spirit of Bianca.

It was natural that, on my arrival in Ireland, the first place I should seek would be Clonmuir Castle, to certify myself as to my brother's fate. From the post-town, hiring a saddle-horse, I proceeded in the direction of the castle. What was my joy when, after passing a few yards up the demesne, I encountered Desmond. In a moment I was in his embrace. Cordial that meeting, and fervent the prayers that went up from me to God, that my brother yet lived.

" Weep not—weep not, Morven," said Desmond; " it is I should weep ;—I should call down on me the curse of heaven and the reproof of a brother, I first wronged, and then sought to murder."

" You !"

"Yes, I—I—I, who sought to wash out the wrong I had done you in your own blood. But come in—come in;—it is our father's roof—"

"It *was*, Desmond," I interrupted, observing his lips quiver and his cheek whiten.

"Well—well—come in, and I'll tell you all."

As I crossed the threshold, with which my boyhood had been so familiar, sad and piercing thoughts went to the very core. The land was of my birth, and the home of my infancy; but where were the faces and voices that, like the gleam of a winter fireside, send a gladness to the eye and a thrill to the heart, that tells us, 'tis our home? Oh! not there—not there. The feet of mourners had trodden these stones since I was here; my father's bier had darkened his own gates with its shadow; and he, who had left a boy, returned now a man, familiar with life's broad chart, scathed by its passions and wounded by its cares.

Desmond, approaching my father's old desk, took down a large document. It was my father's will.

"Here," said he, "is the witness of my shame and the deep wrong I inflicted on an unoffending brother. It is needless to recapitulate the tale of petty jealousies that divided us in childhood, and the memory of which, kindled to animosity in my manhood, induced me to forge a lie and defraud you of your rights. See here; the chieftain would have been false to every sentiment of his ancient blood had he disinherited you, as I rep-

resented.   Here you will find yourself joint heir to the
estates of Clonmuir."

" But my father, Desmond—?"

" Was murdered, as I wrote you.   For some time
the murderer remained in mystery, but at last confessed."

" Who—who—?" I exclaimed.

" That maniac, whom we both saw during the *fête*
at Deer Park."

" She—a—murdress ?"

" It is even so, Morven.   That woman was your
mother.   It beseems not us to judge the dead or censure the errors of a parent.   Seduced by the chieftain,
you were the illicit offspring."

" And where is my mother, Desmond ?"

" Dead," was the answer ; " she did not long survive the confession ; but expired in an asylum in Dublin, whither I had her conveyed."

" Dead—dead," I murmured ; and I seemed on the
instant to stand by the coffin of Bianca, and witness
the last rites that bore her from my sight.

" The unfortunate *rencontre*," resumed Desmond,
anxious to arouse me from the melancholy awakened
by his narrative, " originated in a desire, whose malignity has met its own punishment not only in the
wound (almost mortal) I received, but the still deeper
wounds of agonized conscience it left behind.   I had
been guilty of a lie ; to support which—my God ! par-

don me while I tell it—I sought to take a brother's
life, and with it remove all chances of investigation
that might lead to a detection of my fraud. The
solicitor was bribed to silence; but there was a sting
within me would not be blunted, an ever-crying voice
would not be hushed; and, in the terrible wound I
received at your hands, the lashes of conscience became more relentless from the invisible but infallible
hand that, while it dealt retribution on me, seemed
the more perfectly to avenge you. Availing myself
of the remarkable resemblance between the earl and
myself, and aided by the exceeding gloom of that fatal
morning, I found it easy to become a substitute for
the principal you expected. Morven, I have told you
all. Forgive me, as I trust God has done."

"You are forgiven from my soul, Desmond. But
the De Lacys?"

"Have left Deer Park and gone to Dublin" * * *

"Unwelcome lags the veteran on the stage," saith
rare old Ben. I have no further tale to weave—no
more adventure to relate. Restored to the enjoyment
of my estate, and the friendship of my brother, the
pilgrim, Morven O'Moore, has laid aside his sandal
shoon, and scallop shell; and, as husband of the Lady
Geraldine De Lacy, has found his Mecca in the affections of wedded life and the enjoyments of HOME!

FINIS.

Layard's Discoveries at Nineveh.

Popular Account of the Discoveries at Nineveh. By AUSTEN HENRY LAYARD, Esq. Abridged by him from his larger Work. With numerous Wood Engravings. 12mo, 75 cents.

Lectures on the History of France.

By Sir JAMES STEPHEN, K.C.B., LL.D. 8vo, Muslin, $1 75.

Wesley, and Methodism.

By ISAAC TAYLOR. With a new Portrait. 12mo, Muslin, 75 cents.

A Lady's Voyage round the World.

By Madame IDA PFEIFFER. Translated from the German, by Mrs. PERCY SINNETT. 12mo. Paper, 60 cents; Muslin, 75 cents.

Sixteen Months at the Gold Diggings.

By DANIEL B. WOODS. 12mo, Paper, 50 cents; Muslin, 62½ cents

London Labor and the London Poor,

In the Nineteenth Century. A Cyclopedia of the Social Condition and Earnings of the Poorer Classes of the British Metropolis, in Connection with the Country. By HENRY MAYHEW. With numerous Engravings, copied from Daguerreotypes, taken by Beard, expressly for this Work. Publishing in Numbers, 8vo, Paper, 12½ cents each. Vol. I. ready, Muslin, $1 75.

Chalmers's Life and Writings.

Edited by his Son-in-Law, Rev. WILLIAM HANNA, LL.D. 4 vols. 12mo, Paper, 75 cents per Volume; Muslin, $1 00 per Vol.

Pictorial Field-Book of the Revolution;

Or, Illustrations, by Pen and Pencil, of the History, Scenery, Biography, Relics, and Traditions of the War for Independence. By BENSON J. LOSSING, Esq. With over 600 Engravings on Wood, by Lossing and Barritt, chiefly from Original Sketches by the Author. Publishing in Numbers, 8vo, Paper, 25 cents each. The work will be completed in two vols. Vol. I., handsomely bound in Muslin, is now ready, price, $3 50.

Moby-Dick;

Or, the Whale. By HERMAN MELVILLE. 12mo, Muslin, $1 50

Travels and Adventures in Mexico :

In the Course of Journeys of upward of 2500 Miles, performed on Foot. Giving an Account of the Manners and Customs of the People, and the Agricultural and Mineral Resources of that Country. By WILLIAM W. CARPENTER, late of U. S. Army. 12mo, Paper, 60 cents ; Muslin, 75 cents.

A Dictionary of Practical Medicine ;

Comprising General Pathology, the Nature and Treatment of Diseases. Morbid Structures, &c. By JAMES COPLAND, M.D., F.R.S. Edited, with Additions, by CHARLES A. LEE, M.D. Part XXII. now ready, price 50 cents. In 3 large 8vo vols., Muslin, $5 00 per Vol. Vols. I. and II. now ready.

A Manual of Roman Antiquities.

From the most recent German Works. With a Description of the City of Rome, &c. By CHARLES ANTHON, LL.D. 12mo, Muslin, 87½ cents.

A Manual of Greek Antiquities.

From the best and most recent Sources. By CHARLES AN-THON, LL.D. 12mo, Muslin. (*Nearly ready.*)

Forest Life and Forest Trees :

Comprising Winter Camp-life among the Loggers and Wild-wood Adventure. With Descriptions of Lumbering Operations on the various Rivers of Maine and New Brunswick. By JOHN S. SPRINGER. With numerous Illustrations. 12mo, Paper, 60 cents ; Muslin, 75 cents.

Elements of Algebra,

Designed for Beginners. By ELIAS LOOMIS, M.A. 12mo, Sheep, 62½ cents.

Analytical Geometry and Calculus.

By ELIAS LOOMIS, M.A. 8vo, Sheep, $1 50.

Nile Notes of a Howadji.

With Engravings. 12mo, Paper, 75 cents ; Muslin, 87½ cents.

The Fifteen Decisive Battles of the World,

From Marathon to Waterloo. By E. S CREASY, M.A. 12mo, Muslin, $1 00

A Latin-English Lexicon,

Founded on the larger Latin-German Lexicon of Dr. WILLIAM FREUND. With Additions and Corrections from the Lexicons of Gesner, Facciolati, Scheller, Georges, &c. By E. A. ANDREWS, LL.D. Royal 8vo, Sheep extra, $5 00.

Lamartine's History of the Restoration

Of Monarchy in France. Being a Sequel to the "History of the Girondists." By ALPHONSE DE LAMARTINE. Vol. I., 12mo, Muslin, 75 cents.

Robinson's New Testament Lexicon.

A Greek and English Lexicon of the New Testament. A new Edition, Revised, and in great part Rewritten. By EDWARD ROBINSON, D.D., LL.D. Royal 8vo, Muslin, $4 50; Sheep, $4 75; half Calf, $5 00.

Buttmann's Greek Grammar,

For the Use of High Schools and Universities. By PHILIP BUTTMANN. Revised and Enlarged by his Son, ALEX. BUTTMANN. Translated from the 18th German Edition, by EDWARD ROBINSON, D.D., LL.D. 8vo, Sheep, $2 00.

The Nile-Boat;

Or, Glimpses of the Land of Egypt. By W. H. BARTLETT. With Engravings on Steel and Illustrations on Wood. 8vo, Muslin, $2 00.

Comte's Philosophy of Mathematics,

Translated from the Cours de Philosophie Positive of AUGUSTE COMTE, by W. M. GILLESPIE, A.M. 8vo, Muslin, $1 25.

History of the United States.

By RICHARD HILDRETH.——First Series.—From the First Settlement of the Country to the Adoption of the Federal Constitution. 3 vols. 8vo, Muslin, $6 00; Sheep, $6 75; half Calf, $7 50.——Second Series.—From the Adoption of the Federal Constitution to the End of the Sixteenth Congress. 3 vols. 8vo, Muslin, $6 00; Sheep, $6 75; half Calf, $7 50.

Louisiana:

Its Colonial History and Romance By CHARLES GAYARRE 8vo, Muslin, $2 00.

The Lily and the Bee:

An Apologue of the Crystal Palace. By SAMUEL WARREN, M.D., F.R.S. 16mo, Paper, 30 cents , Muslin, 37½ cents.

The Queens of Scotland,

And English Princesses connected with the Regal Succession of Great Britain. By AGNES STRICKLAND. 6 vols. 12mo, Muslin, $1 00 per Volume. Vols. I. and II. ready.

A New Classical Dictionary

Of Greek and Roman Biography, Mythology, and Geography. For Colleges and Schools. By WM. SMITH, LL.D. Edited, with large Additions, by CHARLES ANTHON, LL.D. Royal 8vo, Sheep extra, $2 50.

The English Language

In its Elements and Forms. With a History of its Origin and Development, and a full Grammar. By WILLIAM C. FOWLER. Designed for Use in Colleges and Schools. 8vo, Muslin, $1 50 ; Sheep, $1 75.

Harper's N. Y. & Erie R. R. Guide:

Containing a Description of the Scenery, Rivers, Towns, Villages, and most important Works on the Road. Embellished with 136 Engravings on Wood, by Lossing & Barritt, from Original Sketches made expressly for this Work, by WM. M'LEOD. 12mo, Paper, 50 cents ; Muslin, 62½ cents.

The English in America.

Rule and Misrule of the English in America. By the Author of "Sam Slick the Clockmaker," "The Letter Bag," "Attaché," "Old Judge," &c. 12mo, Muslin, 75 cents.

The Literature and Literary Men

Of Great Britain and Ireland. By ABRAHAM MILLS, A.M. 2 vols. 8vo, Muslin, $3 50 ; half Calf, $4 00.

A Greek-English Lexicon,

Based on the German Work of Passow. By HENRY G. LIDDELL, M.A., and RICHARD SCOTT, M.A. With Corrections and Additions, and the Insertion in Alphabetical Order of the Proper Names occurring in the principal Greek Authors, by HENRY DRISLER, M.A. Royal 8vo, Sheep, $5 00.

The Recent Progress of Astronomy,

Especially in the United States. By ELIAS LOOMIS, M.A. New Edition. 12mo, Muslin, $1 00.

Cosmos:

A Sketch of a Physical Description of the Universe. By ALEXANDER VON HUMBOLDT. Translated from the German, by E. C. OTTE. Complete in 3 vols. 12mo, Muslin, $2 55.

Bickersteth's Memoirs.

A Memoir of the late Rev. EDWARD BICKERSTETH, Rector of Watton. By Rev. T. R. BIRKS, M.A. With a Preface, &c., by Rev. STEPHEN H. TYNG, D.D., of New York. 2 vols. 12mo, Muslin, $1 75.

Foster's Christian Purity.

The Nature and Blessedness of Christian Purity. By Rev. R. S. FOSTER. With an Introduction by Bishop JANES. 12mo, Muslin, 75 cents.

Elements of Natural Philosophy.

Designed as a Text-book for Academies, High-Schools, and Colleges. By ALONZO GRAY, A.M. Illustrated by 360 Woodcuts. 12mo, Muslin, 70 cents; Sheep, 75 cents.

Lord Holland's Foreign Reminiscences.

Edited by his Son, HENRY EDWARD LORD HOLLAND. 12mo, Paper, 60 cents; Muslin, 75 cents.

Curran and his Contemporaries.

By CHARLES PHILLIPS, A.B. 12mo, Paper, 75 cents; Muslin, 87½ cents.

The Irish Confederates,

And the Rebellion of 1798. By HENRY M. FIELD. Portraits and a Map. 12mo, Paper, 75 cents; Muslin, 90 cents.

The Harmony of Prophecy;

Or, Scriptural Illustrations of the Apocalypse. By Rev. ALEXANDER KEITH, D.D. 12mo, Muslin, $1 00.

The Bards of the Bible.

By GEORGE GILFILLAN. 12mo, Muslin, 35 cents.

Abbott's Illustrated Histories:

The following Works of the Series are now ready: Josephine, Cleopatra, Madame Roland, Xerxes the Great, Cyrus the Great, Darius the Great, Charles I., Charles II., Hannibal, Julius Cæsar, Alfred the Great, Maria Antoinette, Queen Elizabeth, Alexander the Great, William the Conqueror, Mary Queen of Scots. 16mo, Muslin, with Illuminated Title-pages and numerous Engravings, 60 cents per Volume.

Abbott's Franconia Stories:

Comprising Malleville, Beechnut, Mary Bell, Wallace, Mary Erskine. 16mo, beautifully bound in Muslin, Engraved Title-pages and numerous Illustrations, 50 cents per Volume.

Kings and Queens;

Or, Life in the Palace: consisting of Historical Sketches of Josephine and Maria Louisa, Louis Philippe, Ferdinand of Austria, Nicholas, Isabella II., Leopold, and Victoria. By J. S. C. ABBOTT. With numerous Illustrations. 12mo, Muslin, $1 00; Muslin, gilt edges, $1 25.

A Summer in Scotland.

By JACOB ABBOTT. With Engravings. 12mo, Muslin, $1 00

Five Years of a Hunter's Life

In the Far Interior of South Africa. With Notices of the Native Tribes, and Anecdotes of the Chase of the Lion, Elephant, Hippopotamus, Giraffe, Rhinoceros, &c. By R. GORDON CUMMING. With Engravings. 2 vols. 12mo, Muslin, $1 75.

Sydney Smith's Moral Philosophy.

An Elementary Treatise on Moral Philosophy, delivered at the Royal Institution in the Years 1804, 1805, and 1806. By the late Rev. SYDNEY SMITH. 12mo, Muslin, $1 00.

Travels in the United States, etc.

During 1849 and 1850. By Lady EMMELINE STUART WORTLEY. 12mo, Paper, 60 cents; Muslin, 75 cents.

Dealings with the Inquisition;

Or, Papal Rome, her Priests, and her Jesuits. With Important Disclosures. By the Rev. GIACINTO ACHILLI, D.D., late Prior and Visitor of the Dominican Order, &c. 12mo, Muslin, 75 cts.

Leigh Hunt's Autobiography,

With Reminiscences of his Friends and Contemporaries.
2 vols. 12mo, Muslin, $1 50.

Campbell's Life and Letters.

Life and Letters of Thomas Campbell. Edited by WILLIA
BEATTIE, M.D. With an Introductory Letter, by WASHINGTC
IRVING. 2 vols. 12mo, Muslin, $2 00.

Doctor Johnson :

His Religious Life and Death. 12mo, Muslin, $1 00.

Southey's Life and Correspondence.

Edited by his Son, Rev. C. C. SOUTHEY, M.A. Portrait. 8vo,
Muslin, $1 75.

Southey's Common-place Book.

Edited by his Son-in-Law, JOHN WOOD WARTER, B.D. 3 vols.
8vo, Paper, $1 00 per Vol.; Muslin, $1 25 per Vol.

History of Greece,

From the Earliest Times to the Destruction of Corinth, B.C.
146; mainly based upon that of Bishop THIRLWALL. By Dr.
L. SCHMITZ, F.R.S.E. 12mo, Muslin, $1 00.

History of Rome,

From the Earliest Times to the Death of Commodus, A.D. 192.
By Dr. L. SCHMITZ, F.R.S.E. With Questions, by J. ROB-
SON, B.A. 18mo, Muslin, 75 cents.

A Treatise on Popular Education :

For the Use of Parents and Teachers, and for Young People of
both Sexes. Printed and Published in accordance with a Resolution of the Senate and House of Representatives of the State
of Michigan. By IRA MAYHEW, late Superintendent of Public
Instruction. 12mo, Muslin, $1 00.

The Conquest of Canada.

By the Author of "Hochelaga." 2 vols. 12mo, Muslin, $1 70.

Health, Disease, and Remedy,

Familiarly and practically considered in a few of their Relations
to the Blood. By G. MOORE, M.D. 18mo, Muslin, 60 cents.

Hume's History of England,

From the Invasion of Julius Cæsar to the Abdication of James
II., 1688. By DAVID HUME. A new Edition, with the Author's
last Corrections and Improvements. To which is prefixed a
Short Account of his Life, written by Himself. With a Portrait of the Author. 6 vols. 12mo, Cloth, $2 40; Sheep, $3 00.

Macaulay's History of England

From the Accession of James II. By THOMAS B. MACAULAY.
With an Original Portrait of the Author. Vols. I. and II. Li-
brary Edition. 8vo, Muslin, 75 cents per Vol.; Sheep extra, 87½
cents per Vol.; Calf backs and corners, $1 00 per Vol.—Cheap
Editions, 8vo, Paper, 25 cents per Vol: 12mo (uniform with
Hume), Cloth, 40 cents per Vol.; Sheep, 50 cents per Vol.

Gibbon's History of Rome.

History of the Decline and Fall of the Roman Empire. By
EDWARD GIBBON. With Notes, by Rev. H. H. MILMAN and
M. GUIZOT. Maps and Engravings, 4 vols. 8vo, Sheep extra,
$5 00.—A new Cheap Edition, with Notes, by Rev. H. H. MIL-
MAN. To which is added a complete Index of the whole Work,
and a Portrait of the Author. 6 vols. 12mo (uniform with Hume),
Cloth, $2 40; Sheep, $3 00.

History of Spanish Literature.

With Criticisms on the particular Works and Biographical Notices of prominent Writers. By GEORGE TICKNOR. 3 vols.
8vo, Muslin, $6 00; Sheep, $6 75; half Calf, $7 50.

Pictorial History of England.

Being a History of the People as well as a History of the King-
dom, down to the Reign of George III. Profusely Illustrated
with many Hundred Engravings on Wood of Monumental Records; Coins; Civil and Military Costume; Domestic Buildings,
Furniture, and Ornaments; Cathedrals and other great Works
of Architecture; Sports, and other Illustrations of Manners;
Mechanical Inventions; Portraits of Eminent Persons; and remarkable Historical Scenes. 4 vols. imperial 8vo, Sheep, $12 00;
half Calf, $13 50.

The War with Mexico.

By R. S. RIPLEY, U.S.A. With Maps, Plans of Battles, &c.
2 vols. 8vo, Muslin, $4 00; Sheep, $4 50.

Ancient and Mediæval Geography.

For the Use of Schools and Colleges. By CHARLES ANTHO
LL.D. 8vo, Muslin, $1 50 ; Sheep extra, $1 75.

Findlay's Classical Atlas

To Illustrate Ancient Geography. Comprised in 25 Maps, show
ing the various Divisions of the World as known to the Ancient
By ALEX. FINDLAY, F.R.S. With an Index of the Ancien
and Modern Names. 8vo, half Bound, $3 25.

A First Book in Latin.

Containing Grammar, Exercises, and Vocabularies, on the Meth-
od of constant Imitation and Repetition. By Prof. M'CLINTOCK,
of Dickinson College. 12mo, Sheep, 75 cents.

A First Book in Greek.

Containing full Vocabularies, Lessons on the Forms of Words,
and Exercises for Imitation and Repetition, with a Summary
of Etymology and Syntax. By Professor M'CLINTOCK. 12mo,
Sheep, 75 cents.

A Second Book in Greek.

Containing Syntax, with Reading Lessons in Prose ; Prosody,
and the Dialects, with Reading Lessons in Verse ; forming a
sufficient Greek Grammar. By Prof. M'CLINTOCK. 12mo,
Sheep, 75 cents.

The Pillars of Hercules ;

Or, a Narrative of Travels in Spain and Morocco in 1848. By
DAVID URQUHART, M.P. 2 vols. 12mo, Paper, $1 40 ; Muslin,
$1 70.

The Valley of the Mississippi.

History of the Discovery and Settlement of the Valley of the
Mississippi, by the three great European Powers, Spain, France,
and Great Britain ; and the Subsequent Occupation, Settlement, and Extension of Civil Government by the United States,
until the Year 1846. By JOHN W. MONETTE. Maps. 2 vols
8vo, Muslin $5 00 ; Sheep, $5 50.

Moral and Political Philosophy.

With Questions for the Examination of Students. By WILL-
IAM PALEY, D.D. 12mo, Muslin, 60 cents.

History of the Confessional.

By JOHN HENRY HOPKINS, D.D., Bishop of Vermont. 12mo, . Muslin, $1 00.

History of the American Bible Society,

From its Organization in 1816 to the Present Time. By Rev. W. P. STRICKLAND. With an Introduction by Rev. N. L. RICE, and a Portrait of Hon. E. BOUDINOT, LL.D., first President of the Society. 8vo, Cloth, $1 50; Sheep, $1 75.

Gieseler's Ecclesiastical History.

From the Fourth Edition, Revised and Amended. Translated from the German, by SAMUEL DAVIDSON, LL.D. Vols. I. and II., 8vo, Muslin, $3 00; Sheep, $3 50.

History of the Girondists;

Or, Personal Memoirs of the Patriots of the French Revolution. By A. DE LAMARTINE. From Unpublished Sources. 3 vols. 12mo, Muslin, $2 10.

History of the French Revolution.

By THOMAS CARLYLE. Newly Revised by the Author, with Index, &c. 2 vols. 12mo, Muslin, $2 00.

Letters and Speeches of Oliver Cromwell.

With Elucidations and connecting Narrative. By THOMAS CARLYLE. 2 vols 12mo, Muslin, $2 00.

Past and Present, Chartism,

And Sartor Resartus. By THOMAS CARLYLE. A new Edition, complete in One Volume. 12mo, Muslin, $1 00.

Latter-Day Pamphlets.

Comprising, 1. The Present Time; 2. Model Prisons; 3. Downing Street; 4. The New Downing Street; 5. Stump Orator; 6. Parliaments; 7. Hudson's Statue; 8. Jesuitism. By THOMAS CARLYLE. 12mo, Muslin, 50 cents.

Not so Bad as we Seem;

Or, Many Sides to a Character. A Comedy in Five Acts. By Sir E. BULWER LYTTON. As first performed at Devonshire House, in the Presence of her Majesty and Prince Albert. 16mo, Paper, 30 cents; Muslin, 37½ cents.

Sketches of Minnesota,

The New England of the West. With Incidents of Travel in that Territory during the Summer of 1848. By E. S. SEYMOUR. 12mo, Paper, 50 cents; Muslin, 75 cents.

History of the Conquest of Peru;

With a Preliminary View of the Civilization of the Incas. By WILLIAM H. PRESCOTT. 2 vols. 8vo, Muslin, $4 00; Sheep, $4 50; half Calf, $5 00.

History of the Conquest of Mexico,

With the Life of the Conqueror, Hernando Cortes, and a View of the Ancient Mexican Civilization. By WILLIAM H. PRESCOTT. With Portraits and Maps. 3 vols. 8vo, Muslin, $6 00; Sheep, $6 75; half Calf, $7 50.

History of Ferdinand and Isabella,

The Catholic. By WILLIAM H. PRESCOTT. With Portraits, Maps, &c. 3 vols. 8vo, Muslin, $6 00; Sheep, $6 75; half Calf, $7 50.

Harper's Illustrated Shakespeare.

The complete Dramatic Works of William Shakespeare, arranged according to recent approved Collations of the Text; with Notes and other Illustrations, by Hon. GULIAN C. VERPLANCK. Superbly Embellished by over 1400 exquisite Engravings by Hewet, after Designs by Meadows, Weir, and other eminent Artists. 3 vols. royal 8vo, Muslin, $18 00; half Calf extra, $20 00; Morocco, gilt edges, $25 00.

Herman Melville's Works.

TYPEE; 12mo, Paper, 75 cents, Muslin, 87½ cents.——OMOO; 12mo, Paper, $1 00, Muslin, $1 25.——MARDI; 2 vols. 12mo, Paper, $1 50, Muslin, $1 75.——REDBURN; 12mo, Paper, 75 cents, Muslin, $1 00. —— WHITE-JACKET; 12mo, Paper, $1 00, Muslin, $1 25.——MOBY-DICK; 12mo, Muslin, $1 50.

The Country Year-Book;

Or, the Field, the Forest, and the Fireside By WILLIAM HOWITT. 12mo, Muslin, 87½ cents.

Dark Scenes of History.

By G. P. R. JAMES. 12mo, Paper, 75 cents; Muslin, $1 00